# Working with Children Ag and Their Families

This inspiring book shows how Early Years staff can support the best possible practice for children under three and their families whilst making use of the limited funding available. Promoting the idea of infants as powerful learners, the authors focus on 0–3 years as the vital first phase of education and care, which can require a very specific pedagogical approach. They discuss the principles that underpin the practice of working with the youngest children, the critical nature of highly effective pedagogical practice and the important role of family workers in building relationships with parents and the extended family.

*Working with Children Aged 0–3 and Their Families* explores the challenges and responsibilities of working with young children and communicates the 'Pen Green Approach'. Pen Green has become a focal point for Early Years professionals due to its outstanding Early Years provision. The innovative approach chronicled in this book will encourage practitioners to research their own practice and use the outcomes to create a radical, unique and yet highly effective provision for infants, toddlers and their families.

The book will be of interest to Early Years professionals, foundation and undergraduate students, and early childhood educators.

**Tracy Gallagher** is one of the Joint Heads of the Pen Green Centre, Corby, Northamptonshire, UK.

**Cath Arnold** is an Early Years Consultant.

Also available in the *Pen Green Books for Early Years Educators* series

# Working with Children Aged 0–3 and Their Families

The Pen Green Approach

Edited by Tracy Gallagher
and Cath Arnold

Routledge
Taylor & Francis Group

LONDON AND NEW YORK

First published 2018
by Routledge
2 Park Square, Milton Park, Abingdon, Oxon OX14 4RN

and by Routledge
711 Third Avenue, New York, NY 10017

*Routledge is an imprint of the Taylor & Francis Group, an informa business*

*British Library Cataloguing-in-Publication Data*
A catalogue record for this book is available from the British Library

*Library of Congress Cataloging-in-Publication Data*
Names: Gallagher, Tracy, editor.
Title: Working with children aged 0–3 and their families: the Pen Green approach / edited by Tracy Gallagher and Cath Arnold.
Description: Abingdon, Oxon; New York, NY: Routledge, 2017. | Series: Pen Green books for early years educators series
Identifiers: LCCN 2016054603 | ISBN 9781138672598 (hardback) | ISBN 9781138672604 (pbk.) | ISBN 9781315562445 (ebook)
Subjects: LCSH: Early childhood education—Parent participation.
Classification: LCC LB1139.35.P37 W67 2017 | DDC 372.119/2—dc23
LC record available at https://lccn.loc.gov/2016054603

ISBN: 978-1-138-67259-8 (hbk)
ISBN: 978-1-138-67260-4 (pbk)
ISBN: 978-1-315-56244-5 (ebk)

Typeset in Galliard
by codeMantra
Printed and bound by CPI Group (UK) Ltd, Croydon, CR0 4YY

# Contents

# About the contributors

**Andrea Layzell** has her practitioner roots in childminding, moving to work with Early Years Workers as a consultant, project manager, tutor on Early Years qualification courses and in workforce development with local authorities in the north of England. She is passionate about raising the status of Early Years practitioners and her work collaborating with practitioners in thinking about how two-year-olds, particularly those who are disadvantaged, can be best nurtured and supported in their learning in Early Years provision by skilled and well-informed, reflective adults in partnership with their parents. She has supported the professional development of practitioners across the Early Years sector in West Yorkshire and Northamptonshire, and now she works as Workforce Development Leader in Bradford's Birth to 19 Teaching School Alliance based at St Edmund's Nursery School and Children's Centre Services. Andrea has two sons, both adults, who live and work in Leeds. She believes that parenting them is the best, most joyous and satisfying work she has ever done and is exceptionally proud of them both.

**Angela Prodger** comes from a family where she had much younger siblings. Angela knew from childhood that she wanted to work with young children. Initially, Angela qualified as a nursery nurse and later gained qualified teacher's status and has worked in Early Years for more than thirty years. Angela has a passion for working with vulnerable children and their families, and she is a strong advocate for children being able to make their own choices and take appropriate risks whilst supported by adults. Angela is passionate about children having a voice and that children's voices are listened to and respected. Becoming a mother really made Angela think about how young children learn and being attuned to their needs. More recently, Angela has become involved in working with children with special educational needs and/or disability. This work has been challenging and rewarding, but has made Angela think about children's non-verbal communication and how we capture and respond to this. As the current joint head of the Pen Green Centre with Tracy Gallagher, Angela is deeply committed to maintaining parent participation within the Centre and making sure that it strives to be an inclusive service for all.

**Cath Arnold** has been working in the Early Years field for almost forty years, first as a practitioner working directly with children and families, and more recently as a consultant, researcher and writer. Cath is deeply interested in children's thinking and feeling. Her PhD study was on 'Schemas and Emotions' and was a small study of eight children carried out alongside their parents and workers at the Pen Green Centre. Cath is parent of three children and grandparent of six children ranging in age from three weeks to twenty-five years, three of whom have attended the Pen Green Nursery. She has written books and articles about her grandchildren's learning and continues to be intrigued by the uniqueness of each child's journey.

**Cessie Cole (Johannsson)** (MBACP sen accred & UKCP) has been in private practice working with individuals, couples and families as a psychotherapist since she finished her training at the Tavistock Centre in 1990, following teaching work in Adult Education and the Local NHS Child and Family Dept. Her practice is in Cambridge and more recently Rutland, which is how she began work at Pen Green ten years ago. There, her main interest is in the relationships built between infants/young children and their parents. That relational aspect, based on Psychodynamic theory, is how her work informs the teams she works in with families attending the Centre. Pen Green funds Cessie to work in groups at the Centre for one day a week. Cessie helps to have the work at the Centre informed by sound ideas which continually supports practitioners to improve their practice with children and parents.

**Colette Tait** is a Principal Researcher at the Pen Green Research Base in Corby. She lectures on the Foundation Degree, BA and MA in Integrated Working with Children and their Families. Prior to this, she worked at Pen Green for twelve years before leaving to lead a phase two Children's Centre in the county. She has two children, Georgia and Harry, who both attended the Pen Green Nursery, and who are now grown up.

**Elaine Young** has worked with children and their families for over thirty-one years. During this time, she has developed an understanding of relationships within families that continues to grow with each new encounter. Elaine is a parent herself to two children and is enjoying the wonderful delights of being a grandparent.

**Felicity Norton** is a mum of two teenagers and a toddler. She has always worked in the field of Early Years. She has been working at Pen Green for ten years. During this time, Fliss has held responsibility for the undergraduate degree programmes. She has a particular interest in psychoanalysis and group dynamics, as well as working with families. She is passionate about the mental health of infants and adults and the importance of good, robust supervision.

**Judy Potts** started her social work career as an unqualified worker in Scotland. After her three children were born, she became a community mental health worker in rural East Northants and trained as a counsellor. After completing her social work training, she joined Pen Green Centre as a group worker and subsequently led the Family Support team. She was particularly interested in developing partnership working with families, where listening to their experiences, strengths and priorities and forming a joint understanding of possible ways forward was the basis of practice. She really enjoyed working in a multi-professional team with colleagues from Early Years education, health and adult education and valued the opportunities in the Centre for parents to be on their own learning journey, training and developing their skills whilst their own children were in Nursery. Judy became a Deputy Head with responsibility for Safeguarding for the whole Centre. She studied for her Master's degree at the Tavistock Centre, using Psychodynamic perspectives to gain insight into experiences of parenting young children and the processes of child abuse. Now retired, she runs a group for mothers who were sexually abused as children and mentors Early Years practitioners at her local community preschool.

**Kate Hayward** studied zoology and anthropology and trained as a nutritionist, working in health and community development projects overseas in Kenya and Papua New Guinea. She later trained to be a teacher after being involved in the early education of her three children, Tom, Hannah and Emily. She worked at Pen Green for twelve years as a researcher, leading on pedagogical support and professional development programmes including PICL (Parents' Involvement in their Children's Learning) and Making Children's Learning Visible (MCLV) and the MA in Integrated Provision for Children and Their Families (Early Years). She is passionate about parental involvement in children's learning and the transformations that can happen to children's lives when parents and workers listen and learn from each other and the child.

**Kerry McNulty** is the proud mum of her daughter Emie. Kerry enjoys nothing more than spending time with her daughter and having fun together. She is a Senior Family Worker leading the Baby and Toddler Nest provision at Pen Green. She is a strong advocate for the most vulnerable children and ensures they are supported by thoughtful and experienced practitioners. Kerry's strengths also include planning for and providing interesting and challenging pedagogical environments for young children.

**Lesley Hill** is married with two children and the latest magical addition to her family is her wonderful granddaughter. Lesley came to the Centre as a parent nearly twenty-three years ago. She began sessional work in the nursery nineteen years ago. She is currently working full-time as a Family Worker in the Couthie, part of the 0–3 provision. She is passionate about "getting it right" for the youngest children as they begin their journey in the Couthie. She believes that the foundations for building a trusting relationship with children and families begin at that very first meeting and throughout their settling-in period. Lesley's strengths include working hard to ensure children trust her, believe in her and know that she hears them.

**Lorna MacLeod** lives in Corby and is a proud parent of two children. She began working at Pen Green in 1983 as a Family Worker in the nursery and has been able to undertake many learning opportunities, most recently completing her Masters in Integrated Provision for Children and Families. Her current role is the 0–3-year Group Coordinator. She values the importance of group work as a significant route into the Centre, and regards it as an integral part of the offer of services for families. Lorna also coordinates the volunteers at the Centre, offering an in-house training course jointly run with a colleague from HomeStart and providing the link and support to their volunteering placement in the Centre.

**Michele Duffy** has worked with children and their families for over twenty-two years and cares deeply about the quality of education and care that we provide for the youngest children. Michele is passionate about children's well-being and as an Early Years practitioner and leader in the Centre, her aim is to ensure all children have the best possible start in the setting with thoughtful workers who understand how individual children like to play, explore and learn. Michele has a ten-year-old son who attended Pen Green for three years, and she truly believes that the opportunities he was given by deeply thoughtful practitioners has made him the creative thinker he is today.

**Penny Lawrence** has been researching and learning with children, families and staff at Pen Green for almost twenty years. Penny is particularly interested in children's agency and non-verbal dialogue. Her doctoral thesis was on 'Observing and Understanding Decision-Making in Two-Year-Olds'. She worked in pedagogical documentation in the infant-toddler centres and infant schools of Reggio Emilia, Italy for three years. This was in project work, for example on the children's dialogues with materials and with the environment as well as with each other. Penny also made broadcast documentaries of children's initiated experiences for BBC and Channel 4 television in the United Kingdom. Penny is Senior Lecturer in Early Childhood Studies at Froebel College, The University of Roehampton, London.

**Sam Coe** worked at Pen Green for three years in the Baby and Toddler Nest, working with children from nine months to three years. From working in the Nest and with the dedicated team, it gave her the passion and drive to want to go further to promote and support children and their families' well-being. Sam is now employed as a Family Support Worker in a Safeguarding and Care planning team within Northamptonshire.

**Sheena Griffiths-Baker** qualified as a primary school teacher in 1995 and worked for two years as a Reception class teacher in Leicester and Stamford. As part of the government's Sure Start initiative, she joined Pen Green in

2000 under secondment to Lloyds Educare, a community private not-for-profit-run nursery on the Pen Green site. She has worked ever since within Pen Green as a Teacher and Family Worker, completing her MA in Integrated Services for Young Children and Families in 2011. Sheena is passionate about coming to understand how young children learn and how this links with the inner world of emotions. Along with many of the staff team, she has completed an 'Emotional Roots' course run by psychotherapists from the Northern School of Psychotherapy and continues to use these insights in her practice. Sheena has one child who attended Pen Green.

**Tracy Gallagher** For over thirty years, Tracy has worked within the Early Years field. She has been employed as a practitioner working directly with young children and their families and as a lecturer in Early Years, sharing her passion and interest for working with young children. Tracy has worked at Pen Green since 2000 and has been employed in various roles within the Centre. She is currently Joint Head of Centre with her colleague Angela Prodger. Tracy was privileged to take on this role when the previous Director Dr Margy Whalley retired. Tracy has always been passionate about working with young children and their families and is a strong advocate for hearing the voice of the youngest children. Tracy strongly believes in ensuring the needs and wishes of the youngest children are seriously taken in to account. She is also interested in leadership within the Early Years; studying for the MA in Early Childhood Education with Care and the National Professional Qualification in Integrated Centre Leadership (NPQICL) gave her the opportunity to deepen her understanding of the complex role of a leader and how to effectively support practitioners working with very young children and their families. Tracy has learnt, and continues to learn, every day from the youngsters in her family and the children, families and practitioners with whom she has worked during her career.

# Foreword

It is remarkable what a U-turn there has been in public policy regarding the care of babies and under-threes in nursery. In 1945, as the war ended, the official government position, set down in the clearest of terms, was that the best place for under twos 'was at home with their mothers'. Seventy years later, the picture is transformed with a huge expansion of nursery provision in the United Kingdom and internationally. Most nurseries now welcome under-threes for long enough hours to make possible full-time working for parents.

I first started researching what it was like for under-threes in nursery twenty-five years ago. The private nursery sector, in which most of this nursery expansion has occurred, was just beginning its take-off. Yet whilst the availability of nursery places was a relief to parents struggling to balance paid employment with bringing up young children, the idea of such young children attending nursery for such long hours also caused widespread anxiety. The media frequently ran stories asking the same kinds of negative questions: 'Is nursery bad for babies?' In America, the debates between those cast as on the side of the young child and those seen as committed to equality of opportunity for mothers became so passionate they were dubbed the 'infant day-care wars'. Fortunately, this simplistic polarisation has now moved on. Campaigning and research efforts have for a long time been focussed on the much more optimistic question, 'what kind of nursery provides the best opportunities for children and families?'

The principles of respectful pedagogy with young children are now familiar – small group sizes, good ratios, well-trained and supported staff, anti-discriminatory practice, heuristic play and, most of all, consistent, responsive and individual attention from practitioners. In the last two decades of the 20th century and into the 21st century, Elinor Goldschmied, a Froebelian-trained educator, together with her close collaborators, showed how those principles could be turned into practical approaches through her work on the Treasure Basket and the Key Person approach. Contemporary pioneers are continuing to build on Elinor's legacy. Julia Manning Morton was one of the first to document how working with babies and young children in nursery involved the deep personal feelings of practitioners as well as their professional commitment. Jayne Osgood has extended that work, helping us understand better the challenges of offering that commitment to young children in nurseries forced to operate to commercial principles as a dominating concern. Jools Page's work on 'Professional Love' has brilliantly captured the strength of feeling of many practitioners towards the children with whom they work. Sacha Powell and Kathy Goouch have raised the profile of pedagogy with babies through the Canterbury Baby Room Conference Series, and Julian Grenier is developing new models of supervision, including the Work Discussion approach discussed in Chapter 8 of this book. Internationally, there is parallel exciting research work exploring the lives of the youngest children in nursery. For example, Marjetta Kalliala in Finland has shown how welcome are new understandings of the creativity and competence of the youngest children. This way of thinking about young children, whilst not forgetting their dependence too, will hopefully replace old ideas of the young child as vulnerable and simply waiting to be unilaterally shaped and moulded by adults. Linda Harrison and Jenifer Sumsion in Australia have edited a new collection of papers dedicated entirely to rethinking the experiences of infants in nursery, whilst Carmen Dalli and her colleagues in New Zealand have produced a detailed and comprehensive review of the research evidence on high quality provision for under-twos and what high quality looks like.

The reader might be forgiven for wondering, in view of all this work, if there is a place for this book, rooted as it is in the work with under-threes that has evolved at Pen Green. There is a profoundly important place for the book! As the positive contribution that nurseries can make in the lives of families and young children is increasingly accepted, how can we translate all the scholarly work illustrated above into practical day-to-day realities? Academic work, as important as it is, means nothing to babies and toddlers. Inspirational practices, by real practitioners, in real nurseries, in real communities, mean everything to babies and toddlers. And that is what this book documents and supports practitioners to be – inspirational in the way they work with the babies and toddlers in their care, and how parents and young children are supported in groups at Pen Green. The book starts by explaining the principles that underpin the work with young children and their families at Pen Green and then, through the different chapters, shares examples from practice and case studies that outline what this work actually looks like.

This work is not without its challenges, and the book does not shy away from that. For example, we know that respectful skin-to-skin touch is fundamental for babies but still a minefield for practitioners. Why is it so problematic to combine this vital physical holding and touch with effective safeguarding? Key Person practices to facilitate emotional bonds that help babies and young children feel 'Held in mind' (one of Elinor Goldschmied's favourite phrases) but that are not claustrophobic or restrictive of babies' explorations is brilliantly developed in some settings, but why is it not more widespread? Making such close professional relationships with the young children of others is work of the most sophisticated and delicate nature if it is to be respectful of parents' feelings and professional boundaries. Why are so many practitioners still expected to manage this with little, if any, opportunity to talk through their day-to-day relationships with children and families? And why does work with under-threes, despite the efforts of many leaders and managers to raise the status of the work, still have such a 'taken for granted', anyone-can-do-it nature? These challenges are complex and involve many uncertainties. There are not simple standardised solutions. That is why this account of work at Pen Green matters so much. It addresses the day-to-day realities of nursery life and how one leading nursery approaches its work.

Perhaps most important of all, the book explores how practitioners are supported in their work, and it describes the way 'Work Discussion' is used at Pen Green. Work Discussion is a way of talking and thinking together openly about day-to-day work with young children and their families. It is an opportunity for practitioners to talk about their feelings as well as their thoughts without risk of being criticised or blamed when things are not going well. Here, Pen Green is one of a small number of nurseries leading the way in showing that unless practitioners are much better understood and supported in their daily work, it is unrealistic to expect them to manage the complexity and uncertainty that they face daily without risking burnout or a retreat to institutional ways of working and being. It is not a set of simple prescriptions, but it is a respectful and deep thinking book about working in Early Years settings with our youngest fellow citizens and their families. It is very much needed.

Peter Elfer
Principal Lecturer, Early Childhood Research Centre,
University of Roehampton, London.

# Acknowledgements

Cath and I would like to thank all the children, families and staff who have contributed to this book. Without their willingness to share their stories, we would not have the detailed case studies and examples of practice to share with you. Many thanks for each and every one.

We would like to thank all the staff who have contributed to the chapters and the administration support we have had to produce the final book. Thank you. They gave so generously of their time, and their discussions helped us to clarify our thinking.

Finally, thanks to my family and friends who all created a space in their own lives to allow me to accommodate my workload.

This book is dedicated to all the strong and thoughtful women who have influenced me both personally and professionally. Thank you.

Tracy Gallagher

# Introduction

*Tracy Gallagher*

I am deeply interested in working with children under three and their families, and have been throughout my career. I first had the idea to write about our work a number of years ago; since then, we have developed our work in the Centre even further, and it now feels like the right time to share our work with a wider audience. In this book, Cath and I have worked with Pen Green authors to document our work with children under three and their families, sharing experiences from the team and through case study examples.

There are tensions between government policy and quality Early Years practice. The government introduced the Neighbourhood Nursery Initiative in order to help get women back into the workforce without really considering how difficult it would be to provide high-quality provisions for the youngest children. Subsequently, the government has developed the two-year-old offer. Staff at Pen Green were at first resistant to the idea of offering education and care provision for the youngest children for both philosophical reasons and practical constraints. However, over the years, we have worked hard to develop a coherent offer of services for families with children under three years including education and care year-round.

We recognise there are many challenges when taking on work with very young children and with those families facing challenges in our society. We have tried to work out how to use the funding available to support the best possible practice, and as such, we have developed a system for thinking deeply about children aged from birth to their third year.

In practice, work with babies and toddlers is often seen as work that has been done with three- and four-year-olds that has been watered down and made simpler. We want to promote the idea of infants as powerful learners and make it clear that birth to three is the first phase of education and care, which requires a specific pedagogical approach. Support and supervision for staff are an essential aspect of our practice with young children. In this book, we will share our processes for supporting staff and our experience of developing highly reflective teams.

It has been a wonderful experience to meet with authors and produce this book detailing our work at Pen Green. I start in the first chapter considering the principles underpinning our work with children under three years and their families. Colette Tait and I then go on to document the journey of conceptualising and designing a high-quality provision for young children. I believe that pedagogical spaces for young children need to be geared towards their needs and interests and should take into account their relationships with their parents and with workers. Mini 'classrooms' will not do, so designing and developing spaces for infants and toddlers take a great deal of planning and effort, as well as experience and insight. Colette and I describe how we have done this at Pen Green in the 'Nest' and the 'Couthie'.

Michele and I then describe our work with the birth-to-three team, and how we ensured members of staff had a deep understanding of the child development and psychodynamic theories that underpin their work. Cath, Michele and Sam describe the role of the Family Worker, specifically in the birth to three provision. Kerry, Judy and I then add to this by explaining how we support families in the Nest and Couthie that are experiencing challenging circumstances and how we support families across the services we offer in the Centre. We describe the support we offer to improve outcomes for some of the most disadvantaged young children and their families.

Angela and Lesley then describe our documentation paperwork and how the Family Workers work in collaboration with the families to truly hear and celebrate the voice of the child.

Penny and I describe a research project we engaged in with parents and staff where we looked at effective pedagogic strategies for working with under threes. This specific chapter summarises the research project and shares case studies of the families and workers that participated in the project.

Chapter 8 outlines the development of an observational tool, 'consultancy observations', for use when practitioners in Early Years settings have concerns about particular children in their care. This chapter by Colette, Felicity, Sheena and I describes the development of this particular approach and explains how through thinking, reflecting and talking together, staff behaviours change in subtle ways, thus changing the child's experience for the better.

Lorna and Elaine in Chapter 9 acknowledge the critical importance of developing relationships with all the important adults in the child's life and describe how to work in a deep and respectful way in order to develop successful and sustained engagement with parents. At the Centre, we offer families a range of groups to attend across the week and weekend, both within the Centre and offsite. We provide universal, 'non-stigmatised' groups for families to use, as well as more targeted provisions for those families that need more specialist support. We know that for the targeted services to be accessible and acceptable to the most disadvantaged families, they need to have a universal gateway. In this chapter, we outline the range of groups families with children under three years can access, as well as demonstrating the difference the services make for families. Cessie and I then go on in Chapter 10 to describe the Growing Together group, which is a group for parents to attend with children aged from birth to three years. Within the group, parents and workers use video material to study the children's development and learning; it is also critical within the group to consider, with the parent, their relationship with their child. Using a case study and examples from practice, we describe how we do this work.

The final chapter by Kate, Andrea, Michele and I explains the 'Being Two' project, which promotes exemplary early education and childcare for two-year-olds through the development of a national network of Associate Centres. Funded by the Department for Education (2013–15), the aims of the project were to improve the quality of experiences in settings for two-year-olds and their families, and to support better outcomes for the most disadvantaged children. The project was structured to achieve those aims through the promotion and facilitation of thoughtful practice and effective parental involvement in children's learning. 'Being Two' builds on the Pen Green Early Years Teaching Centres model to create Associate Centres that develop collaborative local learning networks.

# Chapter 1

# Principles for working with children under three and their families

*Tracy Gallagher*

In this chapter, I describe Pen Green Centre for Children and Their Families and the principles that underpin our work. The chapter will document the principles of operation, how the principles underpin our work with children under three across the organisation including the education and care provision (Nest & Couthie), as well as the groups for parents to attend with their young children. I discuss the importance of developing reciprocal relationships with parents and share case studies of best practice.

Before I describe the work of Pen Green, I believe that it would be beneficial to mention the early pioneers who have influenced the work of the staff at the Centre. I will also put the work of the Centre into context with a historical perspective of the government policies and initiatives that have had an important impact on our work with young children and their families.

Many educational pioneers have influenced early childhood education, and I recognise that they have had a profound impact on my practice and the practice of my colleagues. Pioneers such as Froebel, McMillan and Isaacs all had a strong belief that the parent's role is a critical one to young children. This belief still underpins our work at Pen Green today. We know from Bruce (1997) that the child's family and sociocultural backgrounds are deeply influential, and children do not leave the sociocultural aspects behind when attending a group or school setting.

Froebel, Montessori and Steiner all believed that when educating young children, we should start with what they can do rather than what they cannot do. Early Years Education and Care at Pen Green encompasses this belief. Our principles are based on placing the child and their family at the centre of all that we do.

Historically, there have been many different attempts at involving parents in the early years, some far more successfully than others. During the Second World War, there was a great increase in early years provision for children to enable women to take up jobs in factories while men were at war; however, as the war ended, many nurseries closed. It was not until the 1960s that involving parents in the early years became a focus once again. Although attempts were made at involving parents at this time, we did not see a true partnership between parents and professionals. The relationship was not usually equal, for example parents were being asked to make costumes for school concerts but not being valued for knowledge they could share with professionals about their children.

It was in the 1960s and 1970s in the United Kingdom and in the United States of America, we saw a trend to set up and offer services in areas of poverty and social disadvantage. We saw an emphasis on compensatory education. The American project Head Start received government funding for two decades in the hope it would break the cycle of poverty (Ball, 1994). It was believed that by placing children in the compensatory education programmes, you would enrich their development and compensate for the poverty they were living in. However, these compensatory education programmes did not recognise the impact of living in poverty, nor did they acknowledge the significant role of the parents and the important influence of family life. Yet, American research would lead us to believe that compensatory preschool education clearly influences later school success (Ball, 1994).

The work of Bronfenbrenner was introduced in the 1970s. He argued that in order to understand human development, we need to understand the entire ecological system in which growth occurs. Bronfenbrenner's theory (1994) identified that the system is composed of five socially organised subsystems that help support and guide human growth. He described interpersonal relationships such as those in families were critical to children's development, as were the links between settings such as home and school. The work of Bronfenbrenner has hugely influenced our work in the Centre and our approach to working in partnership to ensure a strong link between parents and workers.

In the early 1970s, Chris Athey at the Froebel Institute considered parental involvement; the participatory approach to working with parents was completely opposite to the compensatory models that had previously been experienced. Chris Athey directed the five-year Early Education Project at the Froebel Institute. The project valued and respected a close partnership with parents. The staff involved in the project had a strong commitment to sharing theory with the parents, and this influenced going towards a more equal and active partnership. In addition, the child's home life was recognised as important and therefore respected. The analysis and results of this project have had a huge impact on many early years professionals and had a significant influence on our work with young children and their families at Pen Green.

In the 1980s, the early years settings in the United Kingdom still saw separation between the education and care provision for children. It was recognised that at this time, most early childhood services in the United Kingdom were divided into care-focussed or education-focussed (Pascal & Bertram, 2002).

Pen Green was set up in 1983, and in many early years settings at this time, parents were seen as inept and in need of expert guidance from professionals who had all the skills and expertise. This was not the view of staff working at Pen Green; from the onset, parents were valued as important educators of their children (Whalley & The Pen Green Centre Team, 1997, p. 3). The parents, politicians, local authority officers and staff had a vision that there should be a service for children under five years of age, a service that would celebrate their existence and would also offer support to their families (Whalley & The Pen Green Centre Team, 2001). Contrary to the national picture, the staff at the Centre had a strong belief that education and care were indivisible and parents played a key role as their child's first educators. This belief is still at the heart of our work today.

In 1997, the newly elected Labour government strongly encouraged early years settings to involve parents actively in their children's education. Barber (1996) had confirmed the critical role of parents as their children's first and most consistent educators. In August 1997, the government launched its Centres of Excellence programmes following the white paper "Excellence in Schools." The Early Excellence Programmes (DfEE, 1997) had a strong emphasis on amalgamating early education and care. The intention was for Centres to demonstrate good practice in education, childcare and integrated services for children and their families, as well as providing training and a focus for dissemination. Pen Green was designated as a Centre of Excellence and continued to hold firm the beliefs that all parents had a critical role to play as their child's primary educators and the offer of education and care was fully integrated.

Since 1998, the different government agendas have introduced a range of policy initiatives, aiming to have a national coordination of early childhood services. One such initiative was the national Sure Start Programme (DfEE, 1998). The government initiative was set up to support families with children aged from birth to five years living in areas of disadvantage. After many months of discussion, the Corby Sure Start project came to fruition in September of 1999. Pen Green became the lead partner for Corby Sure Start programme. The fundamental aim of the project was to change the way that public services were provided. There was also a clear vision that the project would have a commitment to empowering local people so that the needs of young children and their families could be met. In the Corby Sure Start delivery plan, there was a clear recognition of parents as their children's primary carers and first educators (Whalley, 1999). There was also a strong commitment to having parent representatives on Sure Start boards, making decisions and driving services forward. The National Evaluation summary in 2005 described Sure Start local programmes as representing a cornerstone of the government's drive to tackle child poverty and social exclusion. The Sure Start local programmes were based in areas of disadvantage, and their aim was to improve the health and well-being of young children under four and their families, so that children had a greater opportunity to flourish when they went to school (Barnes et al., 2005).

As well as government policies influencing our work, the Centre has had a strong tradition in keeping up to date with current national and international research and leading early years research projects. The works of Easen et al. (1992), Whalley and The Pen Green Centre Team (1997), Whalley (2007) and Whalley et al. (forthcoming 2017) have explored the importance of involving parents in their children's learning. The research clearly demonstrates the value of working closely with parents, and we continue to believe wholeheartedly in these approaches to working in partnership with parents.

In 2002, "Birth to Three Matters: A Framework to Support Children in Their Earliest Years" (DfES, 2002) was introduced. The intention was to support practitioners in their work with the youngest children. Within the framework, there was an emphasis on working in partnership with parents: 'the role of parents in early years settings has evolved significantly and increasing knowledge about the valuable role parents play in their children's lives has led to an emphasis, by the government, on involving them as much as possible in order to enhance outcomes for children's development' (Langston, 2006, p. 3).

Another critical document was the Labour government's green paper "Every Child Matters" (DfES, 2003). This was published following the Lord Laming inquiry into the death of Victoria Climbie. The programme identified five outcomes for children: Being Healthy, Staying Safe, Enjoying and Achieving, Making a Positive Contribution and Economic Well-being. This was the government's agenda for better outcomes as an entitlement for every child, and at Pen Green, we considered this to be of the utmost importance. The five outcomes reformed the way agencies were expected to work, ensuring that every child was Safeguarded. The intention was clear that practitioners would work collaboratively with parents.

In 2004 at Pen Green, we developed a pedagogical environment for children two years of age and under through the Neighbourhood Nursery Initiative (DfES, 2004). The objective of Neighbourhood Nurseries was to support children under five and their families in the most disadvantaged areas by providing new, good-quality childcare services, so that parents previously prevented from working because of lack of childcare could return to work (DfES, 2004). The development of the new nursery provision at Pen Green for children two years of age and under enabled us to work closely with the youngest children and their families, providing high-quality education with care.

In 2006, we received the designation as School Status which provided us with the opportunity to further expand our provision and offer services to more families within the immediate area, across the town and surrounding villages.

The Early Years Foundation Stage (EYFS) (DCSF, 2008) was introduced following a review of policy; once again an emphasis was placed on partnership working between practitioners and parents. The EYFS focused on care and learning being completely indivisible. The intentions of the framework were philosophically coherent to our approach of working collaboratively with parents and involving them in their children's learning.

Policy and research have continued to influence our thinking at Pen Green. Frank Field's (2010) independent review on poverty and life chances addressed the question of how we can prevent poor children from becoming poor adults. Through his report, he considered the evidence that indicates the earliest years of a child's life are critical if their potential is to be realised in adult life.

He also indicated the importance of involving the community and improving the capacity of local parents to help each other. Graham Allen (2011) identified early intervention as the most effective way of offering services, and the importance of supporting children, young people and families before problems arise. Reports such as those by Field and Allen reflect the thinking of the staff at Pen Green, and the approaches they describe have always been central to the work of the Centre.

Over the years since the Centre opened, we have been involved in a variety of government-funded projects that have enabled us to share our practice and develop innovative ways of working with families and practitioners. In 2014, the revised EYFS (DfE, 2014) identified further requirements for practitioners to work in collaboration with parents. The statutory requirements of the EYFS once again confirmed our approach to involving parents in their children's learning (Whalley & The Pen Green Centre Team, 1997; Whalley, 2007).

At the Centre, the most recent development was in 2014 when we were designated as a Teaching School. The work of the Teaching School enables us to disseminate our work locally and nationally.

Initiatives and policies come and go, but prior to any new development at the Centre, we always reflect on our values and the principles of our work. We always consider what the new development would mean to the children and families accessing our service and ensure any new work is philosophically coherent. This guarantees we remain true to the principles that underpin the practice.

The following table shows a summary of initiatives and documents.

| Initiatives and documents | Year | Influence working with parents |
|---|---|---|
| Head Start – USA | 1960s | A compensatory programme supporting families most at risk; the significant role of parents was not recognised. |
| Urie Bronfenbrenner | 1970s | Bronfenbrenner's work identified the important links between home and settings such as schools. |
| Chris Athey | 1970s | Athey's work recognised parents as making valuable contributions to their children's learning. Theory was shared with parents to develop a more equal relationship between parents and practitioners. |
| Margy Whalley | 1983 | Whalley valued parents as important educators of their children and recognised them as having a critical role to play in the exchange of information relating to children's learning at home and in the setting. |
| Patrick Easen | 1992 | Easen's work recognised the importance of involving parents in their children's learning, valuing parents as the experts in relation to their children. |

| Initiatives and documents | Year | Influence working with parents |
|---|---|---|
| Department for Education & Employment Early Excellence Centres (EECs) | 1997 | EECs promoted in an integrated approach to working with young children, breaking down the division between education and care. Services were intended to meet the needs of families in the local community. |
| Department for Education & Employment Sure Start | 1998 | Sure Start Local Programmes provided high-quality experiences for children in partnership with parents, exchanging information and respecting the contribution parents made. |
| Department for Education & Skills Birth to Three Matters | 2002 | A framework to support practitioners working with children from birth to three years and their families. |
| Department for Education & Skills Green paper "Every Child Matters" | 2003 | The intention of the green paper was to support parents to improve their parenting and in turn improve children's lives through universal services, targeted and specialist support and compulsory action. |
| Department for Education & Skills Neighbourhood Nursery Initiative | 2004 | The Neighbourhood Nursery Initiative was set up to support families in the most disadvantaged areas by providing childcare for families wanting to take up paid employment or training that would lead to employment. |
| Department for Education Early Years Foundation Stage (EYFS) | 2008 | The EYFS set a requirement for settings to allocate children a Key Person and identified that the Key Person must engage and support parents in guiding their child's development at home. |
| Frank Field | 2010 | The Frank Field report recognised the importance of supporting children in the earliest years and recognising the role parents played in their child's learning. |
| Graham Allen | 2011 | The Graham Allen report recognised the importance of early intervention, providing support early before problems arise and valuing the role of parents in their children's learning and future aspirations. |
| Department for Education (Revised EYFS) | 2014 | The EYFS continued to highlight the role of parents and practitioners working in partnership. There was an emphasis placed on supporting parents to understand the importance of supporting their children's learning. |

## Introduction to Pen Green Centre

Pen Green Centre is in Corby, Northamptonshire. The Centre was set up as part of a substantive under-fives initiative and is housed in a 1930s former comprehensive school. At the Centre, we offer high-quality education and care for children and their families. We also offer information and support services for parents through home visiting, group work, health interventions, adult education and training, as well as the professional development, training and dissemination of good practice through the Research, Development and Training Base, and the Teaching School. The principal functions of the Centre have remained constant over the last thirty-three years, although we have significantly developed the accommodation. We have maintained our principles of operation, withstood radical changes in local government, and responded creatively to new legislation and to major demographic changes.

In the Centre, we employ over 130 staff from different professional backgrounds including Early Years, Community Education, Social Work, Health, and Further and Higher Education. It is critical that, as a staff team, we share a common set of values. These values, with the attitudes and expectations of the staff, create the culture of the organisation (Day *et al.*, 1998). The staff team need to have a shared vision and ethos, clear principles that underpin the work and always work across professional disciplines in a way that is philosophically consistent.

## Principles of operation

Our principles of operation outline how we respond to the needs of children and families at Pen Green. We believe that the most effective way of providing coherent education, health and social care services to families with young children is through an integrated Centre such as Pen Green. We want our services to be flexible, responsive, accessible and offered at times that suit families' needs. The services must be driven by the feedback from families, the local data and a diagnosis of what is needed.

We believe that education and care are indivisible, and that the early years curriculum offered is developmentally appropriate for young children, and it recognises the central position of play and language in early learning. We recognise that education begins at birth, and we therefore recognise the key role parents play as their child's first educators and the parents' commitment to their children's early education. We know it is critical to get to know each individual child and their family and always to use the child's interests as the starting point for planning.

We provide services that are respectful of children and parents' individual differences; we value and celebrate ethnic, linguistic and cultural diversity. We focus not only on the education of the child, but we also consider the needs of the families. We offer parent education and adult community education for parents within the Centre.

We have a clear commitment to the staff working within the Centre, and our belief is that the workers need to be highly trained, reflective practitioners with excellent opportunities for professional development. They need to be concerned with empowerment and community regeneration.

## Introducing key principles

The staff members at Pen Green believe that *children, parents and staff should feel strong, feel in control, feel able to question, and feel able to choose*. It is important that staff follow these principles in our education and care settings for children aged from nine months to three years. We support children's independence and autonomy, and you can read more about how the principles that underpin our practice informed the development of these spaces in Chapter 2.

We believe that *parents and children both have rights*, and it is the responsibility of the workers to ensure parents and children are held central to our work. Whalley (2001) on setting up Pen Green clearly had the vision that the Centre would be staffed by a multi-disciplinary team that would not only work with the children but also value working in partnership with parents.

A third key principle is that *parenting is a key concern for both men and women*. We work hard to ensure that all parents are supported and both fathers and mothers have an important role in their child's education and care.

Our fourth principle is our belief in *creating a culture of high expectations for children, families and the staff*. We want children and families to access services that are meaningful for them and support them to flourish and achieve positive outcomes. We want the staff to have high expectations for the children they work with and the families. We also want them to have high expectations for themselves, creating a culture of continuous development, reflection and learning.

## My first experience of Pen Green

When I walked through the door of Pen Green as a student in 1985, I had no idea what to expect. Two of my fellow students had been attending Pen Green for their nursery placement. As part of a project we had been working on in college, we were asked to present a puppet show to a small group of children. Four of us asked to go to Pen Green to present the puppet show. The two students that had been attending Pen Green had spoken fondly of it during our days together in college; I was intrigued to see what it would be like.

I had only been in the Centre for a few minutes when a small wooden block came flying past me. A little boy stood nearby grinning at me. A worker immediately came over to the little boy and bent down to him, she spoke to him for several minutes and I heard her gently saying "You are so good at throwing; shall we go outside and get the balls out? I wonder if we can make some targets for you to throw at". The little boy eagerly agreed and went outside with the worker. I remember admiring the calm way in which the worker spoke to the little boy. I often reflected back on that early experience and had a high regard for the staff member's knowledge of the child. She was attuned to what he was doing and she seemed clear about what her pedagogical role was in supporting the child (Whalley & Arnold, 1997; Lawrence *et al.*, 2015). I later came to learn that the worker was supporting the child's schematic interest (Athey, 2007, 2013; Arnold, 2010). She knew that the child throwing the brick was exploring a strong trajectory schema, and she wanted to support him rather than shut down his efforts to throw. She immediately considered a more appropriate way for him to follow his interest without stopping his desire to throw objects. The staff member was holding the child's interest central and giving him the opportunity to make appropriate choices.

I returned to the Centre in 1994, this time as lecturer in Early Years. I was a course tutor at a local college of Further Education and Higher Education and would encourage the students to attend Pen Green as part of their practical placement experience. I had read a great deal about Pen Green since my initial visit and had used some of their publications as reading material on the courses I taught. The Centre had an excellent reputation locally and nationally, and I wanted the students I was supporting to have the opportunity to observe and learn from the outstanding practitioners in the Centre. I was fortunate that at that time I had the opportunity to visit all my students during their practical work placements; I regularly visited the Centre to observe the students in the setting. I deeply admired the work of the Family Workers in the Centre and respected their approach to supporting children and families. During the period between 1994 and 2000 when I regularly attended Pen Green as a visiting tutor, I began to understand more deeply the ethos, values and principles of the Centre.

It felt to me that I was connecting with like-minded people. It was a meeting of hearts and minds. I realised I shared their beliefs and agreed with the shared ethos within the Centre and how the work of the team helped to create a deeply thoughtful environment. Sergiovanni (1992) describes the heart is to do with what a person believes, values and is committed to, and the head is to do with the theories of practice. The head is shaped by the heart and drives the hand; in turn, reflections on decisions and actions affirm or reshape the heart and head.

## Working full-time at Pen Green

In 2000, I came to work at Pen Green full-time. I coordinated the Early Years services for the Sure Start local programme. My first day was a whole Centre team-building event. It soon became clear to me that it was during events such as this one that a shared philosophy, vision and agreed principles of working with children and families were discussed and agreed.

It remains central to our work today that staff teams have time to come together across the professional disciplines to reflect on their work, valuing and respecting what each other brings. I recognise that sharing philosophies, values and beliefs supports successful collaboration. The shared values and shared practices enable communication and build trust (Childs, 2000). Working in an organisation with shared values and principles assists the coherent offer of the organisation and supports staff to provide a high-quality service for children and their families. We are trying to create synergistic working relationships where staff members are willing to try new things, knowing that their innovation is underpinned by the principles of the organisation.

## The four key principles that underpin the work at Pen Green

To look in more detail at the four key principles, it is useful to illustrate the work with case study examples. At Pen Green, we want children, parents and staff to feel that it is their Centre. We want to create an environment where they feel safe and are able to make choices.

### Principle one

The following case study shows how we support *children, parents and staff to feel strong, feel in control, feel able to question and feel able to choose*. Henry attended the Couthie, and this is the parent's perspective of how his transition through to nursery was thought about and supported.

"It was with great sadness that my son was leaving the warmth of his first nursery experience and the practitioners who had supported his first separation. I first learnt about it when his Family Worker told me that she thought it would be a good idea, as he was spending a great deal of time in the main nursery due to the fact that his friends had transitioned a short time ago. I was amazed and pleased that the environment afforded him to be able to self-transition to another area of the setting and that the practitioners had identified his wants and needs. My son had chosen his practitioner in the other area. This was the person who was Family Worker to his closest friends. Not long after my son had made the decision, both workers came to my family home to meet my son, one to end their relationship and the other to begin theirs. They both worked so hard to support us all during this time that was filled with anxiety. Soon after the visit, I received video and photographic observations from both practitioners, showing me where he spent most of his time. We discussed when he would make the transition and myself and my partner booked time off work to spend time settling him in to the nursery. The first week he spent each morning in this new environment, a change to his two full days. It was felt that the frequency would support him and enable him to get to know the routine, the other children and his Family Worker better. The first morning, he

*(Continued)*

stuck to my side like glue. As the week progressed, he became more confi-dent and I began to leave him. The first time I suggested leaving him, he went back to the 0–3 provision and asked one of the workers to support the separation, knowing that they were very familiar in the separation ritual we had established – one where he went to the door, buzzed me out and kissed me goodbye. After this initial separation, at subsequent separations, my son allowed his new Family Worker to support him. What helped to establish the relationship was her fascination in his learning and develop-ment made evident by the vast quantity of observations I was receiving via the online tool for exchanging observations and her questions to get to know and understand him. A further home visit helped the relationship to form further, and my son became very engaged with her. In addition to all of this, the setting enabled him to take his bike in with him. His bike is a very important part of him. He uses it every day and it is always close by."

### SO WHAT DID WE LEARN?

- The importance of home visits in order to support the relationships between the child, the family and the Family Worker.
- The importance of the relationship between the Family Workers to support the transition of the child.
- Provision of an environment that affords children's autonomy and agency in order for them to self-transition.
- Listening and responding to the child's voice (Henry's interest in the nurs-ery space informed the worker he was ready to make the transition).
- The importance of honest dialogue between workers and parents.

In this case study, Henry was able to feel in control and make decisions about where he wanted to spend his time and with whom. The Family Worker had the confidence to support his decision and help him make a smooth transition from the Couthie through to nursery.

The parent was able to choose the new Family Worker taking the lead from her child knowing he was comfortable and confident with her in the nursery setting.

### Principle two

The work of the staff at Pen Green is to ensure that both children and parents are held central to all the services we offer. Parents have a strong voice in the Centre during the governors' meetings, parent forum meetings, home visits and through daily chats with the staff. I truly believe that it is important for parents to be involved in making decisions about how services are developed and offered. The National Quality Improvement Network (2010) describes the development of services as a joint venture between stakeholders. They explain the involvement of families are crucial if the services are going to meet the needs of a particular community. The following case study demonstrates how the engagement at Pen Green supports *parents and children to both have rights*. A family I worked with provides an excellent example of how a parent was supported by her Family Worker to access services in the Centre and went on to engage in the development of new services for families at Pen Green, making decisions about the new provision and always ensuring her rights were considered as well as the rights of her child. The following case study documents Claire's involvement in the Centre with her second child, James.

"I was pregnant with my second child when Tracey, our Family Worker, told me about the Great Expectations group. I was going to go to the group, I was not confident and I was not sure I wanted to go to the group on my own. Tracey came with me for the first session and stayed with me for about half of the session.

"I also used other groups in the Centre with James. It was good for James as he was socialising with other children; there were no other children in the family that age. It was time for him to play with other children. With James, it was specific focussed time, no house work, no work, just our time together.

"I became involved in the Couthie development (the new nursery space). I started this just after I had James and I met three parents in the group. A working group had been set up to think about the development. They had received an invite to the working group and I hadn't had one. A parent mentioned it to me and I came along. I don't think I really knew what I was coming to. We looked at the development in small chunks. It didn't feel like we had lots of responsibility as the worker did it in a way that broke it down in small chunks. I liked having a say, thinking about why we were choosing certain things and the reasons behind the decisions. It was interesting to think about what had been learnt from the development of the Nest and how we could use this in developing the new space.

"I really enjoyed being involved in thinking about the development of the Couthie and the drop-in space. It was going to be a new, fresh space. It was great to be involved from the start."

## SO WHAT DID WE LEARN?

- The importance of providing support to meet the individual needs of the parent.
- The importance of recognising the valuable input of parents not only in their children's lives, but also what they have to offer the Centre.

- The need to involve parents at their pace.
- The need to simultaneously consider the offer for children and parents.
- The importance of believing in parents to take on new roles and responsibilities and sensitively supporting them to do this.

### Principle three

The staff at Pen Green want to ensure that both mothers and fathers are involved and have a voice in their child's care and education. A high proportion of parents that engage with the Centre are mothers, and they access the services with their children. We have to ensure that the services are accessible for fathers too. We offer home visits to all the children that attend our Nest and Couthie, and we will offer additional home visits to families when they share the care of the children. We offer services on Saturday and Sunday to provide opportunities for fathers to come into the Centre and access the exciting spaces and resources with their children. This is particularly important for fathers who are not able to access the Centre during the week due to work commitments and for fathers that only have access with their children at the weekend.

The following case study of Adam and Alfie demonstrates the principle *parenting is a key concern for both men and women*. Adam clearly explains that he came to Pen Green and knew his role as dad to Alfie was an important one. Adam was aware that experiences may be different for mums than they are for dads, but he felt his role as a dad supporting Alfie's development and learning was understood by the staff. He reflected on his experience of being a dad using services within the Centre:

> "I came to the Growing Together group. My parenting with Alfie was supported in the group. I was always asked "How are you getting on"? I was given the opportunity to talk to staff and have time with the staff. I knew the staff were saying if you need us, we are here and available for you. I noticed the staff offer people the chance to ask for help if they need it. As a dad, you are supported to be with your child. The support isn't just available to mums.
>
> "The staff treat everyone as an individual. Individually you are noticed, and as a dad you are made to feel welcome. Angela (Adam's wife) knew the staff here; it was like home from home for her, as she had used the Centre with Lewis, her older child. When I came, I noticed everyone would make time to speak to me and have conversations with me as Alfie's dad. I didn't have to come with Angela to get noticed.
>
> "I found, as a dad, the 'drop-in' was safe. I felt comfortable. I came to the groups and the drop-in to have a focus with Alfie, and we would be there for an hour or so. We would play, with him leading the way. I followed his interests and I would go where he wanted me to go. The play was definitely child-led. Angela had done Parents Involvement in their Children's

Learning (PICL) with Lewis and she knew how to support his learning. She explained to me about how children learn and develop. At Pen Green, the staff support parents and help them to understand how children learn and develop. Alfie is now three, and more recently I have been involved in wider aspects of the Centre. I attended a consultation event run by the Local Authority. I have been on an interview panel and we appointed a senior leader, and I have recently been appointed as the Parent Director representing Pen Green on a newly-formed Community Interest Company. I look forward, as a dad, to continuing my involvement with supporting Alfie's learning and my role in assisting the work of the Centre."

SO WHAT DID WE LEARN?

- The need for staff to make groups accessible and interesting for dads and mums. Adam felt that the group was as much for him as it was his wife.
- The importance of building relationships with dads in the groups so that they feel included and comfortable.
- The opportunity to give dads time with staff to talk about their child, not putting them under pressure, but as a worker making yourself available at a time that suits the parent.
- The importance of sharing child development theory with dads and mums in the group, making links with the child's learning at home and in the Centre.

## Principle four

The fourth principle that underpins the work of the Centre is to have a culture where we want the best for every child, parent and worker. We want the Centre to be a setting that seriously considers and supports the learning and development of every child, parent and worker.

The following case study explains how we *create a culture of high expectations for children, families and the staff.* This case study identifies how Jemma was encouraged to engage in projects, was valued for her contribution initiating new ideas and supported to take up a role volunteering in the Centre.

"I had been involved in the development of the Couthie and continued to sustain my engagement at the Centre. I was involved right from the beginning in setting up a 'Friends of Pen Green' group. This consisted of a group of parents that held fundraising events and linked with senior staff to represent the voice of the parents across the organisation. The group of parents applied for funding through the Department of Education to
*(Continued)*

explore setting up a charity to help secure the future sustainability of the Centre. As a result of this project I, with other parents, set up a Charitable Incorporated Organisation, '4Corby Children'. The aim was to represent children under five and their families across the town of Corby. I undertook some training and became a volunteer. I volunteered in the breastfeeding support group and then went on to gain paid employment supporting the group work programme. I also put myself forward for the role of governor at Pen Green. I was successfully elected and actively engaged in the role of parent governor. All the time I knew staff members believed in the contribution I could make, and they recognised my journey of development. My eldest child went to school and I became a governor there, too."

### SO WHAT DID WE LEARN?

- The importance of staff having high expectations of parents and valuing their contributions, no matter how big or small.
- The need for staff to get to know parents and find out about their skills and interests (the staff got to know Jemma and respected the contribution she could make to the work of the Centre).
- The importance of staff working with parents as equal partners working on interesting and stimulating projects (Jemma was open to the new learning opportunities and embraced the challenge of setting up the Charitable Incorporated Organisation; this was recognised by staff and effectively supported).
- The importance of staff recognising the valuable contribution parents make to the running of the Centre and creating the vision for the future (Jemma offered her time as a volunteer and a governor, working in the Centre and sharing her aspirations for the future).

In summary, we all have to work hard to ensure that the principles are shared with staff teams, and be certain that they are understood and they underpin our practice. The principles that underpin the work of the organisation need to be evident in the families' experiences. We have to ensure the rhetoric of what is described is the reality for the children and their families. I want all staff, volunteers and students to hold firm to the principles that underpin their work, ensuring that they offer high-quality education and care in collaboration with parents and external partners.

## References

Allen, G. (2011) *Early Intervention: The Next Steps*. London: Cabinet Office.

Arnold. C. & The Pen Green Team (2010) *Understanding Schemas and Emotion in Early Childhood*. London: Sage.

Athey, C. (2007) *Extending Thought in Young Children: A Parent-Teacher Partnership* (2nd edn). London: Paul Chapman Publishing Ltd.

Athey, C. in Mairs & The Pen Green Team (2013) Edited by Arnold, C. *Young Children Learning Through Schemas*. Oxon: Routledge.

Ball, C. (1994) *Start Right: The Importance of Early Learning*. London: Royal Society of Arts.

Barber, M. (1996) *The Learning Game*. London: Victor Gollancz.

Barnes, J., Desousa, C., Frost, M., Harper, G., Laban, D & The NESS Team (2005) *Changes in the Characteristics of Sure Start Local Programme areas – 2000/2001 to 2002/2003*. Nottingham: DfES Publications.

Bronfenbrenner, U. (1994) Ecological models of human development. In *International Encyclopedia of Education* (Vol. 3, 2nd edn). Oxford: Elsevier. Reprinted in Gauvin, M. & Cole, M. (Eds.), *Readings on the Development of Children*, 2nd edn. (1993, pp. 37–43). New York: Freeman.

Bruce, T. (1997) *Early Childhood Education* (2nd edn). London: Hodder & Stoughton.

Childs, M. (2000). Inter-organisational Collaboration in the Information Age. MA Dissertation in Practitioner Research and Consultancy. School of Education, University of Wolverhampton.

Day, C., Hall, C. & Whitaker, P. (1998) *Developing Leadership in Primary Schools*. London: Paul Chapman Publishing Ltd.

Department for Children School & Families (DCSF) (2008) *The Early Years Foundation Stage: Setting Standards for Learning, Development and Care for Children from Birth to Five*. London: DCSF.

Department for Education (DfE) (2014) *The Early Years Foundation Stage: Setting Standards for Learning, Development and Care for Children from Birth to Five*. London: DfE.

Department for Education & Employment (DfEE) (1997) *Excellence in Schools*. White Paper. London: DfEE.

Department for Education & Employment (DfEE) (1998) *Meeting the Childcare Challenge: A Framework and Consultation Document*. London: DfEE.

Department for Education & Skills (DfES) (2002) *Birth to Three Matters: A Framework to Support Children in Their Earliest Years*. London: DfES/Sure Start.

Department for Education & Skills (DfES) (2003) *Every Child Matters*. Green Paper. London: HMSO.

Department for Education & Skills (DfES) (2004) *Working Together: A Sure Start Guide to the Childcare and Early Education Field*. Annesley: DfES Publications.

Easen, P., Kendall, P. & Shaw, J. (1992) Parents and educators: dialogue and developing through partnership. *Children and Society,* vol. 6, no 4, pp. 282–96.

Field, F. (2010) *Foundation Years: Preventing Poor Children Becoming Poor Adults*. London: Cabinet Office.

Langston, A. (2006) *Parents Matter: Supporting the Birth to Three Matters Framework*. Edited by Abbott, L. & Langston, A. Berkshire: Open University Press.

Lawrence, P., Gallagher, T. & The Pen Green Team (2015) Pedagogic Strategies: a conceptual framework for effective parent and practitioner strategies when working with children under five. *Early Childhood Development and Care,* vol. 185, no 11–12, pp. 1978–1994. doi:10.1080/03004430.2015.1028390.

National Quality Improvement Network (2010) *Principles for Engaging with Families*. London: NCB.

Pascal, C. & Bertram, T. (2002) *Early Childhood Education and Acre in the UK*. www. practicalpreschool.com/Resources/Yearbook.pdf (June 18, 2003).

Sergiovanni, T. J. (1992) *Moral Leadership: Getting to the Heart of School Improvement.* San Francisco, CA: Jossey-Bass.

Whalley, M. (1999) *Corby Sure Start Delivery Plan.* Corby: Pen Green Research Development and Training Base.

Whalley, M. (2007) *Involving Parents in Their Children's Learning* (2nd edn). London: Sage.

Whalley, M. & Arnold, C. (1997) *Effective Pedagogic Strategies, TTA Summary of Research Findings.* Corby: The Pen Green Centre for Under Fives and Their Families.

Whalley, M. & The Pen Green Centre Team (1997) *Working with Parents.* London: Hodder Education.

Whalley, M. & The Pen Green Centre Team (2001) *Involving Parents in Their Children's Learning.* London: Paul Chapman Publishing.

Whalley, M. & The Pen Green Centre Team (2017) *Involving Parents in Their Children's Learning: A Knowledge Sharing Approach* (3rd edn). London: Sage.

## Chapter 2

# Setting up the baby and toddler provision at Pen Green

*Tracy Gallagher and Colette Tait*

In this chapter, we describe the conceptualisation and development of our education and care provision for children from nine months to two years at Pen Green – the Baby and Toddler Nest. We go on to describe the development of a second provision, the Couthie, to meet the demand for places and respond to the government's initiative – funding early learning for two-year olds (DFE, 2014).

In 2004, we opened the Baby and Toddler Nest. This was our education and care provision for children under two years of age. We set up a 'steering group' to consider the conceptualisation and planning of the provision. During the year that this took to do, we worked with the steering group members who were experts from the early years field, staff members from the Pen Green multidisciplinary team and parents using the Centre.

We had been designated as a Sure Start Children's Centre in 2004 (DfES, 2004), and part of the 'core offer' for us, as a phase one Centre, was to provide full-day care for children two years and under. We were aware of the conflicting literature and evidence suggesting that the experiences of children in their early years are critical determinants of future progress and attainment educationally and as a member of the social community (Fabian & Dunlop, 2002). We were also mindful of our own beliefs about the youngest children spending significant amounts of time in group care. The research evidence from Bain and Barnett (1986, p. 59) reported, 'If day nurseries persist in their present form they will continue to cause damage to the younger children in their care, particularly the under threes...'. We were concerned that unless the provision was of the highest quality, this type of care for very young children could be detrimental to them and adversely affect their social and emotional development. We wanted to ensure that this would not be the case at Pen Green. We wanted to offer the highest-quality provision, but we had to make sure that we would be financially viable. These two commitments were not easy to reconcile.

## The role of the steering group

The steering group's discussions helped us to widely consider the following:

- the principles that would underpin our practice with a focus on working with younger children,
- our understanding of theoretical frameworks in relation to younger children,

- conceptualising an environment that would be suitable for the youngest children,
- the role of the Family Worker within this provision.

### The principles underpinning our practice

The Centre opened in 1983, and we had clear beliefs that influenced our thinking and underpinned our practice with children and families. We believed

- children, parents and staff should feel strong, feel in control, feel able to question, and feel able to choose;
- that parents and children both have rights;
- parenting is a key concern for both men and women;
- in creating a culture of high expectations for children, families and the staff.

(There is more detail regarding the principles that underpin our work in Chapter 1.)

At the time of developing the Nest, we also considered our attitudes specifically in relation to our work with the youngest children. We knew having highly qualified, reflective practitioners was important, and we wanted to support families with the youngest children living in complex situations. Our aims were to give parents some respite, particularly when they were facing difficult periods, and support parents to return to work, attend training or gain volunteering experience in the Centre.

We believed in providing a high-quality provision that met the needs of families living in disadvantaged circumstances and on the edge of social exclusion. We wanted to ensure that the Nest felt like a haven for them and their children. We agreed that children would be given priority places, particularly the children in our local community, so those living closest to us and most in need of support would be allocated a priority place. We also wanted to ensure we provided a responsive and flexible service to parents who were in need of support to enable them to work or take up a role volunteering.

## Vision and values

In the steering group, it was important to consider what we really believed as a group of early years experts, early years educators and parents working together to conceptualise this development. To gain clarity about what we valued and what we wanted, we undertook a negotiation exercise to consider this.

All steering group members were given six index cards and were asked to write one statement on each card. The statement had to relate to what they *personally* believed were the most important considerations to make with regard to the new provision and across the organisation. There was an emphasis on really considering the needs of younger children, and a wish for participants not to just see babies and young toddlers as small three-year-olds. At the time of developing the provision, the Birth to Three Matters framework defined an aim that was to value and celebrate children, their individuality, efforts and achievements (DfES, 2002). We wanted the staff to recognise the amazing abilities of each individual child and celebrate their achievements.

The group members, once they had completed their six cards, got into pairs. Each person read their statements to the other. No amendments to any of the cards were allowed. The pair then discussed the range of statements to really get to the meaning behind the statement and the words used within them. They then had to negotiate with each other to end up with six statements between them.

Pairs then joined together to repeat the negotiation. Once repeated negotiations had taken place, the group agreed on six values and beliefs that they felt should underpin this development with regard to what children and families attending our setting deserve.

The final six statements were as follows:

Children and families in the 21st century deserve to have

1   A provision that is cognitively challenging, supporting autonomy and mastery, and emotionally supportive;
2   A flexible service that is responsive to family needs, for example

    • Working in collaboration with parents,
    • Documenting children's learning and well-being (Laevers, 1997),
    • Giving priority to families within the local community;

3   A Key Person (Elfer *et al.*, 2003) who is consistent and reliable and who receives ongoing training and professional development;
4   An environment that is stimulating, exciting, challenging and nurturing for all children;
5   A broad routine that contains them emotionally, supports them having fun and enjoyment, and is flexible enough to meet their individual needs;
6   Workers who are committed to knowing about and understanding the detail of a child's life.

It was important that a member of this group was able to liaise with the architect and the builders throughout the process, in order to ensure that the vision and values debated and decided at this stage came to fruition in the finished design.

## Steering group discussions

### The age of the children attending

At the onset, we made a decision to only offer the provision for children from twelve months of age and over because we knew working with younger children was extremely specialist work and we were not prepared to do this unless we knew we could do it well. We also had a local network of childminders who used the Centre and attended training events. The practice of these particular childminders was philosophically coherent with our practice at the Centre. We worked collaboratively with them to advocate home-based care for the very young children and then supported the transition through to our baby and toddler provision when the child turned one year. Our exception to this was the young children for whom life was complex and they were living in disadvantaged circumstances, for instance, those children on child protection plans. In these situations, we would offer younger children sessions in the Nest to give the parents some respite. In addition, we would also work with the parent and child within the Nest environment, supporting them with their developing relationship. The steering group agreed that in these situations, it would be a positive experience to offer the children a place in the Nest.

### Number of sessions

We deliberated for a long time with the steering group members regarding the number of sessions children would be able to attend. We considered the experience for children who could potentially be attending full-time, which meant possibly attending up to fifty hours a week. We also considered what we would expect as a minimum number of sessions appropriate for children to attend. For a child attending full-time, this would mean that they would be in the setting for more hours than their own Key Person (Elfer *et al.*, 2003) and would therefore experience additional separations from their worker as well as their parents/carers. We also considered whether group care was the most appropriate care for very young children. We agreed we would have a range of daily hours and weekly hours available for parents including an eight-hour day, nine-hour day and ten-hour day. Workers would discuss with parents each individual child's attendance plan to agree the most appropriate number of hours for each child.

It was also agreed that to ensure continuity and consistency for children that we would ask parents to book a minimum of two sessions per week. We agreed that anything less than two sessions per week could be difficult for children to establish a routine between home and setting.

### Home visiting

When we opened The Nest, we already had a long tradition of home visiting at Pen Green. Parents told us that they valued this time to offer important information about their child, what their special interests are, who the special people in their lives are and so on. When a place was allocated to a child, the Family Worker would visit the child and their family at home. The home visits are ideal opportunities to exchange information between the parents and the worker in a relaxed setting. The worker can find out about the child's current interests, which will be useful information for planning the environment and planning experiences for the child when in the setting (Manning-Morton & Thorp, 2015). Parents can also use this opportunity to ask questions and find out any information they want to know about the setting.

### Fee structure

We had to consider the fee structure for the provision. Funding through the Neighbourhood Nursery Initiative (DfES, 2004) had been allocated from the Local Authority. This allocated funding enabled us to advertise and market the new provision, purchase resources and equipment and provide a small amount of money to enable start-up costs. The 'reducing scale' model of funding meant that if we didn't fill the spaces in the provision immediately, we had a small amount of funding in reserves to cover the staff costs.

We had to agree on the fee-charging structure and consider fee-charging policies to ensure long-term financial viability and sustainability. We also identified income generation possibilities such as offering training to other early years educators and speaking on visitors' days at the centre to fund staff professional development opportunities.

### Child development and psychodynamic theory informing our practice

The workers in the Nest have a constructivist pedagogy in which "the teacher seriously considers what the child brings to the learning situation" (Athey, 1990, p. 31). The theoretical concepts that underpin the work in the Nest helped staff to think about individual children's development and what they brought to the situation.

The child development theory informing our practice includes the following:

Schema theory (Athey, 2007)

'Schemas are patterns of repeatable actions that lead to early categories and then to logical classifications (Athey, 2007). By understanding children's schemas, we could resource the environment richly to support a range of schemas.'

Involvement & Well-being (Laevers, 1997, 2005)

'Ferre Laevers has spent many years researching how experiences affect children's behaviour, body language, self-worth and sense of self-efficacy. Laevers writes that 'for development to occur, children need to be high on emotional well-being' and 'high on involvement' (Laevers, 1997). It would be important for us to consider and support children's emotional well-being in order for them to engage in deep-level learning.'

Pedagogic Strategies (Whalley & Arnold, 1997; Lawrence *et al.*, 2015)

> 'These are a range of strategies adopted by the adults when working effec-
> tively with children. They include things such as getting down to the child's
> level and acknowledging their feelings.' (For information about our more
> recent work looking at Pedagogic Strategies, see Chapter 7.)

The psychoanalytic theory informing our practice includes the following:

Attachment (Bowlby, 1969)

> 'The concept of attachment describes how adults and children form and
> develop reciprocal relationships (Bowlby, 1969).'

Holding (Winnicott, 1965)

> 'The concept of holding describes the emotional holding parents can give
> their baby by holding him or her in mind (Winnicott, 1965).'

Containment (Bion, 1962)

> 'The concept of containment describes the parent taking in the baby's dis-
> tress, understanding it and responding so that the baby feels emotionally
> looked after, contained (Bion, 1962).'

(More information about the psychoanalytic theory we use can be found in
Chapters 4 and 9.)

Our knowledge of child development theory and psychoanalytic theory
helped us when purchasing equipment and resources. We considered the needs
of the very young children and how we would set up the environment to support
deep-level learning (Laevers, 1997) and children's schematic explorations. We
purchased open-ended equipment to support children's individual interests. We
also considered the type of environment that would be conducive to children
feeling 'Held' and 'Contained' (Bion, 1962; Winnicott, 1965).

## Conceptualising the environment

At the Centre, we have a long-held tradition of supporting professional development opportunities and promoting an environment of reflection and dialogue
where, through observation and reflection, the workers are able to "accumu-
late deep understanding" (Athey, 1990) of individual children's development.
Throughout the planning phase, we supported staff to visit nationally and internationally renowned settings to learn from colleagues and observe best practice
when working with the youngest children. The visits to settings, together with
reflection and discussion, helped the staff to further conceptualise the Pen Green
provision.

Staff visited Bognor, Burnley and London in the United Kingdom and
Denmark, Australia and New Zealand. We saw the following:

- Open spaces that allowed children to freely move around the environment, playing in a solitary fashion or playing with others as described by Bruce (1991) in her twelve features of play
- Resources arranged at low levels to enable children to freely access them
- Environments that enabled the children to independently access the outdoor spaces
- Provision that gave children the opportunity to have first-hand experiences (Bruce, 1991)
- Kitchen areas that were connected to the main nursery spaces so that children could observe meals and snacks being prepared
- Areas for children to rest and sleep that were connected to play areas

In order to think about the kind of environment we wanted to create, we had to have a clear 'image of the child' reflecting 'our values, our aspirations for the next generation, our beliefs about child development, and ... our cultural perspective' (Edwards *et al.*, 1998, p. 296).

We appointed an architect and began to conceptualise the design. This was an adaptation of the existing building which is a 1930s secondary school, with long corridors and rooms off corridors. The new design allowed a small capital project to extend the area. We wanted to make sure that the provision flowed and felt as if it had always been part of the original building. We knew we wanted an environment that supported children's autonomy and decision-making. We wanted children to have real-life experiences just as they would do at home. We also wanted the children to feel connected to their Family Worker throughout the day, using them as a secure base (Bowlby, 1969). We were mindful that children would have already experienced a major transition, separating from their main carer to begin attending the Nest. We know children experience many transitions, and these are critical periods for young children. It is recognised how important it is for children to make smooth transitions, and it is when we get these transitions right that we help children to feel safe, relaxed and comfortable in their new environment (Brostrom, 2002). As we conceptualised the Nest, we wanted to minimise the children experiencing further separations, wherever possible, throughout their day in the Nest, and this thinking had a profound impact on the design that we came up with.

When developing the Nest space, we had to work with the fabric of the existing building and conceptualise a small extension. The main corridor area was part of the original building, and there was very little we could do to alter this layout. We did, however, plan for this to be part of the entrance into the provision. Children would be able to see the Nest as they approached the corridor through the existing Den nursery. Children would also be able to see parents. We knew this would be critical in supporting children to manage separations and reunions as they would be able to wave goodbye as they watched their parents leaving and greet them as they arrived to collect them (Figures 2.1 and 2.2).

(a)

(b)

*Figure 2.1 (a,b)* Children/parents at the gate

*Figure 2.2* Children at the gate

## The kitchen area

The kitchen area was an integral feature to the design of the space as it was designed in a way that would enable children to maintain a connection to their Family Worker. The worker would not have to go off to another area to prepare drinks, snacks or bottles. Similarly, when the food delivery order arrived, the children could have the experience of unpacking the shopping, discussing the items with the worker and handing them over to the worker to be put away, just as the children would do at home (Figure 2.3).

(a)

(b)

*Figure 2.3 (a,b)* Children using the kitchen

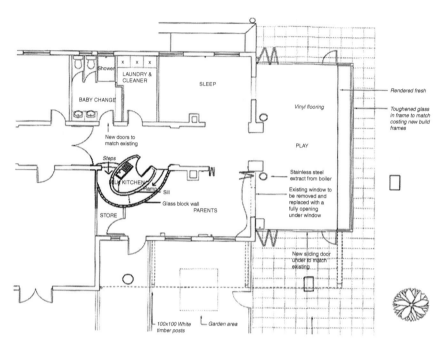

Figure 2.4 The layout of the Nest

The kitchen was designed in the shape of a rugby ball, with a slope up one side and two small steps at the other. The design allowed children the opportunity to practise separations and reunions, by disappearing out of sight behind the kitchen and re-emerging at the other side of the kitchen (Figure 2.4).

We were aware, for some children, it was the first time they had been separated from their main carer, and practising "here" and "gone" may help support them to work through feelings they may have about separating from their parent/carer. We know young children use their schemas to work through emotional events in their life that they do not have an understanding of (Arnold & The Pen Green Centre Team, 2010). This was an opportunity for us to create a space that gave the children the opportunity to feel in control of the process of separating and reuniting with their Family Worker and their peers. Children are able to both circuit the kitchen – disappearing and reappearing in the corridor – and see into the kitchen through the hatch and the glass door, enabling them to pass items into and out of the kitchen (Figure 2.5).

*Figure 2.5* The kitchen

## The play room

The small extension to the existing building enabled us to provide a play room that is divided with part of the room carpeted and used for construction and quiet experiences and an area with vinyl flooring used for messy and wet play and to access the outdoor garden area. The room was designed with low-level drawers that would allow children to access resources themselves. We had a large sandpit built in the wet area and a Belfast sink at the child's level. We knew that having some permanent equipment would help to provide a predictable and containing space with the flexibility to offer additional resources providing opportunities for children to extend their learning and explorations. The idea was that the space would encourage investigation and support cooperation (Figures 2.6 and 2.7).

*Figure 2.6* Sandpit

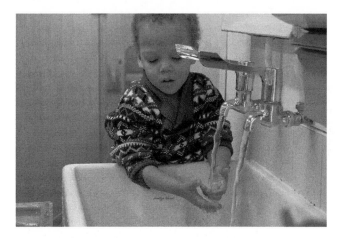

*Figure 2.7* Belfast sink

**Example from practice**

The following observation describes how the physical environment supports children's explorations.

Two children (one aged two years and six months and the other aged two
years and nine months) were playing at the water tray and Belfast sink. They
had various sizes and shapes of bottles and containers. They were deeply involved and interested in pouring from one container to another, filling and

emptying the containers (Laevers, 1997; Athey, 2007). One of the children went over to the low-level drawer situated in the wet area and fetched some lengths of clear tube which he took back to the sink. He used the tube to continue his explorations, pouring the water from a container down the tube and then into a different container. He repeated this with several different sized containers. The second child watched and then after a while joined in using a piece of tube to transport the water from one container to another.

From this observation, we can see how the environment supported the child to make decisions about what he wanted to play with, but also supported his autonomy in selecting additional resources. The child being able to independently select the additional resources enabled him to extend his explorations. By adding the tube, he was able to work out how to not only pour the water from one container to another but also pour the water down the tube, ensuring that it was connected to a container he was filling.

## The sleep room

We designed the sleep room as a space connected to the main play area (Figure 2.8). We wanted to respect each child's individual rhythm and allow them to settle for a sleep and rejoin the group as and when they wanted to. Prior to a child starting, we would discuss with the parents their child's routine and what cues to look for that would indicate their child was getting tired or in need of a rest. To begin with, the workers would look for these cues, comment on them and encourage the children to have a nap or a rest. Over time, the children began to recognise how they felt when they were tired and were able to climb into the sleep baskets. We made the decision to have sleep baskets made rather than traditional cots. Parents had clearly indicated to us that at home children would have snuggled on their lap or rested on the sofa (Figure 2.9).

We wanted to create a soft area where children could take time out to rest or sleep but they could be autonomous about deciding when they wanted to take that time. Through the experience of being supported by the Family Worker, the children are eventually able to recognise the feelings of tiredness and manage them on their own. The sleep room was designed with six sleep baskets; the baskets were designed around the measurements of cot mattresses that comply with all health and safety regulations. The baskets are low to the floor, allowing children to independently crawl in and out. The children tend to have a favourite one they like to use when resting or sleeping. As we follow the individual rhythm of each child, we rarely have more than two or three occupied at the same time. There are no doors on the sleep room; the children are able to go into the sleep room and walk through to the corridor or main play area. Visitors and staff were initially concerned that it might be too noisy for the children to sleep. Staff talked to the children about the sleep room and they soon understood that it

*Figure 2.8* Sleep room from the corridor

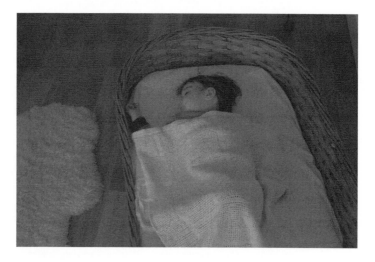

*Figure 2.9* Sleep baskets

was an area to be quiet in. We often find that in the morning children, once they have settled in, will play quietly in the sleep room settling their dolls to sleep or lifting them from the basket to say "hello". However, later in the day when the sleep baskets may be occupied by a sleeping child, the children play in other areas of the Nest. The sleep room was also designed with drapes and small dimmer star lights to soften the environment and create an ambient area conducive to relaxation.

## The windows

We created the space with low-level windows and doors that were connected to the garden areas. We wanted children to be able to observe all that was happening around them; the weather, the vehicles travelling past, the older children in the nursery garden. Parents had said to us if they heard an ambulance or a lorry going past at home, they would pull the curtains back and look out of the window. We wanted the very young children to have these same experiences just as they would at home. The design allowed us to have a panoramic window across the whole width of the extension facing the nursery garden and the road. This enabled children at all times to see what was happening outside (Figure 2.10).

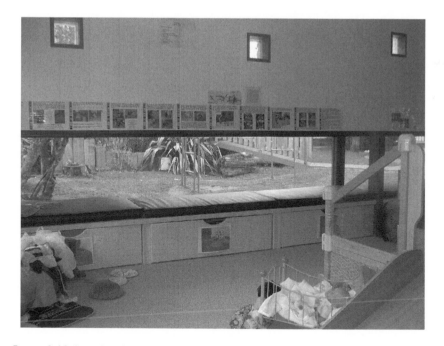

*Figure 2.10* Low level panoramic window

## The parents' room

At the time we conceptualised the Nest, we had twenty-one years' experience of working with children and families in the nursery and therefore knew that the settling-in period was critical for young children. When planning the design of the parent room, we wanted a space with a large window so the parents could see their child interacting with children and staff in the setting. The parents' room would be significant during the settling-in period, as this is an important time when parents and staff can really share information and begin to develop a relationship. Over the course of the two week settling-in period, parents begin to gradually separate from their child by moving away from their child for short periods of time. Over time, the child experiences the feelings of being left by their parent but begins to internalise being 'held in mind', secure in the knowledge that their parent will return (Winnicott, 1965).

## Practical spaces

We developed a laundry room within the provision as inevitably we would be washing and drying clothes for the children. The design of the main play room provided the children with access to the Belfast sink and creative experiences every day. We also needed the laundry facilities to wash the bedding for the sleep baskets after each child had used them for a rest or sleep.

The Nest provision was also designed with a staff toilet, child toilet and nappy-changing facilities. This meant that the environment was self-contained with all the necessary facilities in the Nest area.

### Upholding our vision and values: working with the architect and the builders

Throughout the process, a staff member who had been involved from the beginning was identified as the Project Manager, and this person liaised regularly with both the architect and the builders. We felt it was crucial that the vision that was developed within the steering group was upheld and could be seen in the end result. We had learnt from a previous building project that it was important that there was only one point of contact for the architect and builders. In the previous project, there had been several points of contact and several people able to make decisions. This led to confusion and conflicting advice, making the process more problematic than it needed to be. It was a case of "too many cooks spoil the broth". We were keen to avoid this problem second time around.

There were several points during the process where the Project Manager had to "fight" to ensure that what was wanted by, and for, the children, families and staff was understood by the architect and builders and was able to be realised. This was not always easy!

At one point during the proceedings, the budget was incredibly tight. The architect put forward an argument to change the design of the kitchen (which the children could circuit around and see into easily). As this feature was so important in terms of giving the children the opportunity to play with the concept of "here" and "gone" through circuiting around the kitchen, disappearing and reappearing at the other side, we felt it was imperative it remain. Consequently, we had to find budget savings elsewhere.

## Neutral décor

We were keen to provide a home from home environment, using neutral colours throughout the Nest, creating a feeling of calm. The architect was keen to incorporate bright primary colours and Disney images. The Project Manager had to work closely with the architect explaining how 'a very bright and colourful environment can be very overwhelming for both children and adults who might be feeling anxious and unsure' (Jarman, 2016), and this was not the type of environment we wanted to create.

## The sandpit

We were keen to have a built-in sandpit, made from wood, big enough for children to get into. This was going to be one of the built-in pieces of equipment offering predictability and consistency to the children attending the Nest, helping to create a containing environment (Bion, 1962). The Project Manager had to think on her feet when the builder tried to persuade her not to have a wooden sandpit, which would be tricky to create and relatively expensive. He said, "You can't really have this made from wood as it's next to the sink and it will get wet". After a few moments she responded with, "I am sure it will be fine – aren't some boats made of wood?"

## The role of the Family Worker

We used a Key Person approach (Elfer *et al.*, 2003), but we called our staff Family Workers. The role of the Family Worker was a critical one. We wanted highly skilled, qualified practitioners with a deep understanding of how to support children emotionally and challenge them cognitively. We appointed staff following a rigorous interview process. Parents who had helped to shape our thinking around the Nest were panel members for the interviewing process. During these interviews, parents were vociferous in articulating what they wanted for their children. They wanted an intimate environment where all the staff knew the children well. They wanted a Family Worker who would follow the individual rhythm of each child in their care, and they wanted the children to have real-life experiences just as they would at home. They wanted workers who would develop sensitive relationships with their children and the whole family. (You can read more about how we established the 0–3 team in Chapter 3 and specifically about the role of the Family Worker in Chapter 4.)

## The name of the setting

It was important to us that the name of the provision was appropriate and gave the message we were offering a caring, supportive environment within which young children would have the opportunity to take risks, be cognitively challenged and emotionally supported, allowing them to grow and flourish. We considered names such as "The baby and toddler unit" as this suggested that we would be connected to the main nursery space but still have our own identity. We considered "The baby and toddler base" as this reflected the work of Bowlby (1969) and acknowledged the secure base we wanted to create for the children. We also considered "The baby care centre", but we were concerned this did not reflect our view of care and education being indivisible and totally integrated. After much deliberation, we chose the name "The Baby and Toddler Nest". This we felt represented both the containing (Bion, 1962) space we wanted to create for the infants and toddlers, and also the idea of the "Nest" as a secure base (Bowlby, 1969) from which the children could feel secure and go on to explore the wider environment.

The Nest has now been open for twelve years. We have always worked closely with families over this time to ensure that the provision meets their needs and reflects the experiences that parents want for their young children. We have had a huge demand for places since the Nest opened and have consistently sought feedback about the provision from families, external colleagues and visitors. We use the feedback to inform our evaluation and reflection, influencing change where necessary. We pay close attention to all the feedback, but we are particularly interested when it identifies situations we may not have gotten quite right for families. The critique is really helpful and assists us in continuously reflecting on and improving practice for the children and families and supports us in continuously driving the provision forward.

## Developing a second provision: the Couthie

In 2012, due to the huge demand for places and the change anticipated in the Government's agenda around providing funding for eligible two-year olds, we considered developing a second provision for infants and toddlers. We carried out a parent consultation event. This was led by parents that used services within the Centre at that time. We wanted to ensure whatever new service we developed was what parents in the local community wanted and needed. We invited parents who were already attending the Centre and parents in the local community to express their views regarding the development of new services. We invited families to some open events where they had opportunities to share their views and ideas. The overwhelming response from the consultation was that families in the local community and from across the town would value additional services for children under three and their families. We secured a loan and developed a second baby and toddler provision.

Once again we set up a "steering group" as we had done previously when initially developing the Nest. This time the steering group was comprised of staff and parents who co-constructed the plan for the provision, shared ideas and thoughts about the actual building project and designed the pedagogical space. We were able to draw on much of the learning from opening and running of the Nest for eight years, such as the design of the kitchen and the dining area. We once again worked with the architect to design the pedagogical space. We had been influenced by the work in Reggio Emilia and planned to develop an environment that would be warm and welcoming, supporting children to make relationships and collaborations in the group (Rinaldi, 2001). We wanted a safe, secure environment that was rich and stimulating and encouraged children to develop autonomy and feel challenged.

We wanted the provision to be driven by the needs of the families and the local community. During the development of the second provision, some of the parents who had been involved in the planning with staff had challenged the decision not to take younger children. They argued the case for taking children from nine months, as they wanted to access the provision to return to work after their maternity leave. The parents also explained the complexity of having to return to work and leave their baby for someone else to care for. On reflection, we acknowledged that since opening the Nest, we had worked with young children for eight years and had supported many children under twelve months who had attended the Nest for respite. Over this time, we had worked closely with the families to support them with their children. We had not been offering indiscriminate group care but thoughtful provision that promoted the healthy psychological, social and educational development of children with their families (Bain & Barnett, 1986). We were not separating children from their parents but supporting the whole family so children could thrive with their parents. We felt we were more skilled and able to manage working with younger children than we had been when we opened the Nest. We formed a sub-group consisting of parents, members of the Centre Leadership Team and existing staff from the Nest to reflect on the lessons learnt from the Nest and to conceptualise the second provision. We read research papers and debated the benefits and risks of offering full-day care for children under twelve months of age. Children could gain cognitively and linguistically from opportunities to mix with peers; however, the risks suggested that children could become more aggressive if they did not receive high-quality, consistent support from care givers with whom they had formed secure attachments. This has been more recently highlighted by Blanden *et al.* (2015).

Once again we carefully considered the indoor and outdoor environments, ensuring that the children had access to the garden spaces throughout the day. We

*Figure 2.11* Garden area

knew the importance of having stimulating and challenging indoor and outdoor spaces that provided the children with opportunities to challenge themselves physically and take risks in their play. Manning-Morton and Thorp describe the challenge that two-year olds' development presents to practitioners and parents in keeping adventurers safe whilst enabling them to be independent and take risks (Manning-Morton & Thorp, 2015) (Figure 2.11).

With our experience of successfully running the Nest, we decided to offer the provision to families with children from nine months of age. We set a maximum number of places for babies under twelve months to attend per session and agreed we would not offer full-day care from 8:00 a.m. through to 6:00 p.m. to the youngest children. We would offer shorter days, for example from 9:00 a.m. through to 3:00 p.m., morning sessions from 9:00 a.m. to 12:45 p.m. or afternoon sessions from 1:15 p.m. to 5:00 p.m. asking parents to build up to full-day care over time, giving the very young children time to settle in to the rhythm of attending the setting and adjusting to the separation from their primary carer prior to extending the hours they attend. This transition of increasing the hours they attend over time would help the young baby to adjust to the environment, begin to build a trusting relationship with their Family Worker and securely settle into the new environment. We agreed at this time that we would offer sessions for children from nine months of age in both the Nest and the new provision.

The parents involved in the planning held an event asking other parents to name the new pedagogical space. We wanted a name that once again reflected the containing and nurturing environment we had created. Many names were suggested such as the Nook, the Warren and the Burrow. Parents were linking

*Figure 2.12* The Couthie

the name of the new space with our existing nursery spaces the Den, the Snug and the Nest. The names were made available for voting and the chosen name was the Couthie. This is a Scottish word that we felt honoured the Scottish population who lived in the town and represented the environment we were creating, as "Couthie" means cosy and comfortable (Figure 2.12).

The Nest and the Couthie staff team continue to offer education and care for children from nine months until they transition through to nursery. The staff team continuously evaluate the effectiveness of the provision with children, parents and colleagues, as well as with external consultants. The critical evaluation and reflection (Schön, 1991) assist us in striving to offer the highest-quality provision for the youngest children and their families.

## References

Arnold, C. & The Pen Green Centre Team (2010) *Understanding Schemas and Emotion in Early Childhood*. London: Sage.

Athey, C. (1990) *Extending Thought in Young Children: A Parent-Teacher Partnership*. London: Paul Chapman.

Athey, C (2007) *Extending Thought in Young Children: A Parent-Teacher Partnership* (2nd edition). London: Paul Chapman Publishing Ltd.

Bain, A. & Barnett, L. (1986) *Occasional Paper No 8: The Design of a Day Care System in a Nursery Setting for Children Under Five*. London: The Tavistock Institute of Human Relations.

Bion, W. (1962) *Learning from Experience*. London: Heinemann.

Blanden, J., Del Bono, E., McNally, S., Rabe, B. (2015) *Universal Pre-school Education: The Case of Public Funding with Private Provision*. CEP Discussion Paper No 1352. London: Centre for Economic Performance.

Bowlby, J. (1969) *Attachment and Loss, Volume 1*. London: Hogarth.

Brostrom, S. (2002) Edited by Fabian, H. & Dunlop, A-W. *Transitions in the Early Years: Debating Continuity and Progression for Children in Early Education.* London: Routledge Falmer.

Bruce, T. (1991) *Time to Play in Early Childhood Education.* London: Hodder Stoughton.

Department for Education (DfE) (2014) Early Education and Childcare Statutory Guidance for Local Authorities. London: DfE. www.gov.uk/government/publications (Accessed 16.09.16).

Department for Education & Skills (DfES) (2002) *Birth to Three Matters: A Framework to Support Children in their Earliest Years.* London: DfES/Sure Start.

Department for Education & Skills (DfES) (2004) *Working Together: A Sure Start Guide to the Childcare and Early Education Field.* Annesley: DfES Publications.

Edwards, C., Gandini, L., & Gorman, G. (Eds.) (1998) *The Hundred Languages of Children. The Reggio Emilia Approach – Advanced Reflections.* Westport, CT: Ablex Publishing Corporation.

Elfer, P., Goldschmied, E., & Selleck, D. (2003) *Key Persons in the Nursery: Building Relationship for Quality Provision.* London: David Fulton Publishers Ltd.

Fabian, H. & Dunlop, A-W. (2002) *Transitions in the Early Years.* London: Routledge Falmer.

Jarman, E. (2016) *Communication Friendly Spaces and Transition in the Early Years.* www.elizabethjarmantraining.co.uk (Accessed 09.06.16).

Laevers, F. (1997) *A Process-Oriented Child Follow-up System for Young Children.* Leuven: Centre for Experiential Education.

Laevers, F. (2005) *Deep Level Learning and the Experiential Approach in Early Childhood and Primary Education.* Leuven: Research Centre for Experiential Education. https://vorming.cego.be/images/downloads/BO_DP_Deep-levelLearning.pdf (Accessed 13.09.16).

Lawrence, P., Gallagher, T. & The Pen Green Team (2015) Pedagogic Strategies: a conceptual framework for effective parent and practitioner strategies when working with children under five. *Early Childhood Development and Care,* 185(11–12): 1978–1994. doi:10.1080/03004430.2015.1028390.

Manning-Morton, J. & Thorp, M. (2015) *Two-Year Olds in Early Years Settings: Journeys of discovery.* Maidenhead: Open University Press.

Oxford Dictionary (2016) www.oxforddictionaries.com (Accessed 13.09.16).

Rinaldi, L. (2001) Edited by Gandini, L. & Pope Edwards, C. *Bambini: The Italian Approach to Infant/Toddler Care.* London: Teachers College Press.

Schön, D. (1991) *The Reflective Practitioner.* Aldershot, Hants: Ashgate Publishing Limited.

Whalley, M. & Arnold, C. (1997) *Effective Pedagogic Strategies, TTA Summary Research Findings.* Corby: Pen Green Centre.

Winnicott, D.W. (1960) The Theory of the Parent-Infant Relationship. *The International Journal of Psycho-Analysis,* 41: 585–595.

## Chapter 3

# Establishing the birth-to-three team and building their capacity to work with young children in an education and care provision

*Michele Duffy and Tracy Gallagher*

In this chapter, we explain how we supported practitioners within the Nest provision to settle into their role working with children under three and their families. We go on to outline some of the professional development opportunities we invested in to support the staff in their roles.

## Creating a culture of high expectations

At Pen Green, we are extremely committed to supporting staff with their professional development opportunities. We value the investment of professional development for each person and encourage practitioners to undertake learning opportunities to assist them in reaching their full potential. Our aim is for everyone to work together to provide high-quality education and care for the children and families with whom we work. It is important for us to know at the initial stage of recruitment that practitioners are committed to their own professional development; this shows us they value themselves as learners and understand the importance of continuously improving their knowledge in relation to working with children and their families.

We also encourage practitioners to think deeply about how children develop and learn. We use child development and psychodynamic theory relating to young children to assist us in understanding and thinking about how we most effectively support children's development and learning. At Pen Green, we focus on "professional development" rather than "training", as we believe learning is most effective when it is experiential with opportunities for reflection and development. This process of learning enables practitioners to continuously review their practice and identify areas for improvement. Continuous professional development is crucial to create effective teamwork for the professionals working around the child (Rankin & Butler, 2011, p. 56).

## Recruiting the team

When we first set up the Nest, we knew we wanted to employ experienced and deeply thoughtful staff to work with the youngest children. We set up a rigorous process for advertising and recruiting the staff team (information about the process can be found in Chapter 2).

We agreed all the Family Workers in the Nest and Couthie would be qualified to work with young children at a minimum of level 3. When we initially recruited staff to work with the youngest children, it was important that they understood how to provide a caring and stimulating environment through planning for children, documenting children's achievements and supporting parents by engaging in open and honest dialogue. We recruited staff who had experience of working in a team but were also able to use their own initiative. We recruited knowledgeable, thoughtful practitioners with experience of working with children and their families; we needed to ensure that the staff were confident to work with children and also their parents. These were essential qualities as we wanted staff to make decisions based on our Centre principles as well as plan and provide an exciting and nurturing environment for the children in their care. We needed staff that had absolute confidence in offering full-time education and care for young children under two years in a nursery provision.

> Workers have to make a conscious effort to build a bridge between the Centre and each child's home and family over which information can flow freely both ways, and people too can cross from one side to the other so that there is as much consistency and continuity as possible for the child.
>
> (Goldschmied & Jackson, 2004, p. 199)

We were looking for people who were passionate about working with the youngest children and their families. We wanted to ensure practitioners understood how, and had experience of, supporting parents with settling their child in the early years provision. It was important that the staff were able to empathise with parents; many of the parents were for the first time returning to work or training and were coming to terms with not being with their child every day. The parents had to have absolute confidence in leaving their child in the provision.

We wanted workers to have a deep understanding of child development frameworks; Schema theory (Athey, 2007; Arnold & The Pen Green Centre Team, 2010), Well-being (Laevers, 1997, 2005) and Involvement (Laevers, 1997, 2005). It was also critical for them to understand psychodynamic theories such as Holding (Winnicott, 1965), Containment (Bion, 1962) and Attachment (Bowlby, 1969). The child development theories and psychodynamic theories underpin our practice at Pen Green to help enrich our understanding with regard to children's development and learning and the role of the Family Worker in supporting this. You can read more about these theoretical frameworks in other chapters in this book.

When recruiting practitioners, we wanted to ensure that they had an underpinning knowledge of how young children develop and learn and how to assess and observe the youngest children in a sensitive and supportive way for parents. In our 0–3 provision, we do this through documenting a detailed record of the children's experiences through photographic observations, written observations and information from home. We consider the observations of the child in the setting and those from home and then plan for the child following their interests. We link the observations to the Early Years Foundation Stage (EYFS) (DfE, 2014) and the relevant child development frameworks that we use at Pen Green. All of this detailed documentation helps us support and understand how the children develop and learn. The parents contribute to their child's documentation, and when the child leaves the provision, the family has the documentation to keep and look back on. We call these documents "A Celebration of my Achievement" because we believe it recognizes the successes and accomplishments of each child.

## Introducing the staff to the principles and ethos of the Centre

After the practitioners were recruited, we introduced them to the work of the Centre and supported them to understand the theoretical frameworks we use to underpin our work with the youngest children. We initially had a week together prior to the children starting to give us the opportunity to participate in team-building experiences and have time to get to know each other. The team-building week gave us all the opportunity as a new staff team to think about the visions and values for the provision and to plan and prepare the environment to make it welcoming for children and their parents. The conversations that we shared as a new team helped us to get to know each other and find out about individuals' thoughts, principles and beliefs regarding working with young children. We reflected on our own previous experiences and thought deeply about how we were going to ensure the space for children was a relaxed and fun atmosphere where children could develop and learn. We wanted to create an environment that was emotionally Containing for the children and supported them to be cognitively challenged and take risks in their explorations and play.

> The physical setting should be safe and healthy for children and adults. It should promote children's daily life, feelings of well-being in aesthetic surroundings and learning experiences.
>
> (Pope Edwards & Gandini, 2001, p. 222)

We facilitated the newly recruited practitioners to carry out a vision and values negotiation exercise as described in Chapter 2. Staff were asked to explain what they wanted to offer in the Nest. Some examples of the visions and values statements the newly appointed team believed in at that time were as follows.

In the Nest, we want to make sure that

- Children, parents and staff are encouraged to be all that they can be.
- All children are emotionally and socially supported and cognitively challenged.

- We create an environment that is safe, full of fun and laughter where children and staff are able to make choices and take appropriate risks.

(Staff negotiation notes, June 2004)

'Each of us has his or her own image of the child, which is reflected in the expectation that we have when we look at a child' (Rinaldi, 2001, p. 50). On an ongoing basis, we facilitate the teams to revisit and reflect in detail on their visions and values, understanding each person's image of a child and what they believe is important. We do this as a minimum on an annual basis, and it has become apparent that practitioners are now much more confident during the discussions. As a team, they think more deeply about what each word and statement truly means. They think about their role in supporting the children's development and learning in the 0–3 provision, how they effectively support the parents and how they continuously develop their work as a team. We are always trying to support staff to be leaderful in their role, make decisions about the setting and influence the development of the provision.

During the initial setting up period, we went to visit other outstanding settings where practitioners had been working with the youngest children for some time. This helped us to think about how we 'set up' our provision. It also gave us the opportunity to discuss with other early years professionals any worries or concerns we had about providing long hours of education and care for very young children. We were able to use this time to share our thoughts and ideas with experienced practitioners and leaders. We then returned to the Centre having discussed possibilities and with plans to implement our learning at Pen Green.

As part of our ongoing self-evaluation and development of practice, we continue to visit outstanding settings and learn about early years practice from external colleagues. We also invite leaders and practitioners to visit us at Pen Green helping us to build networking relationships, offering support, advice and share new learning with each other.

## Peer-peer observations

We want the team to feel leaderful, influence the development of practice and bring innovative and exciting ideas to the work with young children. One method we use to help the practitioners continuously reflect and improve their practice is peer-peer observations. We do this on a termly basis. Practitioners video their colleagues with children in the setting. The video is then reviewed in small teams. The use of peer-peer observations helps us to support our pedagogy and helps us to reflect on our day-to-day practice. Practitioners can review the video several times and consider the practice they observe. This self-reflection with colleagues helps to identify areas they could improve in their practice. The video can also be used, with the permission of parents, to share with other professionals. We have seen that the peer-peer observations method has had a positive impact on practitioners' confidence to reflect on and critique their practice, and this is undoubtedly beneficial to the child and setting. When watching the video, the practitioners can clearly see what the child is interested in, and if they are tuned in to the child, the child becomes the focus alongside the practitioner. The practitioners together can discuss the Pedagogic Strategies that are being used and how effective they are in supporting the child or children in the video. This helps us to support children as individuals and with their peers. The ongoing process of peer-peer observations helps practitioners to reflect on the Pedagogic Strategies they are confident in and those they feel less confident about. The practitioners consider how they facilitate and support children's development and learning, which we believe enables us to also work more closely together as a team. We have found the use of video is a great tool to help practitioners analyse themselves, their practice and highlight aspects of their practice they may not even realize they do. The video is shared with families, and this gives the parents a true picture of their child's experience in the setting. Parents frequently feed back to us that having the video to view is a reassurance that Family Workers are effectively supporting the children, and their children are happy and settled in the provision. This process of continuously reflecting on and developing their practice helps the Family Workers to work effectively as individuals and as a team.

The method of peer-peer observations also helps practitioners to reflect on the Pedagogical Strategies that practitioners may not use so often and challenge them to consider why they don't use them and if or how they could. We have found it is important to systematically use the peer-peer observations, as the more regularly the practitioners engage in the process, the more confident they feel to discuss their practice with their colleagues and consider areas to develop. The continuous reflection on their practice and identifying areas to develop helps us to sustain improvement for individual practitioners and the team. The Family Workers are clear that this is not a management assessment tool; it is a process to facilitate reflection and peer discussion.

## Using psychodynamic theory to inform practice

We have found when working with the very young children, it is critical that we use psychodynamic theory to inform our thinking as well as child development theory, which often practitioners are much more familiar with. We use the concepts of Holding (Winnicott, 1965), Containment (Bion, 1962) and Attachment (Bowlby, 1969) to underpin our practice with the youngest children. We believe that it is critical for us to think about the emotional worlds of the young children as well as supporting their cognitive experiences. As Cath Arnold explains,

> When we observe, we are trying to understand what each child is trying to learn about, so that we can tune in to and support their cognitive and emotional concerns.
>
> (Arnold, 2010, p. 14)

When the provision first opened, we had a psychotherapist who would join our weekly staff meeting. He would facilitate us having opportunities for reflection, help us understand the complex worlds of the younger children we were supporting in our setting and help us make the links between the psychodynamic theory and the practice the Family Workers were involved in. We had a strong commitment to the youngest children receiving the best possible education and care from the practitioners and the practitioners having a deep understanding of how to effectively support the youngest children's emotional needs. Through the work with the psychotherapist in the weekly team meeting, we were able to explore the psychodynamic theories and gain confidence in understanding how to support the very young children who attended our education and care provision, for some up to ten hours a day. By having the underpinning knowledge of how to support children's social, emotional and personal development, we are able to more effectively support each individual child. The Family Workers gained a much deeper understanding of the psychodynamic theories and how they would use the knowledge in their day-to-day work.

The following examples from practice show how the Family Workers use the psychodynamic theory in our 0–3 provision.

### Holding (Winnicott, 1965)

In our provision, each child has their own special box. They can put whatever they want in it, for example a transitional object (Winnicott, 1953) from home or a toy from nursery. The nursery offers education and care from 8:00 a.m. through to 6:00 p.m. Monday to Friday, and we open forty-eight weeks of the year. It is important for children to know they are being thought about even when they are not in the setting or when their Family Worker, as Peter Elfer *et al.* (2003) describe 'Key Person', is not there. It is critical that each child knows that they are being 'held in mind'. For example, if the Family Worker is going to be off on annual leave, they will leave a special toy in the child's box for them to find when they arrive in the setting. If a child is off for a period of time, the Family Worker will write a note in the children's celebration of achievements file to say they are missing them but looking forward to seeing them when they come back. This is important for the child to start to understand, along with their parents, that the Family Worker knows and cares for the child and they are in their mind even when they are physically not in the setting.

### Containment (Bion, 1962)

The Family Worker is able to support the child with their different emotions and offer them language to help them gain an understanding of what they are feeling and how they cope with the wide range of the sometimes overwhelming emotions that young children experience. For example, if the child is upset when their parent leaves them in the setting, their Family Worker supports them by using language such as "I know you must be feeling sad that Mummy has gone; it's okay to cry". They may say, "Remember we said bye-bye to Mummy and she always comes back," or they may sit quietly with the child and say, "Shall we have a cuddle together?" The Family Worker may offer a particular toy or comfort if this is something that helps the child to settle. It is important that we acknowledge how the child is feeling and not dismiss the feelings by saying, "Come on now, you are okay" when clearly we can see the child's distress. We encourage the children to express their range of feelings, help them manage their feelings, and name those feelings for the child. This concept of workers temporarily Containing the children's feelings for them comes from the work of Bion. With these experiences, the child will eventually gain an understanding of their emotions and begin to develop their own capacity to manage them. 'This is a long, slow process. .... emotional regulation only gradually increases throughout childhood and adolescence into early adulthood' (Manning-Morton & Thorp, 2015, p. 83).

### Attachment (Bowlby, 1969)

If we are able to support the child by emotionally "Holding" them in mind and "Containing" their emotions, we can begin to develop a relationship where the child feels safe and cared for. The Family Worker will act as an Attachment figure in the absence of the parent. This enables the child to develop a feeling of security in the setting and have a strong foundation for learning.

## Ongoing support

The psychotherapist who initially supported the team continued to join the weekly team meeting for the first few months after the provision opened. Since then, within the Centre, we have gone on to develop different forums for staff to access, thus offering ongoing support. One such forum is the opportunity to work with a child and an adolescent psychiatrist from the Tavistock Institute. We work with the psychiatrist in the Centre each term. The practitioners have the opportunity to meet with him to consider their work, the complex emotions we experience when working with very young children and, if needed, to share anxieties about their work. Advice is offered to the practitioners about their work and how they can most appropriately support the child and their family. Following the work-based discussion with the psychiatrist, practitioners are able to go back into their setting and hopefully feel they are able to more effectively support the child. Having been emotionally Contained themselves equips the staff to have the capacity to consider the emotional needs of the children and parents with whom they work. Permission is gained from parents, and feedback is given to them following the work-based discussion, even though the focus is on practitioners developing their capacity and skills to work effectively with young children.

### Supervision and support

We want to bring out the best in the staff team and fully support them to be highly effective in their role. To maintain the highest standards, we ensure that all practitioners are given supervision every four to six weeks. This is an entitlement for every practitioner in the provision. The supervision session lasts between an hour and an hour and a half, and it takes place on a one-to-one basis with the practitioner's line manager or supervisor. This is an important time for the practitioner to discuss issues without being disturbed or interrupted. Additionally, all practitioners also have an annual appraisal, which gives them the opportunity to identify targets for their work in the year ahead. The supervisor and practitioner together contribute to the setting of appraisal targets. The supervisor then supports the practitioner to recognise their potential and any professional development needs that may have been identified. The appraisal process and six-month review is not seen as a separate tool, but more of an extension to the monthly supervision process. In *The Emotional Competence Framework*, self-awareness is identified as one of the personal competences; this relates to knowing one's strengths and limits (Goleman, 1998). Through the supervision and appraisal processes, staff are encouraged to recognise their strengths and identify areas for further development.

In supervision sessions, it is important for the supervisee and the supervisor to understand the purpose and maintain appropriate boundaries. To do this, we negotiate a mutually agreed contract at the start of the supervision process; this is reviewed annually. It is important that there is a balance between individual and personal support, professional support and discussion of organizational needs and requirements. If workers feel "Held in mind" and emotionally "Contained", they are more able to be in a position to do this for the children and families they work with. If they are cognitively challenged and excited about their own learning and development, then we experience practitioners who are more able to provide a stimulating learning environment for the children. 'Reflective supervision produces reflective practice. This is significant because it can take into account and both value and evaluate any response to a given situation' (Ash, 2000, p. 26).

There are also opportunities for staff to have supervision with the Family Support team, such as with a Social Worker at Pen Green. This process is offered to staff when they are working with particularly complex child protection casework. The additional specialized supervision provides workers with individual time to reflect and discuss matters relating to the specific case they are involved in. It is critical that the supervision is offered by a qualified Social Worker as 'they must know child protection legislation and help staff learn legal phrases ...' (Moore, 2000, p. 58). We want to ensure that all practitioners are equipped and appropriately supported to manage the complex work they are involved in.

### Parent participation

At Pen Green, our underlying philosophy is to work in partnership with parents. We truly value what parents have to say and what information and feedback parents want to share with us. As practitioners, we take feedback very seriously and learn from the parents to influence our practice. One of the ways practitioners do this is to develop trusting relationships with parents and encourage them to provide us with feedback about the successes as well as the things they are not so happy with. This is not about reporting to the lead of the provision but sharing honest feedback with the practitioners who work with their children every day. We encourage parents to have daily chats with Family Workers, and we also ask for feedback using self-evaluation forms. Another method we use is to ask parents to complete a questionnaire just before their child is about to transition in to nursery or leave the Centre. This is an opportunity for parents to provide feedback about what went well and what did not go so well for them or for their child. The practitioners can then consider how they can improve what we offer for parents in the future and appreciate what parents find to be most helpful from our services. The evaluation feedback from parents helps staff to self-evaluate and plan, always aiming to develop a highly skilled 0–3 team that continuously reflect on and improve their practice.

## Conclusion

We value the importance of continuously evaluating our skills and reflecting on the skills of the team as a whole. We believe it is critical to ensure that we build the capacity of all practitioners, encouraging them to have a say in developing our 0–3 provision and making decisions about how the services are delivered. We know it is critical to use the range of different skills and abilities of the team. We also appreciate the importance of offering a diverse range of ways to enable practitioners to develop innovative practice and improve the effectiveness of the team. Rodd describes effective leadership in the early childhood profession. She identifies an aspect of leadership is 'planning for and implementing change in order to improve organisational and professional effectiveness' (Rodd, 1994, p. 5).

Through working collaboratively with staff, we have been able to include them in shaping services, making decisions about the 0–3 provision and influencing the direction of the new provision. Ashman and Green define leadership as

> The responsibility to consider what changes need to be taken in the present that will be best for the future: to prepare for the future.
>
> (Ashman & Green, 2004, p. 3)

We know it is important to effectively distribute leadership to the team, holding them accountable for their work. In our role within the organisation, our intention is to always inspire and develop the potential of all members of the team. We ultimately aim for all practitioners to fully understand their role and to be highly effective in the context of an integrated early years provision.

## References

Arnold, C. & The Pen Green Centre Team (2010) *Understanding Schemas and Emotion in Early Childhood*. London: Sage.

Ash, E. (2000) in Pritchard, J. (Ed.) *Good Practice in Supervision*. London: Jessica Kingsley Publishers Ltd.

Ashman, C. & Green, S. (2004) *Managing in the Early Years: Managing People and Teams*. London: David Fulton Publishers Ltd.

Athey, C. (2007) *Extending Thought in Young Children: A Parent-Teacher Partnership* (2nd edition). London: Paul Chapman Publishing Ltd.

Baby & Toddler Nest Team (2004) *Unpublished Staff Negotiation Notes*. Corby: Pen Green Centre.

Bion, W. (1962) *Learning from Experience*. London: Heinemann.

Bowlby, J. (1969) *Attachment and Loss, Volume 1*. London: Hogarth.

Department for Education (DfE) (2014) *The Early Years Foundation Stage: Setting Standards for Learning, Development and Care for Children from Birth to Five*. London: DfE.

Elfer, P., Goldschmied, E. & Selleck, D. (2003) *Key Persons in the Nursery*. London: David Fulton Publishers.

Goldschmied, E. & Jackson, S. (2004) *People under Three: Young Children in Day Care* (2nd edition). London: Routledge.

Goleman, D. (1998) *Working with Emotional Intelligence*. London: Bloomsbury Publishing.

Laevers, F. (1997) *A Process-Oriented Child Follow-Up System for Young Children*. Leuven: Centre for Experiential Education.

Laevers, F. (2005) *Deep Level Learning and the Experiential Approach in Early Childhood and Primary Education*. Leuven: Research Centre for Experiential Education. https://vorming.cego.be/images/downloads/BO_DP_Deep-levelLearning.pdf (Accessed 13.09.16).

Manning-Morton, J. & Thorp, M. (2015) *Two-Year-Olds in Early Years Settings*. Maidenhead: Open University Press.

Moore, J. (2000) in Pritchard, J. (Ed.) *Good Practice in Supervision*. London: Jessica Kingsley Publishers Ltd.

Pope Edwards, C. & Gandini, L. (2001) *Bambini: The Italian Approach to Infant/Toddler Care*. New York: Teachers College Press.

Rankin, C. & Butler, F. (2011) in Brock, A. and Rankin, C. (Eds.) *Professionalism in the Interdisciplinary Early Years Team*. London: Continuum International Publishing Group.

Rinaldi, C. (2001) in Gandini L. and Edwards C.P. (Eds.) *Bambini: The Italian Approach to Infant/Toddler Care*. New York: Teachers College Press.

Rodd, J. (1994) *Leadership in Early Childhood*. Buckingham: Open University Press.

Winnicott, D.W. (1953). Transitional Objects and Transitional Phenomena. *International Journal of Psychoanalysis*, 34: 1–9.

Winnicott, D.W. (1965) The Theory of the Parent-Infant Partnership (1960). *Maturational Processes and the Facilitating Environment*. London: Hogarth Press.

## Chapter 4

# The role of the Family Worker

*Cath Arnold, Michele Duffy and Sam Coe*

> Evidence is accumulating that human beings of all ages are happiest and able to deploy their talents to best advantage when they are confident that, standing behind them, there are one or more trusted persons who will come to their aid should difficulties arise.
>
> John Bowlby, 1970 (2005, p. 124)

This quote from John Bowlby puts into a nutshell some of why, as educators of the youngest children, we believe that the 'Family Worker' role is essential. In this chapter, we present the following:

- Ideas from Family Workers at the Pen Green Centre about what we mean by the term 'Family Worker'
- Other similar terms used such as 'Key Worker' and 'Key Person' (Elfer *et al.*, 2010)
- The theory underpinning why we believe that young children and their family benefit from being assigned a Family Worker when attending nursery
- What the Family Worker does in the day-to-day life of the nursery and their responsibilities
- What happens when a Family Worker is absent because of sickness or holiday
- A case study illustrating the role of the Family Worker and what we learned from this particular case

## What we mean by the term 'Family Worker'

On joining Pen Green Nursery as Family Workers, we were told that the term is a description of a worker, in nursery, who sees and works with each child, not as an individual, but as part of a family. The group of children that the Family Worker is responsible for is called a 'Family Group'. The Family Group is comprised of children across the age range and, therefore, more accurately reflects a family. The term was also used to 'blur' the roles of Nursery Nurse and teacher, enabling Nursery Nurses to take on more responsibility and not to be viewed as fulfilling an inferior role to that of a nursery teacher.

In a search of recent literature, the term 'Family Worker' seemed to apply mainly to health workers supporting mothers with breastfeeding. As this is a very different role to the one staff at Pen Green are fulfilling for children attending the nursery and their families, we asked Family Workers working across the nursery spaces at Pen Green to help us define the term as used by staff at the Pen Green Nursery. We received definitions from eleven Family Workers. The results were as follows.

---

### What is a Family Worker?

(all eleven mentioned the role as including child and family)

"Someone who works closely with a child and their family including the extended family"
"Supporting the needs of the family"
"Truly knowing child, family and context"
"Being a voice for the individual child"
"Developing a close bond...to be their special person in the setting"
"Building relationships with each child and family"
"Building close relationships and Attachments..."
"Holds the whole family in mind"
"Acts as a 'secure base' for children"
"Build trusting relationships..."

---

As you can see, we are asking Family Workers to invest emotionally in working with families. In order to do this effectively without burnout, workers need sound leadership and regular monthly support and supervision.

## Other similar terms used in practice and in the literature

Similar terms used are 'Key Worker' and 'Key Person'. The term 'Key Worker', though often used in early childhood settings interchangeably with the other two terms, in the recent research literature is mostly confined to working with families or individuals with complex needs (Parr, 2016). It was realised that sometimes families whose children had additional needs were having to interact with and to tell their stories to twenty or more professionals. So, the purpose of having a 'Key Worker' was that this person could be a sort of mediator with other professionals, as well as being a more consistent emotional supporter of the child and family and coordinator of services. Similarly in oncology, the Key Worker can coordinate the treatment and offer emotional support to the family.

'Key Person', on the other hand, is becoming recognised as the special person both the child and family can relate to in the nursery (Elfer *et al.*, 2010; Lindon, 2013). Particularly with regard to babies and very young children, Elfer *et al.* regard 'consistency during each day' to be an important aspect of quality

(2010, p. 3). They use the example of nappy changing and suggest that nappy changing should be carried out by the baby's Key Person, rather than by five different people in one day. They also question whether and support the idea that 'nurseries need to be places where *some* features of the relationship with mothers and fathers are provided for each child?' (Elfer *et al.*, 2010, p. 5).

Adopting a Key Person approach does not mean in any way replacing parents but does mean having a close relationship with individual children. Elfer *et al.* point out that not only the child, but also the parents will 'experience a close relationship that is affectionate and reliable' (2010, p. 18).

Jools Page introduced the concept of 'professional love' after interviewing six mothers making the decision of whether to return to work when their babies were under a year old (Page, 2010). Page sought the views of these six mothers on 'love in childcare' and concluded that 'the type of relationship they craved for their child was in fact in line with my notion of "professional love"' (Page *et al.*, 2013, p. 196). It is rare for the word 'love' to be used unless workers are very confident in their role. However, most professionals would agree that babies and young children need to be loved by people who are close to them, and if they are spending time in nursery, especially from a young age, then we would argue that Key Persons (or in our case, Family Workers) are best placed to take on that role.

## The theory underpinning our approach

### Attachment theory

Bowlby came up with the Theory of Attachment after observing children filmed during temporary separations from their parents (1997). At the time, parents and professionals had very little notion of what was happening for a child at times of separation. The filmed material showed that even fairly secure children could become very distressed when separations were prolonged or they were cared for by a number of different people (www.robertsonfilms.info/young_ children_in_brief_separation.htm).

Bowlby observed that within weeks of their birth, babies 'recognised their primary caregiver' and that they showed a preference for this person (1997, p. 196). He saw this as a survival mechanism displayed by humans as well as animals. He also noticed differences in what he named 'attachment behaviours' as children developed, and we have seen this over and over again since then. At around nine months of age, children demonstrate distress at separation 'more frequently' and 'with more rigour' (1997, p. 200), and towards one-year old, they show 'attachment behaviour towards other adults' (Bowlby, 1997, p. 201). A significant developmental change usually occurs around three years of age when '...most children become increasingly able in a strange place to feel secure with subordinate attachment figures' (Bowlby, 1997, p. 205). Bowlby's original research resulted in different practices being adopted for children spending time in hospitals. For example, as a direct result of his research and films made by the

Robertsons, parents are now usually allowed to stay all day or even overnight in the hospital with their children, depending on the age of the children. With regard to nurseries, for a long time, it was felt that children could cope with the separation at around three years of age. This was considered the appropriate age for children to start attending nursery or playgroup. In our nursery, where we traditionally took children from two years of age, we tried to ameliorate the process for each child by assigning a Family Worker to each child and family, carrying out regular home visits, and having an extended settling-in time of at least two weeks when parents or carers attend with a child until they judge that their child is settled. As well as the initial 'settling-in', parents are encouraged to settle their child each day on arrival, and the Family Worker is usually in a position to help if the parent has to rush off to work or for an appointment.

Bowlby introduced the idea of a 'secure base' from which young children can explore the world. He noted that 'confident exploration comes to an end (a) if a child is frightened or hurt (b) if the mother moves away' (1997, p. 209). We have all seen young children who are preoccupied with their mother's or father's whereabouts and find it difficult to become fully involved if their parent is not close by.

These concepts of 'Attachment' and 'secure base' are important for Family Workers to understand when working with young children. They also help when talking to parents about always saying goodbye to their child, even if that causes distress. As Family Workers, we can talk to children about the fact that their mother or father has gone to work and that, importantly, they will come back. However, if parents try to reduce their own pain and their child's pain by not acknowledging their departure, this is much more difficult for a child and for a Family Worker to talk through with a child. There's a degree of uncertainty (for the child) about what has actually occurred, and this can be more difficult to deal with.

### Companionship

Colwyn Trevarthen extended this concept of 'Attachment' to include 'attachment for companionship and collaboration' (2002, p. 9). Drawing on his own extensive research of young children and their carers, as well as the research of Vygotsky, Bruner, Rogoff and others, Trevarthen noted that 'infants possess a drive to learn meaning *by sensing the interests and evaluations of others*' (2002, p. 4). Trevarthen argued that, as teachers, we need to be alongside children, learning from them about their interests. In terms of the Family Worker role, this can be helpful in articulating our understanding of the ways in which very young children learn.

Rosemary Roberts, in her PhD study, with a focus on 0–3s, coined the term 'companionable learning' to describe the process she observed of building resilient well-being in the youngest children (Roberts, 2007). Roberts pointed out that 'This research has found that companionable learning is about those times when children feel that they are enjoying the full attention of their companions – a kind of "mindfulness"' (2007, p. 278). Roberts further elaborated the concept as 'child and companion learning in sustained episodes of thinking *together*, about areas of mutual interest' (2007, p. 293).

As Family Workers, we need to pay close attention to children's relationships and learning. We also need to engage in mutual interests.

## Transitional objects

Winnicott introduced us to the importance of 'transitional objects' for young children. We have all known young children who like to carry a special blanket, teddy or other special object to bed with them and wherever else they go. Winnicott described these objects as the first 'not-me possession' (1991, p. 4). He explained that they are symbolic of the child's first relationship, usually with the mother and that they are 'a defence against anxiety' (Winnicott, 1991, p. 4). We find it important to respect each child's need to bring their transitional object to nursery, and part of the Family Worker's role is often to keep an eye out to make sure that the object does not get lost or spoilt in any way. 'Transitional objects' cannot be chosen for a child. A child may adopt an object, and it can only change if the child decides to change it (Winnicott, 1991, p. 5). Winnicott stated that 'The object is affectionately cuddled as well as excitedly loved and mutilated' (1991, p. 5). Understanding the importance of a special toy or blanket to a particular child is also supportive of their growing autonomy.

Not all children use a transitional object. Some, however, like to carry something with them from home to nursery or to other carers' homes. Tina Bruce named these 'objects of transition' (2004, p. 140). For this purpose, children might use different objects that are less personal and precious but do help with transitions from one place to another. These objects could be anything from a small toy, carried in a pocket, to a bicycle or buggy, ridden or pushed to nursery.

One of the Family Worker's jobs is to know about how to comfort children when they are distressed, and knowing about their transitional objects or objects of transition can help in comforting children.

## Holding and Containment

Although these concepts are often used interchangeably, Ogden argues that they are different from each other (2004). The concept of 'holding' comes from Winnicott's research. It is best understood by beginning with the physical action of 'holding'. Carers need to physically 'hold' a baby to keep them safe. At first, as well as physically 'holding' their baby, a mother totally identifies with their child's needs, and there is no sense of conventional time. Only the baby's rhythms control the mother's responses. Gradually, the 'holding' becomes the metaphorical Holding of the infant's emotional situation and tolerating the growing separateness from the mother. The mother, by caring for her baby, 'holds' the 'being and becoming of the infant' (Ogden, 2004, p. 1362). As Family Workers, we 'hold' children in mind, caring for them as individuals and remembering what has happened to them previously and who the important adults in their lives are.

'Containing' comes from Bion's work. The adult receives the child's distress or anxieties and returns them to the child in a manageable form. Ogden explains that 'The infant projects into the mother the emotional experience that he is unable to process on his own...' (2004, p. 1357). The mother or carer needs to be emotionally available in order to understand what is being felt by the infant and to articulate the feeling for the child. For example, when a child is distressed when separating from their parent at nursery, as Family Workers, we would comfort them in the way that is preferable to them and articulate what we think is happening for them, which might be "you are really angry when mummy leaves" or possibly "when daddy leaves, you seem to feel sad". We would also reassure them that their mummy or daddy is coming back. Over time, a child would begin to recognise their own feelings.

### The emotional roots of learning

Over the past few years, in partnership with the Northern School of Psychotherapy, we have set up a yearlong course for staff using infant observation, so that staff can learn about and apply psychoanalytic theory to their work. In Chapter 8, we explain how this professional development has developed our practice.

## What does the Family Worker do in the day-to-day life of the nursery?

Again, we asked Family Workers to tell us, and there was a strong consensus in their responses.

---

**What a Family Worker does**

Visits children and their families at home
Greets children and carers on arrival and settles them into the nursery
Spends time playing, encouraging and supporting development
Observes, supports and extends individual interests
Assesses learning
Plans and sets up exciting learning experiences indoors and outdoors for individual children
Changes nappies
Builds Attachment
Works as part of a team
Comforts and loves children
Documents learning through photos and video and completes wonderful celebrations of achievement
Nurtures children's relationships
Makes snacks
Tells stories
Sits with children at lunch
Comforts parents who are upset

Gives time to individual children
Attends meetings
Liaises with other agencies
Safeguards children
Acts as an advocate for children
Holds the child at the centre of everything they do

Taking into consideration what we have written recently about the role, in 2013, Angela Prodger referred to the Family Worker role and stated that it 'would be important to:

- Carry out regular home visits
- Greet the child and carer each day on arrival and facilitate a smooth separation and transition into the setting
- Observe the child's play, interact with and support the play and plan to extend their learning and development in collaboration with parents where possible
- Spend planned time with the child as an individual or in small groups each day'

(Prodger, 2013, p. 22)

What this does not capture is what is described as 'going the extra mile'. The Family Worker system is such that often Family Workers support families outside of Pen Green. They do not resent this because they have built relationships with families that are meaningful and authentic. This emotional investment means that at allocation of places, workers will usually 'claim' siblings of children who have previously attended and been in their group.

## What happens when a Family Worker is on holiday or off sick?

The nature of the work means that Pen Green Nursery is open forty-eight weeks a year and open from 8 a.m. till 6 p.m. each day. Naturally, staff work shifts on a rota basis and also take holiday when children in their group are still attending. These are predictable changes that we can talk with children and their families about. We would try to make sure that the relationship was established before a worker took annual leave. We also set up a 'buddy system' so that Family Workers pair up to ensure that one of the pair is there for children at all times. For example, the pair would be on opposite shifts and only one of the pair would be on holiday at any one period. You cannot, however, legislate for unexpected sickness. One way of introducing some continuity is to have a regular supply person that we can call on at short notice. That way, children are at least familiar with that person and, obviously, children often choose which adult to be with and we would respect their choices.

Children, too, can be off sick unexpectedly. When they are, Family Workers phone to keep in touch, just as we would with a friend who was sick.

**Case Study of Gabriella settling in to the Nest at Pen Green** (part of this case study first presented at a Pen Green Conference in February 2015 by Andrea Layzell, Evita Arnold and Sam Coe) as told by Andrea Layzell

I spoke to Evita (Gabriella's mum) and Paul (Gabriella's dad) at their house one evening after they had finished work, and Gabriella and her sister, Nicole, were in bed. Gabriella's 'Mop' (grandmother) was also part of the discussion. I was particularly interested in how Gabriella's settling in to the Nest had been responsive to her individual needs, as I was aware that it had not been straightforward.

Evita and Paul's previous experience of their older daughter, Nicole, attending nursery provision in the town had not been as positive. They rarely interacted with Nicole's nursery teacher, only entering as far as the lobby to drop her off. At the end of the morning, parents queued up outside, and at the end of the session, the doors were opened and the children were allowed to join their parents outside with no opportunity for dialogue about their session.

Evita and Paul both work, and Mop provided Gabriella's care while they worked. It was a successful arrangement, and Gabriella had developed a strong sense of self in her secure environment. Evita and Paul wanted Gabriella to attend Pen Green as Mop was going to be away in the following February, visiting family in Australia for six weeks. They all recognised the need for Gabriella to be settled before Mop went away.

Evita and Paul came to Pen Green to look at the provision and spaces that were available to Gabriella when she was to start at just over two years. They decided that the Nest was the best space for Gabriella and arranged to start settling-in sessions in October.

When children of any age start at Pen Green, they are allocated a Family Worker, who, as the family's Key Person, will work closely with the child and the family to ensure the close relationship is one that will the best one for the child's progress. Gabriella's Family Worker in the Nest was Sam, who had worked in the Nest for one year and five months and had a Family Group of ten children. Many of Sam's key children attended for part-time hours across the week, some so that their parents could work and others to access their funded two-year-old place. All children are supported to settle in to the new environment with parents or another close adult alongside them, as the adults gradually spend less time in the immediate area but remain on-site for a minimum of two weeks. Sometimes, parents are asked to extend this settling-in time when a child is struggling to settle, though Family Workers will use a range of strategies to support individual children and families.

When Gabriella and her family were allocated to Sam, she arranged a home visit before Gabriella started her settling-in visits. Evita told me that she found this helpful as it gave Sam an opportunity to see how confident Gabriella is at home ...not the shy little girl that is at nursery.

Evita, Paul and Mop all spent time settling Gabriella in to the Nest and, initially, everything went really well and Gabriella settled in to her routine of spending two mornings with lunch in the Nest. Though Gabriella was quiet, she enjoyed her time in the Nest and forged a friendship with another girl attending on the same days.

Mop talked about the gate between the Nest and the Den, understanding that many staff feel it is important for the children to manage their own transitions, friendships and interests by having free access to the Den from the Nest. However, she felt it was important for Gabriella to be in a small, contained space while still settling in and, for that reason, she was keen that the gate was closed (Figure 4.1).

Gabriella missed a couple of sessions when she was ill and, as she attended part-time, this resulted in several consecutive days not coming to the Nest. When she came back, she was much less settled than she had been and struggled to separate from the adult bringing her in. Her friend had moved into the Den and this threw her completely. She returned to needing her teddy and dummy for much longer than she had previously. Both Mop and Paul told me that they thought carefully about Gabriella at this time and recognised they were also struggling with the separation. (Mop recognised that she had had to leave Paul unexpectedly for a short time when he was a baby of six months because her younger sister died as a result of a car accident. Although Paul could not remember this, it had

*Figure 4.1* **The gate between the Nest and the Den**

(*Continued*)

made a difference to their Attachment relationship and it was an event they had reflected on when Paul was an adult. Leaving Gabriella when she was unsettled seemed to bring back those earlier feelings.)

Evita talked about Gabriella's use of her dummy and teddy as transitional objects. Even though she had been happy to put them into her box before she was poorly, during this time, she took comfort from using both for a longer period of time. I talked about my own experience of some nursery staff in settings in the Being Two project feeling that their priority was to get rid of a child's dummy as soon as possible, so that it wasn't a barrier to speech development. Evita was very clear that decisions like this must ultimately belong to the child's parents and that Gabriella's need for her dummy as a support to her emotional security had to be respected.

What really helped Evita and Paul at this time was a video Sam filmed of Gabriella settled and playing in the Nest, which she sent home on a DVD. This was very reassuring. Sam was thoughtful about how she could support Gabriella and undertook another home visit. Mop made a picture book with photos illustrating Gabriella's journey into the Nest each day including the enormous teddy in reception, the fish tank, the rocking horse, a photo of Sam and some photos of Gabriella building and jumping in the Nest, activities she particularly enjoyed at that time. The book supported Gabriella in talking about the Nest and about Sam at home and at Mop's house (Figures 4.2–4.8).

While Gabriella was still feeling unsettled, she was more inclined to reject looking at the book, but the family knew when she was feeling much more settled because she began to enjoy looking at the pictures and talking about her time in the Nest. Evita said that it was helpful in sharing with Gabriella what was going to happen the following day and that the routine and ritual when she arrived at nursery was important to her. Paul said that she followed the same pattern each day but would occasionally introduce a variation, for example when she decided jumping on the big bear was a good idea.

*Figure 4.2* Photos of Gabriella's book

*Figure 4.3* Gabriella looking at the fish as part of her ritual

*Figure 4.4* Gabriella on the rocking horse in the Den on her way to the Nest

*Figure 4.5* Gabriella jumping in the Nest (one of her favourite activities at this time)

(*Continued*)

*Figure 4.6* Gabriella in her favourite car in the Nest

*Figure 4.7* Gabriella with playdough

*Figure 4.8* Gabriella washing her hands

At Pen Green, we use the frameworks of Well-being, Involvement and Schemas alongside an awareness of the Pedagogy used by adults to support children's learning. We use these frameworks to carefully reflect on each child alongside their parents. Evita and Mop attended an open evening that Christmas and had a good look at the documentation, which was of a high standard. They also took Gabriella's Celebration of Achievement home for Paul to look at, as he was working that evening.

Mop said that when she picked Gabriella up from the Nest, she asked what Gabriella has been interested in that day, rather than whether she has had a sleep or what she has eaten, although they are important bits of information to share too. Sam described that Gabriella's current interest was playing with water. This matched what Mop experienced at her house where Gabriella would loudly protest when it was time to leave the water in the sink to go out. Evita told me about Gabriella's conversations at home and how she talks about children at nursery, but Evita is not entirely certain that these are real children! We talked about the value of exchanging this type of information and how it would help Sam plan effectively for Gabriella's time in the Nest.

What finally helped Gabriella to become more settled was her mum dropping her off. Even at the age of two, she knew that Evita had to go to work and that that was non-negotiable. Evita explained that she and daddy had to go to work, Nicole had to go to school and that the Nest is 'Gabriella's work'. She could understand and accept this. She still cried at first, which Evita found really hard, but she explained how all the staff in the Nest were really happy to hear from Evita when she rang to check that Gabriella had settled, which she invariably had. Gradually, it became OK for Mop or Paul to drop her off.

At this point, Evita, Paul and Mop wondered whether it would help to increase the number of sessions Gabriella attended the Nest. When they discussed this with Sam and Michele, Michele suggested that perhaps the rhythm of two longer days would be easier for Gabriella to get used to and would help prepare her for when Mop was away for six weeks. So, they increased her hours to 9 a.m. to 3.30 p.m., and this worked well and was a good preparation for attending a few days a week from the following February.

Towards the end of the year, Gabriella, along with friends from the Nest, began to go through the gate to access the Den even staying in the 'big' nursery for a couple of hours and having a story at group time with a Family Worker from the Den. This was a sign that Gabriella was feeling more confident and 'at home' in the nursery. It also meant that workers from the Nest and Den were working together so that giving children that amount of freedom was manageable.

After a year in the Nest, Gabriella transferred to the Den and was allocated to Shelley as a Family Worker. Shelley made a visit to Gabriella's home prior to the transfer in order to get to know Gabriella and her family and visited again, later in the year, when she knew Gabriella quite well.

*(Continued)*

> The transition seemed to work well as Gabriella could still see Sam, from the other side of the gate this time, and could go back and visit whenever she wanted to. The family found Shelley 'brilliant and so helpful'.
>
> "If you ever asked her for anything, she would help you. On the last day, she arranged a special party for Gabriella because we were going away and Gabriella would miss out on the (leavers') party. She made it a special day for Gabriella with cake – she didn't need to do that and we really appreciated it!"

## Concluding remarks

You could see from this case study that each Family Worker was treating Gabriella as an individual: visiting the family at home prior to Gabriella starting to attend nursery, working hard to welcome the whole family into the nursery to help her settle in, responding by visiting her at home when she became unsettled, making a film to send home to reassure her parents that she did become settled during the session and enjoy herself, and supporting her to move into the Den when she was ready. During the year Gabriella spent in the Den, a secure online learning journal was introduced, which the whole family enjoyed viewing and contributing to.

## References

Bowlby, J. (1997) *Attachment and Loss Volume 1*. London: Pimlico.

Bowlby, J. (2005) *The Making and Breaking of Affectional Bonds*. Oxon: Routledge Classics.

Bruce, T. (2004) *Developing Learning in Early Childhood*. London: Paul Chapman.

Elfer, P., Goldschmied, E. & Selleck, D. (2010) *Key Persons in the Nursery*. Oxon: Routledge.

Lindon, J. (2013) *The Key Person Approach: Positive Relationships in the Early Years*, Practical Pre-school, London.

Ogden, T. (2004) On Holding and Containing, Being and Dreaming, *International Journal Psychoanalysis*, 85, 1349–1364.

Page, J. (2010) Mothers, work and childcare: Choices, beliefs and dilemmas. Unpublished PhD thesis, University of Sheffield.

Page, J., Clare, A. & Nutbrown, C. (2013) *Working with Babies and Children from Birth to Three*. London: Sage.

Parr, S. (2016) Conceptualising 'The Relationship', in Intensive Key Worker Support as a Therapeutic Medium, *Journal of Social Work Practice: Psychotherapeutic Approaches in Health, Welfare and the Community*, 30 (1), 25–42.

Prodger, A. (2013) Sharing Knowledge with Families Using Our Nursery: The Family Worker Role. In Whalley, M., Arnold, C. and Orr, R. (Eds.) *Working with Families*. Oxon: Hodder Education.

Roberts, R. (2007) Companionable Learning: The Development of Resilient Well-being from Birth to Three, Unpublished PhD study, University of Worcester in association with Coventry University.

Trevarthen, C. (2002) Learning in companionship, *Education in the North: The Journal of Scottish Education*, New Series (10), 16–35.

Winnicott, D.W. (1991) *Playing and Reality*. East Sussex: Brunner Routledge.

## Chapter 5

# Supporting families in challenging circumstances

## Extending the 'Key Person' role

*Kerry McNulty, Judy Potts and Tracy Gallagher*

In this chapter, we describe how we work in partnership with families to support vulnerable children in our nursery setting and through the wider Family Support services available in our Centre and outside.

The Family Worker role is firmly embedded in our nursery. It is an experienced Key Person role (Elfer *et al.*, 2003), extended and enhanced to provide Family Support. At the heart is the trusting reciprocal relationship carefully built between parents and their child's worker. We believe that parents are equal partners. Patrick Easen and his colleagues wrote about sharing theories with parents: 'Educators learned from parents about individual children and parents learned from educators about child development theory'. This 'developmental partnership' had the children's learning as the focus (Easen *et al.*, 1992). Parents are the experts on their own child, their strengths and vulnerabilities, their interests and their personalities. The worker is the expert in child development and helps to create an optimal learning environment for the child outside of the home.

We believe that parents want the best for their child. We believe that our commitment to, and the joy and love of, their unique child and their family fosters a special trusting relationship, a bedrock that allows a mutual exploration of wider family issues including vulnerability and possible responses.

We describe what this work with families with vulnerabilities looks like in our nursery and integrated Centre. We include the 'voices' of the child and families through case studies that identify the support families have received and the difference it has made.

Governors and the Centre Leadership Team have made a commitment to offering 50% of places, in the Nest and Couthie (our provision for the youngest children), to the most vulnerable children in our community; these will include families with children currently working with Social Services and engaged in multi-agency meetings. We prioritise the allocation of places to children eligible for two-year funding, children who are Looked After by the Local Authority, Children on Child Protection Plans, Children in Need, Children with Early Help Assessments and Children with SEND.

Our 0–3 provisions, the Nest and Couthie, have both priority places and fee-paying places. No matter how the places are funded, all the children are together in an environment that enables them to freely move around the thoughtfully planned Pedagogical Spaces. Our focus is on providing all children with the opportunity to feel safe whilst gaining independence and support for their development and learning. On average, we have eighty children on roll attending the Nest and Couthie, and 50% of these children will be considered to be receiving a priority place. This means that Family Workers can have up to eight children with high levels of need in their Family Group at any one time. Each of these children will receive a thoughtful service responsive to the family's unique vulnerabilities.

We also have Nurture Group Workers, located within the Couthie, who provide more intensive Family Support for families with greater vulnerabilities or more complex needs, or where there are Safeguarding issues. Places are allocated from referrals from Social Services, Health Visitors, Family Support Workers or other early years practitioners. Nurture places are provided to four families with children aged from twelve months to two or three years who live anywhere within the town and surrounding villages. The young children attend the nursery for two sessions each week. The two Nurture Group Workers provide appropriate, intensive Family Support within a multi-agency context on a weekly basis. The children attend the Nurture Group up until they are two if they then access their two-year funding; however, some children stay on until they access their three-year funding. If families are local to Pen Green, then they may access their two-year funding, whereas families further afield may stay longer until they feel confident to access a place nearer their home. Further details of this specialized role and a case study are described later in this chapter.

## Our approach to involving parents in their children's learning

For every family with a child starting in our setting, we go and visit the family in their own home before the child starts nursery. We arrange a time to visit that suits both parents where possible and appropriate. This is to ensure we hear the voice of each parent, listening to their thoughts and feelings around their child starting our setting. This gives us a detailed insight into their child's interests and family life.

Following on from the first home visit, we build on this relationship through reciprocal dialogue in the following ways:

- Ongoing home visits
- Daily chats with the parents when they drop the child off or collect them
- Parents sharing information from home that can be added on to the weekly planning sheets
- Parents suggesting ideas to be added on to their child's individual planning sheet (Possible Lines of Direction – PLOD)
- Online tool for exchanging photographs and video between home and setting
- Making Children's Learning Visible assessments

(Chapter 4 gives more information about the role of the Family Worker, and Chapter 6 explains how we celebrate the voice of the child.)

We believe that enabling parents to become involved in supporting and extending their children's learning is a critical aspect of the role of the Family Worker, and we know that when we do this effectively, children achieve more and are happier (Meade, 1995).

Parents want to see that we have heard their voices and we use their information to plan for their child. An example of this is when we send something home to parents via the online information-sharing tool, and we are thrilled when they respond to us. We must also 'hold in mind' (Winnicott, 1965) that when parents initiate this process and send something to us in the setting, we must always take the time to thoughtfully respond, acknowledging and acting on their information. In all the relentless demands of family life, it can be a huge achievement for a parent to find time to describe, photo or video something their child has said or done, send off to their Family Worker, get a response and realise the value of the contribution they have made.

The following example shows how a parent was supported to set up a secure account allowing her to receive and send observations of her daughter using an online tool. This reciprocal exchange of information enabled the parent to link her children's interest and experiences at home with those in the setting.

Joanne had been attending a group at Pen Green with her daughter Chloe since she was a few months old. The group supports parents to develop their relationship with their young child. Tracy was one of the group leaders in the group that Joanne and Chloe attended. Chloe had a hearing impairment and received support from Portage and occupational therapists.

When Chloe was two, she started attending the Nest provision through a two-year funded place. Joanne continued to bring Chloe to the group and chat with Tracy, the group leader. In the Nest, Christine was Chloe's Family Worker. Christine had talked to Joanne about sharing information through the online tool. Joanne was hesitant about saying to Christine that she didn't know how to do that, so she spoke to Tracy, who she was more familiar with. Tracy helped Joanne to set up the password for the secure account and explained how to send photographs and observations. Together Joanne and Tracy talked about sharing photographs of Chloe with Christine. Joanne had so many photos and was unsure which to pick. Tracy helped her choose ones which illustrated Chloe's particular interests, such as Chloe dressing up, as this was something she loved to do at home. So, on the Friday afternoon in the group, Joanne was able to select and securely send photos of Chloe to Christine. On Monday, when Chloe arrived for her session in the Nest, Christine had set up the dressing up clothes, creating a stage out of wooden blocks in front of a large mirror. From the images Christine had received from Joanne, she knew that this was something Chloe was deeply interested in.

Joanne was thrilled to see that Christine had used the images of Chloe to inform her thinking and had set up a particular experience knowing it would be of interest to Chloe. Christine was able to continue the exchange by sharing observations of Chloe in the Nest with Joanne, which Joanne loved to see.

## Assessments and interventions

We continuously observe and assess the children within the Nest and Couthie. We keep a detailed record called a Celebration of My Achievements for each child. Every term we make a more detailed assessment of the children's learning and development alongside the parents. We call this process Making Children's Learning Visible (MCLV). Working in collaboration with the parents gives us a deeper insight into the abilities and competencies of the child within the home environment. We then use this information with our evidence and professional judgement of what we have observed in the setting. We review the assessment and consider the progress the child is making. After looking deeply at the child's MCLV, we thoughtfully produce action plans to target specific interventions to support each child's learning and development. We work closely with the centre SEND Coordinator to consider the needs of Children with SEND and how we provide the most appropriate support at the earliest age.

## Our work with vulnerable children in our nursery

There are many factors contributing to families struggling to meet their children's needs, for example:

A family living with mental health concerns
A family member within the home misusing/abusing alcohol and/or drugs
Domestic violence between parents
Parents caring with children with additional needs
A parent with a disability
A parent in prison
A family living in poverty
A family living in poor housing or with poor living conditions
A parent living with a severe illness

In the last ten years, governments have tried to support families living in challenging circumstances by formulating policies based on research findings of the interventions which make the most positive difference for children.

In 2008, the Cabinet Office published *Reaching Out: Think Families*. The key messages from this publication were as follows:

- The greater the number of different parent-based disadvantages in a family, the greater the negative impact on the child.
- The family needs to be at the centre of service planning and delivery.

- Effective intervention often requires a coordination of child and adult services with one professional coordinating.
- The approach needs to build on family strengths and promote resilience.

Also, in 2008, Springate, Atkinson and Straw *et al.* published a research report on "Narrowing the Gap", a policy designed to promote the development of children living in difficult circumstances.

They said,

> In general, the evidence demonstrates that interventions focused on children in their early years have the potential to improve outcomes that are fundamental to their future life chances, and to narrow the gap between disadvantaged and other children. Improvements in cognitive development, social/behavioural development, and health outcomes can be achieved in the short-term, and there is some evidence that these outcomes can be sustained into later life.
>
> Four cross-cutting themes are identified as contributing to successful practice. These are the involvement of parents; the delivery of interventions that are of high quality, delivered by qualified and skilled professionals; interventions that are able to meet the specific needs of the individual child and, if appropriate, their family; and interventions that help build constructive relationships between adults (staff and parents) and children.

In 2011, Graham Allen produced a report, "Early Intervention, The Next Steps," which argued that not intervening early in families with young children, aged 0–3, facing adverse circumstances, was deleterious to the future of these families and led eventually to much more expensive interventions. He said,

> Early Intervention is an approach which offers our country a real opportunity to make lasting improvements in the lives of our children, to forestall many persistent social problems and end their transmission from one generation to the next.

He said that the central objective of Early Intervention was 'to provide a social and emotional bedrock for the current and future generations of babies, children and young people by helping them and their parents (or other main caregivers) before problems arise'.

Our county, Northamptonshire, has published guidelines, "Making Children Safer, Northamptonshire Thresholds and Pathways (Oct, 2015)", to ensure all early years settings deliver on these policies and offer a coordinated approach across agencies and disciplines. This document describes the levels at which families are operating and defines the responses to particular levels of need (Figure 5.1).

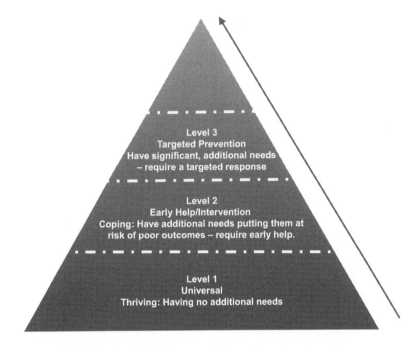

**Examples of services:**

| Level 4 | Level 3 | Level 2 | Level 1 |
|---|---|---|---|
| CAHMS Specialist (Community) and Highly Specialist (inpatient) Services<br>• Community Paediatricians<br>• Specialist Looked After Children Service<br>• Children's Continuing Care<br>• Children in Need Team<br>• Youth Offending Service (also Level 3)<br>• Social Workers | • CAMHS Primary Mental Health Workers<br>• Community Paediatricians<br>• Early Help and Prevention Service<br>• Youth Offending Service<br>• Children's Centres (also Level 1 & 2)<br>• Connexions / Horizons<br>• GPs<br>• Social Workers | • Health Visitors (also Level 3)<br>• School Nurses (also Level 3)<br>• Therapy services<br>• Children's Centres<br>• Schools and colleges<br>• Educational Psychology Service (also Level 3)<br>• Midwives<br>• Portage Team<br>• GPs | • Health Visitors<br>• Family information service<br>• Children's centres/libraries<br>• Schools and colleges<br>• CYP Public Health nurses<br>• Midwives<br>• GPs |

*Figure 5.1* Levels of need – vulnerability matrix
Source: Northamptonshire County Council

Family Workers must operate within the structures laid out in these frameworks and practice guidance.

Within our Centre, our Nursery-based interventions place an emphasis on 'narrowing the gap' for our most vulnerable children. We put rigorous plans in place to ensure that we are effectively supporting the child's development and learning, helping them to make progress and catch up with their peers.

For instance, all children who receive priority places are offered set sessions each week. Each Family Worker is highly attuned to what is currently happening for their families and can therefore offer additional sessions if necessary.

When we first meet families, they may not have any additional support and may never have shared their worries and concerns. Conversely, they might already be involved in multi-agency processes. These will include Early Help Assessment (EHA), Children in Need (CIN), Children with Child Protection Plans (CPP), Looked After Children (LAC) and Children with Special Needs and Disability (SEND). We will need to understand with the family and the agencies involved what vulnerabilities exist, what plans are in place and how we can be included in them. We often hear the phrase 'hard-to-reach families'. We always try to ask ourselves the question, "Are *our* services difficult for some families to get involved in?" We consider, "How do *we* support parents to have a voice when they often feel unheard in many other situations?"

Whatever the referral route or level of concern for the vulnerable child, the initial home visit is the same as for any other family. This ensures that families who are struggling with complex challenges and who often feel disempowered are just like all the other parents, active participants in sharing their knowledge about their child.

Additionally, if the family are already involved with other agencies, we talk that through with them at this stage as well.

## So, what is it that enables an initial home visit to develop into a trusting honest relationship?

Parents have said the qualities they need from their Family Worker are as follows:

- "Somebody who shares honestly their concerns about our child or our family"
- "Somebody who listens authentically and genuinely tries to understand things from our point of view"
- "Somebody who seems non-judgmental"
- "Somebody who doesn't blame"
- "Somebody who acknowledges our strengths and the ways in which we are being successful"
- "Somebody who doesn't get other agencies involved without discussing this first with us"
- "Somebody who has faith and hope in us even when we are not doing terribly well"
- "Somebody who will never give up on us"
- "Somebody who can bear our pain and anger"
- "Somebody who actually does what they say they are going to do and tells us why if they can't"
- "Somebody who really wants to understand our family's culture, lifestyle and traditions"

We develop this trusting relationship through our daily chats with parents when they are dropping off and picking up their children and through further home visits when appropriate.

## Tensions

Tensions can arise in these relationships when:

- Parents' perspectives on their child's needs are very different from the worker.
- Parents' priorities are very different from those of the worker.
- Workers are struggling to balance the needs of the parent and the rights of the child.
- Workers have real concerns about whether the care or home circumstances are good enough but parents dispute this.
- Workers need to talk about Safeguarding issues such as domestic violence, drug and alcohol misuse and parents are not acknowledging these factors.

These difficulties can be overcome through the strength and trust of the relationship that has already been built up and the parent's belief in the worker's enthusiasm and dedication to their child, and the honesty of the relationship so far.

We want parents to become involved and excited about their children's learning and development, but we also understand how hard this can be when they may be preoccupied with living in complex situations and facing disadvantage.

Sometimes, a family's reluctance to work with us stems from previous negative experiences of services. This may be because they felt let down by services as a child or, more recently, they have felt dismissed and/or judged by services. Parents who have been brought up in other countries and cultures may fear any form of perceived state intervention or misunderstand agencies' roles. It can take patience and persistence on our part for families to trust the services that we provide.

## Family Worker offering Family Support

Family Workers with vulnerable children in nursery have a range of options of what enhanced services they can offer in the integrated Centre:

Respite care
Family Support Worker
Group work – universal offer and targeted support
Transport
Adult education training, return to work, employability
HomeStart

Many of these families would not have the confidence to access these services independently. We can underestimate the barriers that prevent families accessing relevant services. Some of these barriers are as follows:

- Low self-esteem – parent's inner voice telling them, "this isn't for the likes of me"
- Concerns about being different in culture, background, religion or ethnicity
- Not knowing the 'rules' of the group or service or how to behave
- Feeling that they should be able to cope on their own or are a failure for seeking/accepting 'help'

Again, the quality of the relationship with their trusted Family Worker may enable a dialogue where the family talk about their fears and anxieties about seeking or accepting further services. The Family Worker can then offer specific support in accessing the services.

## Early Help Assessments (EHAs)

We work closely with families, trying to ensure that our support is responsive to their needs and is offered in a timely manner. We want to support families at an early intervention level, trying to prevent concerns from escalating and therefore statutory services becoming involved. On home visits, throughout the settling-in period and when engaged in daily chats, Family Workers will share with parents what Early Help Assessments are and how they can help with support for the family.

Traditionally within Pen Green, the Centre's Family Support Team has led on the EHAs and Nest and Couthie Family Workers have attended the meetings. However, we recognized that the Family Workers often had the strongest relationship with the family and were well placed to advocate on behalf of the family. We also acknowledged that families were more open to sharing sensitive information within this already established relationship of openness, honesty and trust. So, more recently, the Family Workers have taken a lead role in facilitating the meetings and coordinating the relevant professionals coming together. This change has been carefully planned with appropriate training to ensure that the Family Workers have the necessary skills and confidence to take on this lead role, always knowing that members of the Family Support Team are available if they need them.

An EHA helps both the parent and Family Worker to identify any additional support the family may need. It gives the time and space for parents to voice their feelings in a safe and secure environment. It gives Family Workers the time to challenge in a sensitive and respectful way if needed. EHAs facilitate multi-agency working and give all practitioners involved with the family the time to coordinate the support around the family. EHAs can also open different windows for families, assisting them to access a variety of different services such as housing, welfare rights, health, counselling, schooling and legal advice.

The following case study explains one parent's experience of having an EHA to facilitate multi-agency working. The process enabled the parent to access a range of services to support her and her family at a particular time when they were in need of additional help.

Lilly lives at home with her mother Leanne, father Tom and older sibling Henry. She attended the Couthie from the age of two and has now made a happy transition into Nursery. When Lilly was two, her mum Leanne was given the devastating news that she was suffering with bowel cancer. This was a very traumatic time for the family, and Leanne's health problems caused her to take time off work. Whilst life was turned upside down, it did mean that Leanne was able to spend more time with Lilly on the days she was feeling well. It was at this point Leanne decided to access Pen Green Centre. When talking about her reasons for her initial visit to the Centre, Leanne explained that she didn't feel well enough to give Lilly the opportunities for play and exploration she had previously been able to provide at home. Leanne talked about how she felt when she first visited Pen Green. She looks back on it as a very positive encounter at a difficult time, and talked about how visiting the Centre made her feel. "I was overwhelmed by how warm and welcoming everyone was to me and to Lilly".

Leanne and Lilly began accessing the Social Toddler Group on a Tuesday afternoon, which was run by the Centre's Health Visitor (Jo) and an Early Years Practitioner (Kerry). When talking about the group, Leanne described it as being "a chance to rest and know that Lilly is still happy". She went on to say "I built strong relationships with the two workers in the group and felt I could open up and explain my situation to them, trusting that they would support me in the group if I needed it. I didn't think for one minute that they would be able to support me and my family to the extent they did". As Leanne began chemotherapy and the weeks went by, she became increasingly tired. Despite this, she continued coming to the group. It was at this point Leanne explained that it was becoming difficult for her to get out of the house. The possibility of the family being entitled to two-year funding for Lilly to attend the 0–3 provision was discussed; however due to their family income, it became apparent that this would not be available to the family. With Leanne feeling unwell and tired, life was becoming more difficult. She also began preparing herself emotionally for major surgery. It was at this point that she was offered an Early Help Assessment (EHA) by Kerry and Jo, the staff at Social Toddler Group. Leanne talked about her first EHA meeting and described it as a positive and helpful experience. "I felt comfortable as on my first EHA, it was just me and Kerry, the Early Years Practitioner. She listened as I told her how I was feeling and what support I felt I needed. The EHA meetings went on to include a Family Support Worker and Health Visitor. During these meetings, I was able to talk about how I was feeling and explain what support I needed. I was then offered support and advice regarding applying for the two-year funding application, and this left me feeling relieved. Within a week, Lilly's application was accepted and she was offered a place in the Couthie, the 0–3 Provision at Pen Green".

The EHA meetings with the multi-agency team supported Leanne and her family to access two-year funding, which gave Leanne the important time she needed to rest at home whilst Lilly was in the education and care provision at the Centre. Leanne said, "I was so pleased and felt so lucky to have been offered this. I was then approached by Kerry at the group who told me that, as she worked in the Couthie, she was going to be our Family Worker. This meant I didn't have to explain my situation to anyone new and that Lilly didn't have to build a relationship with someone new, which had always been a worry of mine. Kerry knew me and Lilly so well that leaving her in a new setting didn't seem to scare me at all anymore. Kerry came to our home to visit and I was so pleased she could meet the rest of the family and get a bigger picture of what life was for me and Lilly". Lilly started attending the Couthie at Pen Green after two weeks of settling-in. She attended three mornings a week, which gave Leanne the time to attend appointments and continue with her course of chemotherapy at home. This hadn't been possible whilst Lilly was in the house and so made such a difference to Leanne. Her diagnosis with cancer and her subsequent treatment and operations meant that she would often spend long periods of time in hospital away from Lilly. She explained that Lilly's time in the Couthie provided "the time to rest and resume strength for precious time with Lilly".

Lilly thrived at nursery. She loved exploring and experimenting with the range of resources available to her. She would often choose a small toy or a small animal and repeatedly cover it with play dough, carefully covering the whole area and then uncovering it, seemingly interested in totally 'enveloping' the object. Arnold and The Pen Green Team (2010) describe 'Enveloping' as 'enveloping or covering oneself, an object or space'. Being in the setting gave Lilly the time, through her play, to explore something being there but not being visible; it appeared that she was trying to understand the emotions she was experiencing in relation to the absence of her mum. Through Lilly's schematic play, she was not necessarily talking about her mum going in to hospital and therefore 'not being there', but she was repeatedly investigating disappearing and reappearing. Lilly seemed to be making sense of the periods of separation she had from her mum and was gaining a greater understanding of all that was going on for her.

Leanne reflected on Lilly's time in the Couthie, "Kerry would always phone me and tell me about Lilly's day at nursery, which was so reassuring for me as I missed her so much. She would send Lilly's pictures to the hospital and kept links with me through a secure online system for

*(Continued)*

exchanging information. It was so reassuring that when I wasn't there she had 'Her Kerry' looking out for her – well, for all of us! Kerry would offer Tom extra sessions for Lilly to attend the Couthie to make sure he could get to work or care for me after operations. She would even do Lilly's hair when Tom was finding it a little tricky. Kerry offered me extra home visits at the times I was feeling unwell or had just returned home. The support we were offered as a family was inspirational and gave me the chance to get through a very difficult time in our lives, so much so it has inspired me to want to do the same. Now that I am on the mend and feeling much better, I have started a new journey through the Pen Green Centre studying the Level 3 Early Years Educator qualification".

Family Workers must be able to work collaboratively and share information appropriately with colleagues from other teams and disciplines outside the Centre, building professional networks of support by linking closely with Social Care colleagues, Health Visitors and other Early Years specialists. Family Workers also need to be effective members of Team Around the Family (TAF) meetings, case conferences and core group meetings. Family Workers, like all workers in the Centre, are required to meet beforehand with parents who are going to attend such meetings, listen carefully to their perspectives, help the family prepare what they want to say, and share honestly their professional perspective – what they will be saying at the meeting, whether detailing encouraging improvements or voicing concerns for the child's well-being, progress or family circumstances.

Not only are these meetings often very daunting for the family, but also for the Family Worker, who needs to feel confident about putting forward their unique perspective, even if it is a minority view, and, where appropriate, advocating on behalf of the family. These skills require appropriate training and support and supervision.

Finally, we give further details of the work of the most intensive Family Worker role – Nurture Group Workers, who work in close collaboration with their professional colleagues, often from Health and Social Services. Our Nurture Group is run by two very experienced Family Workers who have specialist skills both in supporting our county's most vulnerable young children in the nursery setting, and in delivering well-planned, rigorous intervention that supports families' individual needs.

They act as the 'Key Person' (Elfer et al., 2003) to the children whilst in the Couthie. They collect the children from the home and bring them in to the Couthie for their sessions. So, this ensures that the children access their Nursery provision regularly and are seen in the family home every week. The workers also visit each family on alternate weeks to offer additional support. In addition to the direct work they do with the families in the home, they also support families to attend appointments and groups. The role of the Nurture Group Workers also requires them to attend meetings such as TAF, case conferences and core groups.

Their role is as diverse as the needs of each unique family; they may be sending a family a text reminder to put their bins out, offering practical work in the family home or being alongside the parent to attend a solicitor's appointment. The workers have to be extremely flexible and responsive to the needs of each individual family, always working alongside the family, prioritising their needs.

The following case study describes a family that accessed the Nurture Group provision at Pen Green. The case study is of Mathew and his children Lacey and Kian, and it describes how this family overcame a tragic time in their life, used the services offered to them and became strong.

---

Mathew is the dad of two children, Lacey and Kian. They have been accessing the Nurture Group service for three years. Mathew is the stepfather of Lacey and the biological father of Kian.

The family had been referred to Nurture Group via Health Services. The referral highlighted concerns regarding their mother Tammy not engaging with supportive services. At the point of referral, Tammy was establishing a family home while Mathew was staying with his parents. When the Nurture Group Workers first became involved, Lacey and her unborn brother were on Children Protection Plans due to their mother's health needs and how this impacted on her capacity to parent. The role of Nurture Group had been defined within the Core Group as 'supporting positive engagement with professionals and providing a safe, nurturing environment for Lacey'.

Mathew tragically lost his partner and the mother of his children fifteen months after the Nurture Group Workers started working with the family. This was an extremely painful time for Mathew, who now found himself a single father of two very young children, homeless and fearful that he would lose the care of his daughter. The extended family, Mathew and the children were full of grief after losing someone whom they loved, and who loved them dearly. The Nurture Group staff had established a strong relationship with all members of the family and clearly Tammy's loss shocked them also. This sorrowful change in situation created a different level of involvement from the nurture workers, and meant their emotional connection to the family became strengthened. As professionals, they had to be aware of their own emotions, as they were mourning alongside the family whilst still trying to provide a safe and Containing relationship with Mathew and the children.

Mathew's love and commitment to his children had always been evident, but following the loss of Tammy, he showed strength and determination. Mathew had clear ideas on how he would manage parenting and support them to understand the loss of their mother. At the times that this led to conflict within the family, the Nurture Group Workers offered objective advice and facilitated conversations to enable the family to remain

*(Continued)*

connected and strong. Mathew faced a long and complicated course of action to gain full parental responsibility for Lacey. During this process, he also began to secure a new permanent family home. The Nurture Group staff provided gentle, respectful care for both the children and Mathew. They continued regular home visits, Kian also began attending sessions with his sister to allow Mathew to have time alone, and they offered practical assistance, for example sourcing furniture for their new home and regular transport to and from the setting. Their aim remained to support and Hold the family, to enable Mathew to establish daily routines and get through the difficult and at times frightening legal processes and to reinforce Mathew's efforts to create happy, loving experiences for his children.

The family is now settled in their new home and is part of their new community. The children enjoy regular visits with their grandparents, Lacey has moved on to her preschool and Kian continues to be part of the Nurture Group. Mathew is a strong father figure who has hopes and aspirations for his family. The staff and family journey evolved from a supportive service into a Containing, loving professional relationship. The Nurture Group staff believe that the family will always hold a firm place in their hearts.

When thinking about how Nurture Group supported Mathew, he has said that "After everything that has happened with Tammy, I was really glad to have the help of Katherine and Laura and their support made a difference. It helped the children to deal with what had happened and made a difference to us as a family. It also helped them to have somewhere to play and to have fun."

From Mathew's experience, we have learned how important it is for the staff to have an open and honest relationship with the families with whom we work. It is critical that workers are consistent with families to enable, over time, trusting relationships to develop. Having strong relationships means that the workers are more effectively able to support the family through the challenging times as well as the periods when life is less complex.

## Support for Family Workers carrying out extended Family Support roles

Family Workers, particularly those with additional Family Support responsibilities, need to feel safe, confident and skilled in these aspects of their job. They receive in-house Safeguarding training regularly and training in lone working. There is a robust home visit procedure for logging where they are going, and a system of safety calls while out home visiting. These help staff to be mindful of their responsibility for keeping themselves safe.

Workers need to be both qualified and experienced to carry out this complex work. Additionally, they need, and must be given, appropriate supervision time to plan for home visits and reflect on experiences. The extra demands on them include anxieties about Safeguarding, and being exposed to parents and young children experiencing pain, neglect and abuse. At the Centre, there is always a senior member of the Family Support team available to consult on Safeguarding issues. Centre leaders and those with supervisory roles need to have a deep understanding of the psychological processes that could affect their workers while carrying out this work, understanding the effects of adversity and deprivation on the emotional states and subsequent actions of young children, parents and workers. Workers who have experienced traumatic childhoods or are currently experiencing distressing circumstances could find memories or echoes of their own experiences being reawakened by exposure to the deprivation and difficulties being currently experienced by the family they are working alongside. This could lead to defensive avoidance of that family's pain, or an over-identification resulting in feeling overwhelmed. Both reactions could reduce the effectiveness of the service they provide to the family. Skilled supervision can tease out these possible reactions to the work, ensure that the work with the family continues unaffected, and the worker gains insight and relief from their distress. Additionally, young children and adults experiencing pain and trauma can relieve themselves of their awful feelings by projecting them on to their worker. Again, a skilled supervisor can help the worker gain insight into these processes, become experienced in not taking in these projections but, by noting the effect they have on them, understand at a deeper level what the parents and children are experiencing and thereby be more effective in responding to their emotional state and circumstances.

Additionally, at Pen Green, leaders and workers carrying out complex Family Support are invited to undertake a period of study at the adjoining Research and Training Base. This course, The Emotional Roots of Learning, facilitated by a team from the Tavistock Centre, The Northern School of Child and Adolescent Psychotherapy, provides training in Infant Observation, and the emotional impact of work with young children on workers. Course participants also bring situations from their current practice which are 'stirring up' their feelings. There is more information about this work in Chapter 8.

## Conclusion

In this chapter, we have tried to show how, within the setting of the universal nursery provision, the Family Worker role can be extended to provide additional support to young children and their families experiencing significant challenges. The bedrock of this work is the absolute belief that parents and Early Years Practitioners are equally valuable in supporting the child's development and learning. The role of the worker is to work alongside the parents and build trusting relationships. The relationships established between practitioners and parents are based on having open and honest dialogue, and these are established through working closely and intensively with families building a strong trusting foundation. The mutual respect inherent in these relationships provides the basis for families facing challenge and adversity to explore these factors with their Family Worker and to see how they impact on their child. We have to be careful to consider the individual needs of each child and their family, and tailor the offer to most appropriately meet their needs. Throughout this work, it is critical that reflective supervision is consistently offered to staff to enable them time to process the emotional impact of the complex work they are engaged in.

## References

Allen, G. (2011) *Early Intervention: The Next Steps*. London: Cabinet Office.

Arnold, C. & The Pen Green Team (2010) *Understanding Schemas and Emotion in Early Childhood*. London: Sage Publications Ltd.

Cabinet Office, Social Exclusion Task Force (2008) *Think Family, Improving the Life Chances of Families at Risk*. London: Crown.

Easen, P.P., Kendall, P. & Shaw, J. (1992) Parents and Educators: Dialogue and Developing Through Partnership. *Children and Society* 6 (4), pp. 282–296.

Elfer, P., Goldschmied, E. & Selleck, D. (2003) *Key Persons in the Nursery: Building Relationship for Quality Provision*. London: David Fulton Publishers Ltd.

Meade, A. and Cubey, P. (1995) *Thinking Children*. Wellington: New Zealand Council for Educational Research.

Northamptonshire County Council (2015) *Making Children Safer: Northamptonshire Thresholds and Pathways*. www3.northamptonshire.gov.uk/councilservices/children-families-education/help-and-protection-for-children/protecting-children-information-for-professionals/Documents/NCC114615_Thresholds%20and%20Pathways%20June%202014_AW3.pdf (accessed 31 October 2016).

Springate, I., Atkinson, M., Straw, S., Lamont, E. & Grayson, H. (2008) *Narrowing the Gap in Outcomes: Early Years (0–5 years)*. Slough: NFER.

Winnicott, D.W. (1965) *The Maturational Processes and the Facilitating Environment*. London: Karnac Books.

## Chapter 6

# Celebrating the voice of the child

*Lesley Hill and Angela Prodger*

In this chapter, we describe how staff work with children and their families to capture 'the voice of the child' from initial home visit, transition into the setting and throughout the child's time in the setting. We describe how we plan for children and use documentation to acknowledge the voice of the child.

## Getting to know you

In the Centre, all staff are committed to getting to know children and their families. All children are visited in their homes prior to starting in the setting. This allows the Family Worker to get to know the child in their home context. The initial home visit to a family is the most important visit, as this is where the foundations of the relationship and trust with the child and their family begin. 'What we want for all children is for them to be rich in potential, strong, powerful, competent and, most of all, connected to adults and children' (adapted from Malaguzzi cited in Edwards, Gandini & Forman, 1998, p. 42). On a regular basis, staff come together to think about their 'Image of a Child' and how they will support all children to be all that they can be.

The child is never seen as separate from their family. Family Workers acknowledge and celebrate where each child has come from and use information from home to start planning for the child's transition into the setting.

## Initial home visit

Family Workers make contact with the family to introduce themselves and arrange a home visit at a time that is convenient for the child's parents. This is sometimes the first time that the Family Worker has met the child and their family. For some families, this can be an anxious time, as they are uncertain about what the home visit will entail. On the initial visit, there is a need to complete documentation but more importantly to get to know the child in their familiar surroundings. Family Workers will use their professional judgement to gauge whether the parent(s) need some more time to complete the necessary paperwork and give the parent(s) the chance to talk. Similarly for the child, they may be keen to engage with the Family Worker and invite them to participate in their play, but for some children, this experience can feel a bit intrusive and they are more reluctant to engage. The Family Worker needs to read the subtle cues and nuances of the child and adapt their engagement style to meet the needs of each child. Children will engage in their own way and in their own time, and as adults, we need to recognise the importance of this and accept it.

## Using documentation to capture the voice of the child on the initial home visit

On this first home visit, Family Workers use a pro forma to gather information about the child.

First, the Family Worker tries to gather information about who lives in the house and their relationship to the child. We believe that this information is important, as these adults are the people who will be significant for the child and have an influence on the child's life. Second, we ask about pets, as they often play a special part in young children's lives too. Third, we have found that many families have family names and words that have a special meaning for their children. The Family Worker would discuss with the parents whether they would like their family names and words to be used in the setting. For children, to hear familiar words and the use of a family name can offer some reassurance when making the transition from home to the setting. Fourth, for some children, it is important to have visual images of the significant people in their life. This can also include pets. With permission from parents, the Family Worker would take some photographs or ask the parents to provide photographs which could be put into a book and shared with the child during their time in the setting. This simple resource gives the Family Worker a chance to talk with the child about the familiar people in their lives and is another way of offering a sense of reassurance and security.

## Settling-in

When a child is starting in the setting, Family Workers gather information about how the child likes to be comforted. This could be a cuddle from an adult, to the use of a special blanket, teddy bear or toy (transitional objects, Winnicott, 1953). Transitional objects play a significant part in young children's lives and help children to be able to manage their feelings and to self-regulate. Some parents may be anxious about their child's special toy or comforter being lost in a setting. This in turn can make staff feel worried and to have a tendency to store the special toys out of reach. The important thing to remember is that children will be using these transitional objects as

# Initial Home Visit

Date................................

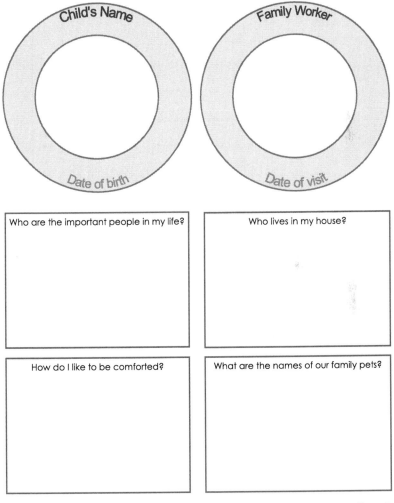

Child's Name

Date of birth

Family Worker

Date of visit

| Who are the important people in my life? | Who lives in my house? |
|---|---|
| | |

| How do I like to be comforted? | What are the names of our family pets? |
|---|---|
| | |

*Figure 6.1* Initial home visit sheet

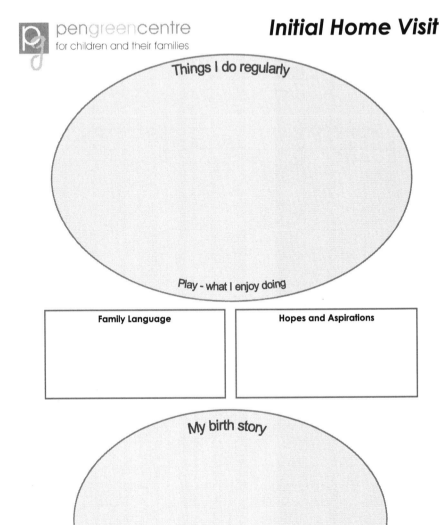

Figure 6.1 (Continued)

# Initial Home Visit

## What does my week look like?

| Monday | Tuesday | Wednesday | Thursday | Friday | Saturday | Sunday |
|---|---|---|---|---|---|---|
| | | | | | | |

Figure 6.1 (Continued)

pengreencentre
for children and their families

# *Initial Home Visit*

| General Health | Favourite foods/drinks |
|---|---|
| | |

**Medication/Allergies**


**Immunisations**

**Sleeping and waking patterns**

Favourite TV/computer programmes and DVDs

Favourite rhymes and books

Child's interests and family interests

*Figure 6.1 (Continued)*

pengreencentre
for children and their families

# Initial Home Visit

**Photographs or other information gathered at initial home visit**



*Figure 6.1* (*Continued*)

a substitute for their main caregiver; therefore, it is essential that they have free access to their special objects to support them in times of transition or when feeling emotionally Uncontained. There may be a particular way a child likes to be comforted by the special people in their life. It is important that the Family Worker knows this so that they can offer the child some continuity through replicating similar holding or rocking patterns and rituals in the setting.

If a child hurts themselves or has a sleep whilst in the setting, knowing how to comfort them the way they are comforted at home can play a significant role in their recovery.

When children start in the setting we ask that a significant adult spends two weeks settling the child into the setting. This gives the child time to get to know the new environment and begin to make relationships with staff whilst still having the security of a trusted, familiar adult. During this settling-in time, parents also have the opportunity to get to know staff and to observe practice in the setting. Staff are able to talk to parents about their child and what they like to do, where they like to go and what they like to play with. We start to build a picture of the child's interests and what excites them. Parents and staff share experiences and start to work together. Parents are invited to participate in 'key concept' sessions where they are introduced to the theoretical frameworks which staff use as a lens for looking at individual children's development and learning. This opportunity for dialogue and interaction between staff and parents gives parents the chance to share their specialist knowledge, and show that they are the expert on their own child (Easen *et al.,* 1992). It helps to create a shared language and meaning when discussing individual children, as well as being a catalyst for change in our practice and knowledge.

The following example is a case study of a child and his mother settling in to the setting.

Tiago began his settling-in several months prior to his transition into the Couthie. Flavia, Tiago's mother, began this journey with him well in advance of his initial settling-in date by bringing him into the setting for regular short periods of time and staying to play with him. Flavia had previously negotiated that Tiago's Family Worker would be Lesley. Flavia and Lesley, when possible, would sit together on these visits, chatting and playing with Tiago. Lesley was not always available to spend time with Tiago due to her commitment to other children in the setting; however, Flavia still wanted Tiago to spend time in the space to help him become more familiar with having lots of children around him, seeing other staff members and most importantly having time with his mum to get the feeling of the space he was going to be in. (This was an unhurried luxury that Flavia was able to offer Tiago. It is not always possible for parents to begin their child's settling-in so many weeks in advance, but we would certainly welcome it if it was possible.)

Flavia explained, "Lesley invested a lot of time to settle Tiago; from day one, she was really tuned into him, understanding his needs, being caring and sensitive. This really helped him to settle. I started settling-in really early on to ensure Tiago was familiar with the space, children and adults".

A home visit was arranged between Lesley and Flavia where the necessary paperwork was completed. Tiago was becoming more and more familiar with Lesley. He even allowed Flavia to go into the kitchen without him, staying with Lesley in the sitting room. Flavia commented how significant this was, as he hadn't done this with anyone else before.

Flavia said, "Tiago has settled really well in the Couthie; he has developed a lovely relationship with Lesley, feeling safe and loved, knowing she is his secure base". Bowlby (1969) writes about how babies use the mother as a 'base from which to explore' (p. 302).

Over the two-week period in the summer when the Centre was closed, Tiago went to Portugal with Flavia, Trevor, his father, and Aron, his older teenage sister. Flavia is Portuguese, and they were visiting her parents, Tiago's grandparents. Flavia has spoken to Tiago in both Portuguese and English since he was born.

Flavia commented, "Tiago loved being surrounded by all the people that love him".

When Tiago came back to nursery, he was unsettled and didn't want to separate from his mum.

Flavia reflected, "This was a difficult time for both of us. I felt sad that I had to let him go after spending 24 hours with him for two whole weeks, and I felt sad that it was also upsetting him to separate from me".

Tiago needed to be very close to Lesley, not wanting to leave her side. He indicated this very clearly by being upset whenever Lesley needed to move around the setting. This was a change from how Tiago had been prior to his holiday, and we needed to understand what was going on from his perspective. Lesley and Flavia spoke about Tiago's distress and how best to manage this for him and for Flavia as his mother. Trevor, Tiago's father, was also feeling anxious about Tiago. He said, "When we came back from Portugal, I felt that Tiago, having spent every hour with me and Flavia, was struggling to be apart from us, not wanting to leave our sides, which is hard to watch. But I think the great bond he has with Lesley helped him settle quickly and also made me and Flavia feel at ease".

Lesley gave Flavia and Tiago lots of reassurance and made sure that she was available to help 'Hold and Contain' Tiago at times of transition or when he was struggling emotionally. The concept of Holding is described as the emotional Holding parents can give their baby by Holding him or her in mind (Winnicott, 1965). Containment can be described as the parent taking in the baby's distress, understanding it and responding

*(Continued)*

in a way that the baby can feel emotionally looked after and Contained (Bion, 1962).

Lesley said, "Tiago and I come as a package for the time being. He is communicating to me clearly how he needs to be with me, so that is what is going to happen".

Flavia explained, "I trusted that he had a safe and secure relationship with Lesley and knew that he needed time to resume it".

Gerhardt states, 'If caregivers are well attuned to the child, they will be able to acknowledge the child's current emotional state' (Gerhardt, 2004, p. 51).

One particular morning within this first week back when Flavia announced that it was time for her to leave, Tiago became upset, letting his mummy know that he was going to miss her but signalling that he was okay to be left with Lesley by stretching his arms out to her.

Flavia commented, "Lesley tried to ensure that she was getting it right for Tiago. That was really reassuring for me as a parent".

Lesley and Flavia had daily chats, discussing what was going on for Tiago and what he was trying to tell us. At the end of this first week when Flavia picked Tiago up, he was really happy to see her and they had a big cuddle. Tiago then signalled that he wanted to go to Lesley, stretching his arms out to her. Flavia passed him over, and he gave Lesley a big cuddle too. Flavia and Lesley both agreed that they felt that Tiago was trying to tell them that his week had been hard, but he had gotten through it.

Flavia was pleased and reflected, "Lesley was there for him".

Tiago has settled back into the Couthie again now. He is happier to go off exploring independently and is much more comfortable in his space again.

Flavia said, "Lesley played a big part in this by allowing him to be dependent on her; that's what he needed for most of the time, to be supported by a loving, caring adult. Attachment Theory says that babies and children need to be dependent to become independent. That's exactly what happened for Tiago. He is now more independent because he had a long time being dependent on Lesley".

During the settling-in period and when parents first leave their children in the setting, the child's Family Worker completes a 'Getting to Know You' pro forma. This document has been adapted from the work of colleagues in New Zealand (Carr *et al.*, 2000). Staff use this documentation to focus on how well they know each child using five specific questions from the child's perspective as prompts:

- Do you know me?
- Can I trust you?
- Do you hear me?
- Is this place fair for me?
- Do you let me fly?

**pengreencentre**
for children and their families

# *Getting to know you*

My first day.....................................

**Do you know me?**

**Do you let me fly?**

**Do you hear me?**

Do I feel strong?

Unique child

Can I choose?

positive relationships

Do I feel in control?

Enabling environments

**Adult pedagogic strategies**

**Well-being**

**Involvement**

**Schemas**

Development and learning

Can I question?

**Can I trust you?**

**Is this place fair for me?**

*Page 1*

Figure 6.2  Getting to know you

**Family Voice**

*Figure 6.2 (Continued)*

This information is shared with the child's parent and forms part of the child's Celebration of My Achievement record. For staff, this sometimes highlights that children need more time to transition and that staff and parents need to think together to make sure that the child is being 'Held in mind' and their emotional needs supported appropriately. This often means staff acknowledging the child's pain and distress and talking to them about it. When parents leave their children in the setting, all staff will encourage the parents to say goodbye to the child. Some parents are reluctant to do this as they do not want to upset their child when they appear to be settled. Staff talk to parents about the importance of the child knowing that their parents have left and not turning to look for them and then feeling a sense of abandonment. During this process, staff will make themselves available to support the child and the parent if this is distressing for them, too.

## Child's interests

Family Workers observe children in many different ways, mainly through narrative and snapshot observations. We also use photographs and video recording to support our documentation of children's development and learning. This way of capturing children's development and learning also helps Family Workers and parents to reflect on what a child or a small group of children have been doing and what their current interests might be. Family Workers make time to engage in daily dialogue with parents, grandparents and carers, as this gives Family Workers the opportunity to find out more about what the child is currently interested in doing at home.

Information from home is used to plan for children in the setting and forms part of the child's development and learning journal (Celebration of My Achievements file). When trying to understand each child's interests and preoccupations, Family Workers will use schema theory (Athey, 1990, 2007) and Well-being and Involvement signals and scales (Laevers *et al.*, 1997, 2005). Chris Athey describes schemas as 'patterns of repeatable actions that lead to early categories and then to logical classifications' (Athey, 1990, p. 36). Ferre Laevers refers to well-being and involvement as the two process variables that tell us how children are doing. Laevers and his team developed a tool to help us to identify deep level learning. This tool can be used in a setting and at home (Laevers *et al.*, 1997).

## Information from home

We work closely with parents and carers to help us plan for their child when they attend nursery. If we know what the child is doing regularly at home, we can plan similar interests for them in nursery. On our initial home visits, we have opportunities to talk to parents about their child's current interests and what they like playing with.

> Nothing gets under a parent's skin more quickly and more permanently than the illumination of his or her own child's behaviour.
>
> (Athey, 1990, p. 66)

We are also able to meet the child, see them in their familiar surroundings and observe what they are playing with. This helps us to plan for their initial settling-in sessions and set out similar resources that we think might be of interest to them. For instance, if a parent tells us that their child is mad about cars and plays with them all day long, we can set out the garage and vehicles for them to explore when they come to nursery.

## Planning sheets

Family Workers plan for children's development and learning on a daily basis using their personal and professional knowledge of individual children, alongside daily observations, to inform the planning for the following day or session when the child will next attend. Information from home is also used to plan meaningful experiences for children in the setting. For some children, it is really important that they have time to revisit experiences and have the opportunity to explore, experiment and discover, giving the child the chance to assimilate and accommodate their prior learning. Planning is not about next steps and moving children on, but more about close observation and reflection on what the child is curious about and what they want to learn. Through the use of schema theory, Family Workers are able to plan meaningful opportunities for children based on what a child is intrinsically motivated to do at home and in the setting.

## Celebration of My Achievements file

All children in the setting have an individual file, 'A Celebration of My Achievements', with information and evidence about their achievements. Staff in the setting gather information about the child over time through narrative observations, photographs, work produced by the child, learning journeys, information from home, anecdotal evidence and summative assessments of the child's development and learning. These files belong to the child, and parents can choose to access them freely in the setting. Parents are encouraged to contribute to their child's documentation and can take their child's file home to share with family and friends. Children also like to look through their files and some children make a conscious contribution to what goes in to their Celebration of My Achievement file. For some children, it is a lovely way to revisit and talk about previous experiences, giving their perspective on what took place and what is important to them.

## Possible Lines of Direction

This is a tool that Family Workers use to document and plan possible individual development and learning opportunities for children in the setting and at home. Family Workers start with a child's current interest at home and in the setting and recent observations to map ideas against each area of the Early Years Foundation Stage (DfE, 2014). The information collated on the Possible Lines of Direction

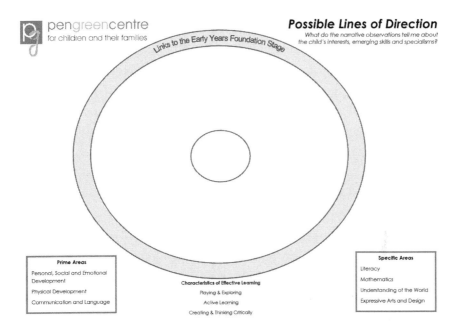

*Figure 6.3* Possible Lines of Direction (PLOD)

(PLOD) is used as a medium-term plan. By recording the child's play, interests and schematic explorations, we are able to build up a picture of the individual child and where they are on their learning journey. Information and ideas from the PLOD are used in daily planning and planning for special visits and outings.

## Sharing information with parents

Family Workers in the setting use a secure online journal app to document children's experiences in the setting. This information is shared with parents and other significant adults in the child's life, for example grandparents, aunties and uncles. Using technology to share children's experiences can capture children in 'flow' (Csikszentmihalyi, 1992, p. 74). Csikszentmihalyi describes flow as a feeling of '"being carried along", a sense of discovery, a creative feeling of transporting the person into a new reality.'

This information can be sent to parents immediately, almost allowing parents to be a 'fly on the wall' in the setting. It can also be used for children to revisit and share their learning at home and in the setting. All parents are encouraged to sign up to the app and share information and learning from home as well as commenting on the information that has been shared by Family Workers. When there is a reciprocal exchange of information from home to setting and from the setting to home, children will experience continuity and a consistent approach to their development and learning.

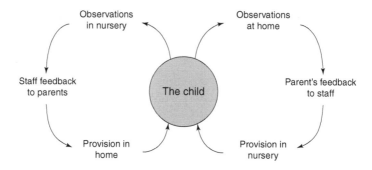

*Figure 6.4* Pen Green Loop

## Peer-peer observations

The Ofsted Early Years Framework has an emphasis on the importance of observations of children and practitioners.

Peer-peer observations happen on a termly basis whereby Family Workers video one another's practice and watch it back together to critique themselves and their practice. Family Workers use the Pedagogic Strategies as a framework for these reviews (Lawrence & Gallagher, 2015). You can read more about the revised Adult Pedagogic Strategies (2013) in Chapter 7.

The idea of peer-peer observations is to enable the Family Worker to look closely at his/her own practice with time to think deeply about what is going on for the child and themselves in the video vignette. To complete this alongside a colleague enables discussions to evolve around the child's interests, sharing knowledge about individual children and exchanging ideas based on what a child's play and investigation may have been about. Family Workers alongside colleagues have the opportunity to complete future individual planning for the child which would be recorded on a PLOD pro forma.

Etherington (2004, p. 19) describes reflexivity as

> An ability to notice our responses to the world around us, other people and events, and to use that knowledge to inform our actions, communications and understandings.

Initially, this process can feel quite a daunting experience, but the more regularly it happens, the more honest and open Family Workers can be with each other. This said, it is important that you are comfortable with the colleague filming you. It is important that you have trust and respect within your team and can ask for the filming to be stopped at any time.

The importance of these reviews is to have time to reflect and dialogue about your practice with colleagues. This should be a positive experience for all participants and the engagement based on trust and honesty. Through this process, we hope to improve practice for all participants.

The following example is of a peer-peer discussion with a focus on Tiago. Staff carefully considered Tiago's needs, gaining multiple perspectives to help one another to gain a better understand and knowledge of the child. It is also an opportunity for staff to jointly discuss the implications for practice (Cherryholmes, 1993).

When Tiago started in the setting, he was nine months old, and at home, he co-slept with his parents during the day for naps and at night. It was important for Tiago that this was replicated as much as possible in nursery for him. By understanding his needs and his routine at home, Lesley was able to mirror this in nursery. If we are to truly represent the child's voice, it is important that we understand the child's home context. When using the Pedagogic Strategies framework the staff team discussed.

Adult Pedagogic Strategies 2 – Linking experiences: The adults are aware of the child's experience with other adults at home and in the setting.

To begin with, Tiago would need two naps during his day. He was rocked to sleep in Lesley's arms and would stay in her arms to sleep peacefully until he woke. This meant that Lesley was sitting with Tiago, sometimes for two-, one-hour periods, during the day, taking her away from being physically available for other children. Lesley felt the need to discuss this with the other members of the team. The peer-peer approach was used to engage in an honest dialogue with the rest of the team.

Adult Pedagogic Strategies 6 – Adult Attitudes: The adult is aware of the impact of his or her own attitudes and beliefs and how these will affect the child's learning.

Time was taken to talk through Tiago's needs, Lesley's approach, feelings of the team and the overall impact this may have.

Lesley believed that Tiago's sleep pattern at home needed to be mirrored in nursery throughout the day; this also means the way he slept, too. The team had a meaningful discussion around the ethos of following a child's home pattern and the importance of understanding

(*Continued*)

how this can support a child to feel more settled and secure in the nursery environment. This lead the discussion onto the importance for Lesley to hold Tiago whilst he slept, as during the day at home, he would sleep on his mother. Tiago needed to do this in nursery, too; he had experienced no other way of taking his daily naps. The staff team discussed the need for Lesley to be emotionally and physically available for Tiago, as he needed that close, intimate contact to allow him to rest and sleep.

> Adult Pedagogic Strategies 8 – Using the Body: The adult affords learning experiences using the body ranging from using slight touch to whole body experiences if appropriate. The adult knows how individual babies and children like to be held, rocked and comforted.

The team talked through their own feelings about this approach and the fact that Lesley would make herself available to Tiago when he needed to sleep. This is where peer-peer respect and honesty counted; staff needed to talk openly, ask questions and consider the impact on their practice.

Staff discussed the implications for their practice and how best to manage this situation. Picking up on Lesley's other children whilst she was with Tiago was the main point. It was agreed that staff would share the responsibilities and Hold the other children in mind from Lesley's group.

Over time, Lesley began to notice that Tiago was pulling at his mummy's scarf, or trying to kick it off his legs and feet. When Lesley talked to Flavia about this, she confirmed that Tiago no longer used the scarf at home. He did not like being covered with her scarf or blankets any longer. He was now beginning to communicate this to Lesley in nursery, too.

Later, he began to show signs of being uncomfortable in Lesley's arms. Whereas previously he had appeared happy to snuggle into Lesley, using her body for comfort and security, he had started to pull away slightly and resist her embrace. He would take longer to fall asleep and Lesley felt that he was not so comfortable or restful. Lesley spoke to Tiago's mum and she again confirmed that he was doing a similar thing at home. She explained that Tiago would fall asleep in her arms but then lay on the sofa until he woke. Lesley began to do this in the setting, allowing Tiago to fall asleep in her arms before transferring him to one of the sleep baskets. Lesley immediately noticed that Tiago was taking his naps more peacefully again.

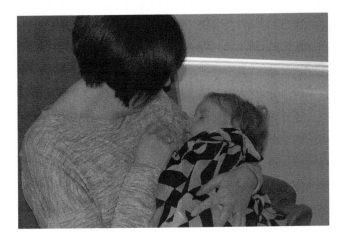

*Figure 6.5* Tiago and Lesley

## Parents' involvement in their children's learning

In the setting, all staff work closely with the important adults in a child's life. Daily dialogue with parents forms part of the setting's routine. Staff want to know how the child has been at home and to learn as much as possible about what the child is interested in. For some parents, having an opportunity to have an informal discussion about their child on a regular basis is important. For other parents, it is more beneficial to have time in their own home to talk about their child. Staff are mindful that fathers and extended family play a significant role in children's lives and try hard to engage them in dialogue as they can give a different perspective on the child. There is no one-size-fits-all; therefore, staff have to find alternative ways to engage with all parents. We believe that all parents will engage in their own way in their own time.

## Capturing the child's voice through non-verbal communication

When working with the youngest children in our setting, staff tune into children's non-verbal communication, paying close attention to their body language, eye contact and gestures. Children will start to make relationships and communicate with peers and adults through non-verbal communication, and this needs to be documented and celebrated. Most of our communication is non-verbal; therefore, a lot can be learnt from young children's non-verbal communication.

## Conclusion

At Pen Green, we honour and celebrate the voice of the child through a variety of different methods. We find it is helpful to have a repertoire of methods to find the most appropriate one for each individual child and their family. We work in close collaboration with the parents to ensure that we fully understand the young child's home context. We strive to understand how the young children we work with are communicating with others and finding out about the world around them.

## References

Athey, C. (1990, 2007) *Extending Thought in Young Children: A Parent-Teacher Partnership.* London: Paul Chapman.

Bion, W. (1962) *Learning from Experience.* London: Heinemann.

Bowlby, J. (1969) *Attachment and Loss, Volume 1.* London: Hogarth.

Carr, M., May, H., Podmore, V., Cubey, P., Hatherly, A., & Macartney, B. (2000) *Learning and Teaching Stories: Action Research on Evaluation in Early Childhood. Final Report to the Ministry of Education.* Wellington: New Zealand Council for Educational Research.

Cherryholmes, C. (1993) Reading Research. *Journal of Curriculum Studies,* 25(1), 1–32.

Csikszentmihalyi, M. (1992) *Flow: The Psychology of Happiness.* London: Rider.

Department for Education (DfE) (2014) *The Early Years Foundation Stage: Setting Standards for Learning, Development and Care for Children from Birth to Five.* London: DfE.

Easen, P., Kendall, P. & Shaw, J. (1992) Parents and Educators: Dialogue and Developing through Partnership. *Children and Society,* 6(4), 282–296.

Edwards, C., Gandini, L. & Forman, G. (1998) *100 Languages of Children* (2nd edition). Westport: Ablex Publishing Corporation, 49–97.

Etherington, K. (2004) *Becoming a Reflexive Researcher – Using Ourselves in Research.* London: Jessica Kingsley Publishers.

Gerhardt, S. (2004) *Why Love Matters: How Affection Shapes a Baby's Brain.* London: Routledge.

Laevers, F., Vandenbussche, E., Depondt, L. & Kog, M. (1997) *A Process-Oriented Child Monitoring System for Young Children.* Belgium: Centre for Experiential Education.

Laevers, F., Debruyckere, G., Silkens, K. & Snoeck, G. (2005) *Observation of Well-Being an Involvement in Babies and Toddlers.* Belgium: Centre for Experiential Education.

Lawrence, P. and Gallagher, T. (2015) *Adult Pedagogic Strategies – Professional Development Learning Materials.* Corby: Pen Green Centre.

Winnicott, D.W. (1953) *International Journal of Psychoanalysis,* Volume 34, Part 2. London: Tavistock Publications.

Winnicott, D.W. (1965) *The Theory of the Parent-Infant Relationship (1960) in the Maturational Processes and the Facilitating Environment.* London: Hogarth Press.

## Chapter 7

# 'Pedagogic Strategies'

## A conceptual framework for effective parent and practitioner strategies when working with children under five

*Penny Lawrence and Tracy Gallagher*

(A version of this chapter was published in the journal *Early Childhood Development and Care* 2015 DOI 10.1080/03004430.2015.1028390)
In this chapter, we explain a research project in which we identified adult Pedagogic Strategies; these are ways in which adults already engage to support children's learning effectively. The strategies themselves make a conceptual framework. The Pedagogic Strategies framework was first developed by parents and practitioners for working with children aged three to five years at Pen Green Centre (Whalley & Arnold, 1997). At Pen Green, we have created several frameworks to support the development of practice. We focus on professional development rather than training as we see the introduction to these frameworks as part of an ongoing process of reflection and review. This chapter focuses on the 2013 revision of the adult Pedagogic Strategies framework to encompass work with children under the age of three.

## What is effective pedagogy?

In their longitudinal study Researching Effective Pedagogy in the Early Years (REPEY), Siraj-Blatchford *et al.* (2002) sought to broaden the definition of pedagogy from 'the practice of teaching' to consider the environment and the process of play while retaining a core of instruction: '*Pedagogy* refers to that set of instructional techniques and strategies which enable learning to take place and provide opportunities for the acquisition of knowledge, skills, attitudes and dispositions within a particular social and material context' (Siraj-Blatchford *et al.*, 2002, pg. 28). Their research suggested that particular differences in philosophies or curriculum priorities were not the main contributing factors to educational performance, so a setting may be effective without it being related to one approach or another. There is, nevertheless, a case for considering the underpinning values that define pedagogical effectiveness beyond economic effectiveness or outcome measures (Weikart, 2000): 'Pedagogy needs explicitly to be seen to encompass a spirit of enquiry and professional dialogue about *why* we do what we do' (Kinney, 2005, pg. 4). The Pedagogic Strategies project at Pen Green aimed to develop locally what Coles (2002) calls 'professional judgment'.

We wanted a framework that would provide staff with opportunities to review their practice, consider the aspects of their work they do well and identify how to make improvements.

Internationally, Bertram and Pascal (2002) reviewed the Early Years pedagogical approaches of twenty different countries. They found a substantial consensus on reciprocal interactional pedagogy, 'adopting a flexible range of teaching and learning strategies according to the needs of the children' (Bertram & Pascal, 2002, Section 3.6, pg. 22). Within the Effective Early Learning Project (EEL), Pascal and Bertram (1997) drew on the work of Rogers (1983) to think about the ways in which, as adults, we interact with young children in order to facilitate their learning in dynamic relational processes. This latter work informed the Pedagogic Strategies research project with parents and practitioners that we carried out at Pen Green.

## What are adult Pedagogic Strategies?

Adult Pedagogic Strategies are how adults effectively support children's learning and development. They are *not* a "to-do" check list. They are effective strategies that are embedded in our practice. Noticing them, reflecting on them, and observing and recognising the children's learning and development enable us to work more effectively and critically reflect on our own development as pedagogues (Carr, 2001). They complement and integrate our work with other frameworks, the Early Years Foundation Stage (DfE, 2012) and the Teacher's Standards for qualification and continuing professional development (National College for Teaching and Leadership, 2013) as EYPs, EYTs and Qualified Teachers in Early Years and primary.

### The pedagogy of parents and the local context

The role of parents has been extensively researched and yet has developed relatively recently in terms of pedagogy. In a literature review of developmentally appropriate practice and play-based pedagogy, Walsh *et al.* (2010) did not consider the potential of parents beyond a role limited to the time of transitions for the child, although they called for a more open-minded evidence-based approach to understand pedagogy in the Early Years. An exceptional case within the REPEY findings did indicate the potential of home-based pedagogy. It described a situation where the effectiveness of the practitioners in the setting was limited, yet the cognitive outcomes for the children were excellent:

> It was less the staff's interventions and more the parents' proactive behaviour towards their children's learning in the embedded, cultural context of the home, that provided a good basis for sustained shared thinking [...] the parents prepared themselves to provide a 'potent home-based pedagogy' on a daily basis!
>
> (Siraj-Blatchford & Sylva, 2004, pg. 726)

There can be no presumption that it is the setting that improves the teaching potential of the parents. The cultural contexts for children's learning vary, as will the extent to which children may learn through observation of their parents and practitioners (Rogoff *et al.*, 1993). The construct of parents having a 'natural pedagogy', rather than what may otherwise be referred to as sensitive interaction or a high level of engagement, remains to be explicitly validated and current understanding of it is limited (Sage & Baldwin, 2012). Nevertheless, the value of working with parents' pedagogy is that it includes what the children learn within their home and within their culture. Local knowledge construction aligns with England's Department for Education (DfE) (2014a) call for educational communities to generate evidence of effective practice that is owned at the setting level. At a local level, the Pedagogic Strategies project at Pen Green had also identified 'Principles of Engagement with Under Threes' (Tait, 2007) established by parents and staff in our area.

## The methodological approach to the research

### Phase 1 methodology

In 1997, we invited parents to take part in a small study, funded by the then Teacher Training Agency (now the National College of Teaching and Leadership), to consider the Pedagogic Strategies that both workers and parents were using (Whalley & Arnold, 1997). We began by introducing a group of parents to the work on Adult Style which was being used in the EEL (Pascal & Bertram, 1997).

At first, the Pen Green workers and parents used the EEL framework to discuss what they were seeing on several video sequences of adult/child interactions. The children were three to five years old. Workers then spent time video-filming this group of parents, each with their own child, settling them into nursery and then supporting them in their play. The same children were then filmed with their Family Worker from the nursery. All the parents and workers met and looked at the video material together and subsequently began to reflect on and analyse what were effective teaching strategies that were being used. From this detailed analysis, we arrived at a framework of effective adult teaching strategies used by both parents and nursery staff.

### Phase 2 methodology

More than a decade after the original research, the review of the Pedagogic Strategies was an opportunity for us to respond to the increased number of children below the age of three that we were now working with at Pen Green. Therefore, in 2012–2013, a second working group of parents and staff was formed. We decided to repeat the method we had used in 1997 filming parents each with their own children and then filming the same children with their Family Worker. The parents and workers would once again meet to reflect on and analyse the video clips.

## Participatory approach

The decision to use participatory research in case studies aligns with our commitment to working with families and Family Workers (Desforges & Abouchaar, 2003; Langford, 2010; and Whalley *et al.*, in press). More than a method, it is a decision about an entire approach to research (Kindon *et al.*, 2007). In order to research *with* people, not *on* them (Heron & Reason, 2001), within a socially constructivist perspective (Creswell, 2012), we deliberately sought parents from the setting to take a participatory role in meaning-making in 'a participatory process concerned with developing practical knowing' (Reason & Bradbury, 2008, pg. 4), and the resulting selection of participants can be seen as a strength in terms of validity. They contributed their knowledge and their values (see the Shared code of ethics section).

## Participants

Six mothers decided to participate after due consideration of the time commitment involved. The process of self-selection was also an ethical selection to ensure that the burden for participants would be manageable (BERA, 2011). They were not representative of individuals who have less inclination or availability to participate. The selection process proved to be successful as the participants did not withdraw from the study because of time issues and remained engaged throughout the research. There were six mothers out of sixteen families, over a third of the families using the provision for children under three at the time (the Nest). We considered this to be a large enough number to inspire confidence in our findings. Sourcing data with our participants was more important than the number of participants.

The participants reviewed their initial discussions and, through the group's own processes of quality control, decided to ensure increased male participation in the study. There had been no fathers present in the discussions, although they had seen the video clips that had been sent home for viewing. The case studies were extended to include two additional families from which the fathers could participate more fully.

## The case study approach

The participants did not form a sample, but case studies. Valuable findings can be made from a small number of case studies, and the generalisability can be increased by the strategic selection of cases to provide rich information. 'Random samples emphasizing representativeness will seldom be able to produce this kind of insight; it is more appropriate to select some few cases chosen for their validity' (Flyvbjerg, 2006, pg. 13). The rationale for selecting a case study approach derives from the situated nature of our enquiry, 'its real world context' (Yin, 2014, pg. 8). A case study also allows for the use of tacit knowledge by those who interpret the findings (Simons, 2009). Trustworthiness (Lincoln & Guba, 1985) and authenticity (Guba & Lincoln, 1989) are evidenced by confirming results with participants and through the high level of their involvement.

## Visual analysis

Video episodes provide for a multi-modal reading of the interactions between the children and adults. For example, the modes of gesture and gaze, as well as vocalisations, are important for children's learning (Goodwyn *et al.*, 2000; Raikes *et al.*, 2014; Topping *et al.*, 2013), and the research team drew on the works of Flewitt (2006) and Norris (2004, 2011) to interpret these.

Each child was video recorded by a practitioner or the researcher with his/her parent while involved in a learning experience, and was also recorded with his/her Family Worker. The research group met over a series of early evening sessions to discuss the short (three- to five-minute) episodes. Two stages of analysis were derived from visual anthropology (Collier, 2001). The first was an open viewing initial stage of the whole experience of the episode. Rather than starting with a list of themes or codes and then applying them, comments were noted in the open viewing, identifying images or critical sequences in the episode for the second stage, a detailed interpretation. This was an inductive process drawn out of the observations. Our closeness to the visual material countered the risk of seeking to confirm pre-existing theories (Flyvbjerg, 2006). The project employed appreciative enquiry, drawing value from what we saw and from each other's evaluations (Gergen, 2001; Reed, 2006). Themes emerged through dialogue and comparison between the video clips. The themes were reported back to the broader staff team and were developed into strategies in dedicated continuing professional development meetings. There had been more than one possible interpretation and way of structuring the strategies, and this whole staff evaluation was a key stage in constructing and embedding the knowledge collectively in our practice (Kindon *et al.*, 2007).

## Shared code of ethics

The project complied with the British Educational Research Association ethical guidelines (BERA, 2011). As democratic a relationship as possible was sought between the researcher, staff and parents (Nolen & Vander Putten, 2007), using the project setting's own ethical policy. These were relational ethics in an ongoing relationship with the participants. We shared concern for the children's learning and development and concern for each other's experience. We saw a range of reactive attitudes (Strawson, 1962) which were meaningful to and demonstrated between all the participants in the study: the practitioner's consideration of how one family's response to a video episode may affect another family, the practitioner's reflection on her own practice, the researcher's awareness of her presence and the potential changes caused to the children and staff experience, and the parents' responses to a close study of their child.

To be clear, the main and overriding responsibility for the conduct of the project was the researchers'. However, as a research group, we were developing judgement not only of effective pedagogy, but also of how we conducted ethical relationships in our setting. Eshleman (2014) situates these judgements on principles within our practice: 'Their justification refers back to an account of the reactive attitudes and their role in personal relationships, *not to some independent theoretical account of the conditions on being responsible*' (online). Our developmental partnership (Easen *et al.*, 1992) was within an ethical space for sharing values and evaluation of pedagogy. It demonstrated 'a particular attitude that leaves open the possibility for ethical reflection' (Ramaekers & Suissa, 2011, pg. 198), rather than a parenting intervention to instruct parents or for them to feel they ought to develop expert knowledge. Leading the research, we were mindful of our diverse roles and knowledge bases, neither assuming nor intending that parents and practitioners were or ought to become the same.

Power issues were addressed by the distribution of decision-making. In addition to the researcher, practitioners recorded each other's practice and led their own contribution. The setting manager did not decide what the observations should include. Parents discussed and decided what and when to record in their interactions. For example, they selected the time of day to record that allowed for the most typical interaction between adult and child. At the interpretation stage, the participants chose which clips to focus on. The parent of each child led the discussion, and the researcher and team manager were conscious to facilitate all participants, at all staff leadership levels, to have time within the meetings. In addition, practitioners were able to give feedback within regular supervision with their line manager. In the second phase of the research, we considered how we heard the parents' contributions, we decided to include more individual communication to check transcripts and exchange feedback through phone calls and email. The voice of the participants could therefore be heard both in the group and outside it to allow time and convenience for reflection on the study.

## Findings

### New strategies

There was a degree of continuity with the original strategies identified by the first research cohort in 1997, and two newly identified strategies emerged (see Table 7.1). For example, the pre-existing first strategy, 'Subtle intervention: The adult watches and listens to what the child is doing before intervening', was also identified in 2013. There was some adaptation of original strategies. The team leader for children below three years valued what she called 'the synergy and synchrony between staff and between staff and parents'. The children's experience is with and between the adults who have awareness of each other, both within the same period of time as the child moves between adults in the setting, and asynchronously between days and between home and setting. Although the

*Table 7.1* The revised adult Pedagogic Strategies (2013)

1. Subtle Intervention – The adult watches and listens to what the child is doing before intervening.
2. Linking Experiences – The adults are aware of the child's experience with other adults at home and *in the setting*.
3. Acknowledging – The adult acknowledges the child's presence, emotions and capability by

   • being physically close to them including using touch if appropriate to make contact (see also Strategy 8),
   • tuning into the child's facial expressions and vocal intonation, including playfulness and teasing.

4. Working with the Child's Initiative and Agency – The adult considers what the child is bringing to each interaction, checks out the child's meaning and gives the child time to respond or to question. The adult encourages the child's curiosity and ability to make choices including taking appropriate risks.
5. Adult Learning – The adult is committed to his/her own learning. S/he is open to play and learn alongside the child, encouraging new learning for both child and adult.
6. Adult Attitudes – The adult is aware of the impact of his or her own attitudes and beliefs and how these might affect the child's learning.
7. Using Language – The adult knows about the child's home vocabulary and offers new information to the child, including preparation for what is about to happen and describing what has just happened, and language to support the child's actions.
8. Using the Body – The adult affords learning experiences using the body ranging from using slight touch to whole body experiences if appropriate. The adult knows how individual babies and children like to be held, rocked and comforted.

'in setting' aspect of the child's experience may have been understood to be in place in the pre-existing strategies, it was not stated explicitly. The second strategy was revised to incorporate it, 'Linking Experiences: The adults are aware of the child's experience with other adults at home and *in the setting*', whereas before the links had been stated as between home and setting.

The two new strategies that emerged in 2013 were 'acknowledging the child's presence' and 'using the body', an embodied pedagogy, with the following definitions.

### Acknowledging

'The adult acknowledges the child's presence, emotions and capability by: being physically close to him/her including using touch if appropriate to make contact; tuning into the child's facial expressions and vocal intonation, including playfulness and teasing'. An example of acknowledging was when a practitioner, Sarah, used speech, touch, gesture and gaze to let two children, Oscar and Polly, each knows that she is paying attention to them when they both wanted to use the same push-along trolley at the same time.

## Using the body

'The adult affords learning experiences using the body ranging from using slight touch to whole body experiences if appropriate. The adult knows how individual babies and children like to be held, rocked and comforted'. An example of using the body was when Dawn allowed Danny to recline back extending his full length to relax and read a book in her arms.

The following case study demonstrates the different Pedagogic Strategies used with a child, in the first example by his Family Worker and in the second example with his mother.

## Case study of Dawn with Danny

In the first part of the case study, a Family Worker, Dawn, interacts with Danny (twenty-eight months) using the following Adult Pedagogic Strategies: Subtle Intervention (1), Acknowledging (3), Working with the Child's Initiative and Agency (4), Using Language (7), and Using the Body (8).

---

Danny had just settled at the play dough when his attention was drawn to another child, Jenny. Dawn watches with him (Strategy 1). He is then involved in balancing the rolling pin, which Dawn acknowledges (Strategy 3), 'Ooh look at that!', putting down the flattened dough which she had been holding for him.

Danny gives Dawn the rolled and folded dough. She acknowledges (Strategies 3 and 4), contextualises and extends his language (Strategy 7):

DANNY:  Roll it.
DAWN:  Roll it! Like a sausage roll.
      She then offers him alternative directions that the imaginative play could take (Strategy 4),
DAWN:  Thank you. Does it need cooking? Does it need to go in the oven? Or is it cooked already? [Pause]
DAWN:  Shall I put it in the oven on a plate, or can I eat it now?

There is a pause in which Danny smiles and makes eye contact with Dawn. She interprets his use of his body verbally 'Can I eat it now?' and with the use of her own body lifting and pretending to eat the roll (Strategies 3 and 8). She sustains eye contact, smiles and draws in her shoulders in a complicit movement towards Danny. When she offers the roll back to Danny, he meets it carefully with the rolling pin.

---

## The second part of the case study is Nina with Danny

Nina interacted with her son, Danny (thirty months), using the following Adult Pedagogic Strategies: Subtle Intervention (1), Acknowledging (3), Working with the Child's Initiative and Agency (4), Adult Learning (5), Using Language (7), and Using the Body (8).

---

Nina is aware of how Danny is using his body pointing, curling and re-curling his fingers, to indicate his interests and explore objects ('What are you showing me?') (Strategies 3 and 8). She responds to Danny's question about the treasure basket (Strategy 4). She acknowledges Danny's presence, emotions and capability by being physically close to him and letting him make contact with her hair with the brushes (Strategies 3 and 8). She also tunes into Danny's facial expressions and vocal intonation, including playfulness and teasing with the objects they find in the basket, such as the curtain rings and the metallic foil (Strategy 3).

DANNY: 'I like that one'
NINA: 'Yeah!'

Nina is working with Danny's initiative and agency (Strategy 4) checking his meaning and encouraging his curiosity and using language to support the child's actions ('Noisy, isn't it?') (Strategy 7).

Nina's timing is tuned to Danny's as they experiment looking through the rings (Strategies 1 and 5). Her movements are paced to match his as they explore using touch. Her close proximity and body position make an intimate space for their interactions (Strategy 8).

---

## Discussion and involving fathers

### The experience of the participants

The project found many aspects of the new strategies resonated in our analysis of the episodes recorded with the male participants.

### The following example is of a parent, Darren, and his reflection on 'Acknowledging' and 'Using the Body'

Darren reflected on video episodes of his interactions with Oscar. He met with Penny, the researcher, and Sarah, Oscar's Family Worker. The video viewing discussion raised Darren's awareness. He recognised the use of touch in the family's own culture. He was prompted to record Oscar's older brother, Michael, caressing Oscar's head early in the morning.

DARREN: I've seen it again with his hair and I put my finger out for his hand.

PENNY: Has anything surprised you?

DARREN: I was surprised when we looked back at the video I noticed how many times I touched his hair.

PENNY: What do you think that's like for Oscar when you do that?

DARREN: I think it's soothing for him to realise that I'm there and it gives him security that if he looks round, I'm there.

SARAH: Like both touch and acknowledging together.

PENNY: What about the value for you as the parent?

DARREN: I've noticed it around the house and at Dads' Group. I always seem to touch Oscar's hair all the time. Since we did the last video, I've noticed it a lot more.

The use of video revealed surprising aspects of interactions for people who have worked in a setting or been a parent for years. A process of diffraction or transformation of perspective on what otherwise had been considered known occurred. Video case studies were, therefore, an appropriate tool for reviewing practice as Iedema (2014) found in his video reflections with medical practitioners and patients: 'people often saw beyond what was displayed on the screen out across the organisation, back into the past, or forward into the future, linking what was shown to what was known' (2014, pg. 198). The use of the body was identified through our raised awareness of multi-modal interactions. Darren reconsidered what he knew of his own family culture in the light of the research discussion. However, Darren's finding does not correspond with Iedema's conclusion that

> while our multimodal analyses of interaction may identify bodily and behavioural peculiarities, these issues may not be easily communicated to those in the footage. Our findings may confront, precisely because they delve below the level of everyday consciousness, accessing the more embodied, and therefore normalised and naturalised aspects of existence.
>
> (2014, pg. 209)

Darren's realisation was his own, direct, readily explored and demonstrated in this research process. The participants' reflection on their practice showed that while not all strategies are in use at any one time, the strategies were readily recognised by each of the participants as forming part of their own pedagogy. Similar processes of recognition were found through video reflection in Cremin et al.'s (2006) study of pedagogy in relation to fostering agency and possibility thinking.

The REPEY project noted some deficit in the responses of adults with regard to their own practice: 'The child-minders were not able to articulate explicitly their pedagogical understandings' (Siraj-Blatchford et al., 2002, pg. 113). By contrast, the experiences of the participant parents in this research project indicated articulate and considered understanding of the findings and the implications for the community. Sue, Sally's mother, spoke of her experience: 'Regarding the themes that have emerged in the Pedagogic Strategies, I think the process is crucial to the development of the setting. I think we [parents] do all of this [strategies] all the time and through this [discussion] we learn the reasons'.

### The new strategies: acknowledging and using the body

#### Acknowledging

Acknowledging relates to attunement, affirmation, accompanying, recognition, connection, and inter-subjectivity. Why should being noticed be an important part of these processes?

> What is it about being noticed that is important? Is it simply that when we are noticed we notice that we have an impact on the world – that we are effective? Or is there something special about being noticed by other minds?
> (Reddy, 2008, pg. 40)

Being noticed is fundamental for the child to interact and be involved and connect with others. Knowing that one has been noticed is the essence of inter-subjectivity (Stern, 1985; Trevarthen, 1998). Inter-subjectivity in turn is the ground in which Attachment grows (Stern, 1985). Acknowledging the child's presence is saying 'You're here'. There are arguments (Dalli *et al.*, 2011a; Stern, 2004) to suggest that these moments of inter-subjectivity, of encounter between self and other, construct a sense of identity in the young child. We identified many instances of the adult noticing the child who approached him or her and the child knowing that s/he had been noticed, that his/her presence was acknowledged.

Presence is both physical and emotional. Physically, the adult could acknowledge presence in close proximity through touch or through creating an interactive space (Payler, 2007) by the orientation of his/her body to the newly arrived child (this relates to the other new strategy – using the body).

The adult could also acknowledge over distance through speech and through eye contact. It could happen without overtly intervening in the child's experience by *active listening* (Rinaldi, 2001), by using facial expressions and through alertness to the child's presence (Goodfellow, 2008). Acknowledging the physical presence does not happen only at the beginning of an interaction, but also throughout an episode; the experience can be acknowledged from a child's perspective. For example, the Family Worker, Anna, asked one child who was watching the others on the slide, 'Can you see that, Henry?'

Beyond the physical presence and perspective of the child, the adult is also tuning into the emotional state and cognitive interest of the child responding to his/her expressions and actions. Acknowledgement is the foundation stone for attunement that is the key concept of quality identified in Dalli *et al.*

(2011b): 'pedagogy with under-two-year-olds is realised in the establishment of attuned interaction between children and their caregivers who are present, supportive and responsive to the interactional cues of the infant and toddler' (2011b, pg. 4). It is a strategy that does not require extensive resourcing or time. As Sam, another mother, reflected, it was about 'Presence, acknowledging presence as well as feelings. I didn't have to do a lot'.

As the fundamental basis for the learning relationship, and for the child's developing sense of identity, acknowledging as the initial part of inter-subjectivity could be the focus of significant further research: 'there are few investigations of the pedagogical role of the teacher in this area of under-two-year-olds' inter-subjective experience' (Dalli *et al.*, 2011b, pg. 76). Acknowledging could be identified in other cultures as connecting to the other person and as part of the inter-connectedness of learning; for example, in the Maori context of 'whanaungatanga', where people are intimately connected to everyone else (Tamati, 2005).

Strategies are not completely separate. The categorisation only serves to clarify what is, in practice, interlinked. The acknowledging strategy underpins and complements the first 'Subtle Intervention' strategy. The English REPEY study also found that in the most effective pedagogy, shared purpose is founded on attunement to the perspective and knowledge of the child before intervening (Siraj-Blatchford *et al.*, 2002, pg. 725). We found that the strategy of acknowledgement often co-occurred with the use of the body and touch, resonating with Johansson's description of inter-subjectivity,

> A pedagogical encounter with the child's life world [...] involves approaching and trying to understand the child's whole being. Bodily experiences and expressions, as well as ways of relating to others constitute the components of a child's very existence in the world, and are as such significant for learning.
>
> (Johansson, 2004, pg. 11)

Acknowledging relates to the image we have of the child as a person and the stance we take to relating to that person: 'underpinning professional capabilities is a philosophy which describes an adult who seeks to connect with the essence of the child' (Atherton & Nutbrown, 2013, pg. 14). Acknowledging works within what Nutbrown calls 'a learner and person centred ethos' (2006, pg. 125). Brennan (2005) calls this a 'culture of tenderness' when teachers help young children feel at home with love, patience, humour and personal attention. For Singer and de Haan (2007), part of the teacher's role is creating a 'we-feeling' of togetherness. Greeting and giving attention to each child are a simple starting point for this relational pedagogy. In Elfer's (1996, 2007) research, family interactions were described as 'intimate and spontaneous' and in-setting interactions as 'more professional and planned' (2007, pg. 169). Acknowledging and using the body raise questions about intimacy that perhaps need to be answered locally, at the setting level. Is there a place for more 'family-like' effective pedagogic strategies, intimacy and spontaneity in Early Years settings? When parents in this study were asked to rank the Pedagogic Strategies, they prioritised wanting their child to have acknowledging and touch and contact (using the body) when in the setting, as that is what they would have had at home.

## Using the body

Young children learn using movement, physical actions and tactile experiences. They have many modes of making meaning in addition to developing speech (Flewitt, 2006). In Multiple Intelligence Theory, Gardner (1983, 2006) sets out many forms of intelligence, whereas Malaguzzi (1998) thought intelligence is single but using many *languages*/modes of expression. Both include using the body as part of an educational experience. An effective pedagogy will use and provide for the children using these many modes of participation (Bae, 2010). The project participants used touch at a finely controlled level, allowing their fingers to be guided by children to trace over the text and images on the page, or to explore the geometry of a watch-strap. They used their whole bodies, making themselves into a base for the children as a chair, a chaise lounge, a harbour or platform.

The adults also interacted using their whole bodies expressively, as when Sarah skipped along a corridor with children. An embodied pedagogy that integrates the body and mind, acknowledging the physical presence and experiences of the children and using the same modes of communication as they do, is called for internationally (Bresler, 2004; Chodarowski & Egan, 2008; Hocking *et al.*, 2001; O'Loughlin, 2006).

*Figure 7.1* A child using a worker as a 'seat' to share a story

The pedagogic strategy 'using the body', like the Key Times training for 'the physical as professional' (Manning-Morton & Thorp, 2006), could ensure appropriate provision for the children rather than the alternative 'no touch' policies (Tobin, 2004) that neglect the needs of the children and, in our case, the preferences of parents. Developing good physical and mental health is supported through sensitive and responsive holding and rocking, as well as embodied learning, often in games (Tait, 2007). Trevarthen and Aitken (2001) suggest that physically rhythmic movements can be part of inter-subjective interactions, encouraging emotional, cognitive and social growth if they are attuned. The *way* in which these physical interactions take place is significant for the child's positive sense of self (Gerhardt, 2004).

*Safeguarding.* One outcome of the project was to provide targeted Safeguarding training for staff to support safe, healthy intimacy in interactions with children. Safeguarding can be seen in two different ways: keeping children safe, and Safeguarding their well-being by ensuring that children have good experiences to flourish. Early childhood settings can combine these two important aspects; however, leadership needs to be equally confident and competent in both areas. Leaders must themselves be well trained and very clear about their robust policies, procedures and practices, and national statutory responsibilities (DfE, 2013).

### Implications, applications and limitations of the study

The Pedagogic Strategies link to and complement other frameworks. In England, they integrate with Positive Relationships used in guidance for the curriculum (Early Education 2012) and the professional standards for Early Years teachers (National College for Teaching and Leadership, 2013). Practitioners' workloads are subject to pressures in many early childhood contexts (DfE, 2014b, pg. 6; Easthope & Easthope, 2000). To introduce a framework for effective pedagogy in addition to the statutory requirements that practitioners fulfil would be an untenable proposition were the principles, practice and processes unrelated. Moreover, workload is not the only consideration of quality of experience for Early Years Practitioners. Hargreaves and Hopper (2006) propose that the status of Early Years professionals would be increased by emphasising the pedagogical elements of their specialist expertise. Formosinho and Figueiredo (2014) see the 'Pedagogy-in-Participation' approach as an asset rather than an imposition, and one that builds capacity for working with cultural diversity. The Pedagogic Strategies project has built staff capacity for working in the local community through appreciating cultural values and practices that have come from that locality.

The new revised framework of Pedagogic Strategies was agreed in whole staff meetings by the project setting staff. After this stage, the Pedagogic Strategies framework was integrated into continuing professional development. It forms part of the peer-peer observation review process for all practitioners working with under and over threes. The Early Years Inspection Handbook (Ofsted, 2015) has a strong emphasis on observation of young children and practitioners. During the inspection process, the inspector will focus on how well adults care for children and consider the impact of what the adults do on children's learning and development. Inspectors are required to make one or more joint observations to gain an insight into the effectiveness of the provision's professional development programme for practitioners. The Pedagogic Strategies approach will support practitioners in responding to Ofsted inspector's questions and lines of enquiry about how they are ensuring and developing quality Early Years education in their setting.

## What did we learn?

There have been extensive reviews of what constitutes quality in Early Years pedagogy. What is distinctive about this project is the parent and practitioner developmental partnership co-constructing strategies that are local, relevant and owned by the participants. The findings show a high degree of consistency with the findings of the major studies. This project recognised the extensive pedagogy that parents have with their children and identified two strategies that are particularly important for children under three: acknowledging and using the body. Although there is a need for further research into the pedagogical role of the educator in inter-subjectivity, this project demonstrates how acknowledging interweaves with the use of touch in safe, healthy intimacy with children, and more broadly shows the value of an embodied pedagogy. The project team would recommend that all Early Years staff teams have opportunities to enquire into their own pedagogy, the values and priorities in their settings, and that they should do this with the families in their community.

## References

Atherton, C. & Nutbrown, C. (2013). *Understanding schemas and young children: From birth to three.* London: Sage.

Bae, B. (2010). Realizing children's right to participation in early childhood settings: Some critical issues in a Norwegian context. *Early Years, 30*(3), 205–218.

Bertram, T. & Pascal, C. (2002). *Early years education: An international perspective.* London: Qualifications and Curriculum Authority.

Brennan, M. (2005). "They just want to be with us" young children learning to live the culture: A post-Vygotskian analysis of young children's enculturation into childcare settings. Wellington: University of Wellington (dissertation).

Bresler, L. (2004). Prelude. In L. Bresler (Ed.), *Knowing bodies, moving minds: Towards embodied teaching and learning.* Dordrecht: Kluwer, 7–11.

British Educational Research Association (BERA). (2011). *Ethical guidelines for educational research.* London: BERA. Retrieved from www.bera.ac.uk/wp-content/uploads/2014/02/BERA-Ethical-Guidelines-2011.pdf (Accessed 23 January 2015).

Carr, M. (2001). *Assessment in early childhood settings.* London: Paul Chapman Publishing.

Chodarowski, A. & Egan, K. (2008). The body's role in our intellectual education. In J. Kentel & A. Short (Eds.), *Totems and taboos: Risk and relevance in research on teachers and teaching.* Rotterdam: Sense Publishers. Retrieved from www.ierg.net/ assets/documents/publications/IERGBodyrole.pdf (Accessed 2 December 2011).

Coles, C. (2002). Developing professional judgment. *Journal of Continuing Education in the Health Professions, 22,* 3–10. doi:10.1002/chp.1340220102.

Collier, M. (2001). Approaches to analysis in visual anthropology. In T. Van Leeuwen & C. Jewitt (Eds.), *Handbook of visual analysis.* London: Sage, 35–60.

Cremin, T., Burnard, P. & Craft, A. (2006). Pedagogy and possibility thinking in the early years. *Thinking Skills and Creativity, 1*(2), 108–119.

Creswell, J. (2012). *Qualitative inquiry and research design: Choosing among five approaches* (3rd ed.). London: Sage.

Dalli, C., Rockel, J., Duhn, I., & Craw, J. with Doyle, K. (2011a). *What's special about teaching and learning in the first years?: Summary report.* Wellington: Teaching Learning Research Initiative. Retrieved from www.tlri.org.nz/sites/default/files/projects/ 9267-Dalli/9267_summaryreport.pdf (Accessed 27 January 2014).

Dalli, C., White, E., Rockel, J., Duhn, I., with Buchanan, E., Davidson, S., Ganly, S., Kus, L. & Wang, B. (2011b). *Quality early childhood education for under-two-year-olds: What should it look like?: A literature review.* New Zealand: Ministry of Education. Retrieved from www.educationcounts.govt.nz/_data/assets/pdf_file/0009/89532/ 965_QualityECE_Web-22032011.pdf (Accessed 27 January 2014).

Department for Education (DfE). (2012). *The early years foundation stage: Setting standards for learning, development and care for children from birth to five.* London: DfE.

Department for Education (DfE). (2013). *Working together to safeguard children: A guide to inter-agency working to safeguard and promote the welfare of children.* Retrieved from: www.gov.uk/government/uploads/system/uploads/attachment_data/file/281368/ Working_together_to_safeguard_children.pdf (Accessed 23 January 2015).

Department for Education (DfE). (2014a). *Early education and childcare research priorities and questions.* DfE, DFE-00090-2014. Retrieved from www.gov.uk/government/ uploads/system/uploads/attachment_data/file/288192/Early_education_and_ childcare_research_priorities_and_questions.pdf (Accessed 23 January 2015).

Department for Education (DfE). (2014b). *Teachers' workload diary survey 2013: Research report DFE-RR316.* Department for Education. Retrieved from www.gov.uk/ government/uploads/system/uploads/attachment_data/file/285941/DFE-RR316.pdf.

Desforges, C. & Abouchaar, A. (2003). *The impact of parental involvement, parental support and family education on pupil achievements and adjustments: A literature review.* Research Report 443. London: DfES.

Early Education. (2012). *Development matters in the Early Years Foundation Stage (EYFS).* London: Early Education.

Easen, P., Kendall, P. & Shaw, J. (1992). Parents and educators: Dialogue and development through partnership. *Children & Society, 6,* 282–296. doi:10.1111/j.1099–0860.1992. tb00395.x.

Easthope, C. & Easthope, G. (2000). Intensification, extension and complexity of teachers' workload. *British Journal of Sociology of Education, 21*(1), 43–58.

Elfer, P. (1996). Building intimacy in relationships with young children in nurseries. *Early Years, 16*(2), 30–34.

Elfer, P. (2007). What are nurseries for? The concept of primary task and its application in differentiating roles and tasks in nurseries. *Journal of Early Childhood Research, 5*(2), 169–188.

Eshleman, A. (2014). Worthy of praise. In D. Shoemaker & N. Tognazzini (Eds.), *Oxford studies in agency and responsibility, Volume 2: 'Freedom and resentment' at 50*. Oxford: Oxford University Press, 216–242.

Flewitt, R. (2006). Using video to investigate pre-school classroom interaction: Education research, assumptions, and methodological practice. *Visual Communication, 5*(1), 25–50.

Flyvbjerg, B. (2006). Five misunderstandings about case-study research. *Qualitative Inquiry, 12*(2), 219–245. doi:10.1177/1077800405284363.

Formosinho, J. & Figueiredo, I. (2014). Promoting equity in early years context: The role of participatory educational teams. *European Early Childhood Education Research Journal, 22*(3), 397–411.

Gardner, H. (1983). *Frames of mind: The theory of multiple intelligences*. New York: Basic Books.

Gardner, H. (2006). *Multiple intelligences: New horizons*. New York: Basic Books.

Gergen, K. (2001). Appreciative inquiry as dialogue: Generative and transformative. *American Psychologist, 56*(10), Oct 2001, 803–813.

Gerhardt, S. (2004). *Why love matters: How affection shapes a baby's brain*. Hove and New York: Brunner-Routledge.

Goodfellow, J. (2008). Presence as a dimension of early childhood professional practice. *Australian Journal of Early Childhood, 33*(1), 17–22.

Goodwyn, S., Acredolo, L. & Brown, C. (2000). Impact of symbolic gesturing on early language development. *Journal of Non-verbal Behavior, 24*(2), 81–103.

Guba, E. & Lincoln, Y. (1989). *Fourth generation evaluation*. Newbury Park, CA: Sage.

Hargreaves, L. & Hopper, B. (2006). Early years, low status? Early years teachers' perceptions of their occupational status. *Early Years, 26*(2), 171–186.

Heron, J. & Reason, P. (2001). The practice of co-operative inquiry: Research 'with' rather than 'on' people. In P. Reason & P. Bradbury (Eds.), *Handbook of action research: Participative inquiry and practice*. London: Sage, 179–188.

Hocking, B., Haskell, J. & Linds, W. (2001). *Unfolding bodymind, exploring possibility through education*. Rutland, VT: Resource Centre for Redesigning.

Iedema, R. (2014). A participatory approach to analyzing visual data: Involving practitioners in visual feedback. In S. Norris & C. Maier (Eds.), *Interactions, images and texts: A reader in multimodality*. Boston/Berlin: de Gruyter, 195–212.

Johansson, E. (2004). Learning encounters in preschool: Interaction between atmosphere, view of children and of learning. *International Journal of Early Childhood, 36*(2), 9–26.

Kindon, S., Pain, R. & Kesby, M. (2007). *Participatory action research approaches and methods: Connecting people, participation and lace*. Abingdon: Routledge.

Kinney, L. (2005). *Let's talk about pedagogy: Towards a shared understanding for early years education in Scotland*. Learning and Teaching Scotland/Scottish Executive. Retrieved from www.educationscotland.gov.uk/images/talkpedagogy_tcm4–193218.pdf.

Langford, R. (2010). Critiquing child-centred pedagogy to bring children and early childhood educators into the centre of a democratic pedagogy. *Contemporary Issues in Early Childhood, 11*(1), 113–127. doi:10.2304/ciec.2010.11.1.113.

Lincoln, Y. & Guba, E. (1985). *Naturalistic inquiry*. Beverly Hills, CA: Sage.

Manning-Morton, J. & Thorp, M. (2006). *Key Times: A framework for developing high quality provision for children from birth to three*. Maidenhead: Open University Press.

Malaguzzi, L. (1998). History, ideas and basic philosophy: An interview with Lella Gandini. In C. Edwards, L. Gandini & G. Forman, (Eds.), *The hundred languages of children: The Reggio Emilia approach – advanced reflections.* London: Ablex Publishing Corporation, 49–98.

National College for Teaching and Leadership. (2013). *Teachers Standards (Early Years).* www.gov.uk/government/publications. (Accessed 13 September 2016).

Nolen, A. & Vander Putten, J. (2007). Action research in education: Addressing gaps in ethical principles and practices. *Educational Researcher, 36*(7), 401–407.

Norris, S. (2004). *Analyzing multimodal interaction: A methodological framework.* Abingdon: Routledge.

Norris, S. (2011). *Identity in (Inter)action: Introducing multimodal (Inter)action analysis.* Berlin/Boston: de Gruyter.

Ofsted. (2015). *Early Years Handbook.* www.gov.uk/government/publications/early-years-inspection-handbook-from-september-2015 (Accessed 15 September 2016).

O'Loughlin, M. (2006). *Embodiment and education: Exploring creatural existence.* Dordrecht: Springer.

Pascal, C. & Bertram A. (1997). *Effective early learning: Case studies of improvement.* London: Hodder and Stoughton.

Payler, J. (2007). Opening and closing interactive spaces: Shaping four year-old children's participation in two English settings. *Early Years, 27*(3), 237–254.

Raikes, H., Roggman, L., Peterson, C., Brooks-Gunn, J., Chazan-Cohen, R., Zhang, X. & Schiffman, R. (2014). Theories of change and outcomes in home-based Early Head-Start programs. *Early Childhood Research Quaterly, 29*(4), 574–585. doi:10.1016/j.ecresq.2014.05.003.

Ramaekers, S. & Suissa, J. (2011). Parents as 'educators': Languages of education, pedagogy and 'parenting'. *Ethics & Education, 6*(2), 197–212.

Reason, P. & Bradbury, H. (Eds.). (2008). *The Sage handbook of action research: Participative inquiry and practice (2nd ed.).* London: Sage.

Reddy, V. (2008). *How infants know minds.* Cambridge, MA: Harvard University Press.

Reed, J. (2006). *Appreciative inquiry: Research for change.* London: Sage Publications.

Rinaldi, C. (2001). A pedagogy of listening. *Children in Europe, 1,* 2–5.

Rogers, C. (1983). *Freedom to learn for the 80s.* New York: Merrill Wright.

Rogoff, B., Mosier, C., Mistry, J. & Goncu, A. (1993). Toddlers' guided participation with their caregivers in cultural activity. In E. Forman, N. Minick, & A. Stone (Eds.), *Contexts for learning: Sociocultural dynamics in children's development.* New York: Oxford University Press, 230–253.

Sage, K. & Baldwin, D. (2012). Exploring natural pedagogy in play with preschoolers: Cues parents use and relations among them. *Education Research and Perspectives, 39,* 153–181.

Simons, H. (2009). *Case study research in practice.* London: Sage.

Singer, E. & de Haan, D. (2007). *The social lives of children: Play, conflict and moral learning in day-care groups.* Amsterdam: SWP.

Siraj-Blatchford, I., Muttock, S., Sylva, K., Gilden, R. & Bell, D. (2002). *Researching effective pedagogy in the early years.* London: Department for Education and Skills, Research Report 356.

Siraj-Blatchford, I. and Sylva, K. (2004) Researching pedagogy in English pre-schools. *British Educational Research Journal, 30*(5), 713–730.

Stern, D. (1985). *The inter-personal world of the infant.* New York: Basic Books.

Stern, D. (2004). *The present moment in psychotherapy and everyday life.* New York: W. W. Norton & Company.

Strawson, P. (1962). Freedom and resentment. *Proceedings of the British Academy, 48,* 1–25.

Tait C. (2007, 29th August – 1st September). 'Principles of engagement with under threes'. Paper presented in symposium at the European Early Childhood Education Research Association Conference, Prague.

Tamati, A. (2005). Ma tou rourou, Ma toku rourou – The concept of Ako: Co-construction of knowledge from a Kaupapa Māori Perspective. In C. Scrivens (Ed.), *Early Education,* 37. Palmerston North: Department of Social and Policy Studies in Education, Massey University College of Education, 23–32.

Tobin, J. (2004). The disappearance of the body in early childhood education. In L. Bresler (Ed.), *Knowing bodies moving minds, towards embodied teaching and learning.* Dordrecht: Kluwer, 111–125.

Topping, K., Dekhinet, R. & Zeedyk, S. (2013). Parent-infant interaction and children's language development. *Educational Psychology, 33*(4), 391–426.

Trevarthen, C. (1998). The concept and foundations of infant inter-subjectivity. In S. Bråten (Ed.), *Intersubjective communication and emotion in early ontogeny.* Cambridge: Cambridge University Press, 15–46.

Trevarthen, C. & Aitken, K. (2001). Infant inter-subjectivity: Research theory and clinical application. *Journal of Child Psychology and Psychiatry, 42*(1), 3–48. http://dx.doi.org/10.1017/S0021963001006552.

Tripp, D. (2012). *Developing professional judgement.* Abingdon: Routledge.

Walsh, G., Sproule, L., McGuinness, C., Trew, K. & Ingram, G. (2010). *Developmentally appropriate practice and play-based pedagogy in early years education: A literature review of research and practice.* Belfast: CCEA. Retrieved from www.nicurriculum.org.uk/docs/foundation_stage/eye_curric_project/evaluation/Literature_Review.pdf.

Weikart, D. (2000). *Early childhood education: Needs and opportunity.* Paris, UNESCO: International Institute for Educational Planning.

Whalley, M. & The Pen Green Team. (forthcoming 2017). *Involving parents in their children's learning* (3rd ed.). London: Sage.

Whalley, M. & Arnold, C. (1997). *Parental involvement in education: Summary of research findings.* London: Teacher Training Agency.

Yin, R. (2014). *Case study research* (5th ed.). Thousand Oaks, CA: Sage.

## Chapter 8

# Consultancy observation

## A methodology to promote group reflective capacity

*Colette Tait, Felicity Norton, Tracy Gallagher and Sheena Griffiths-Baker*

This chapter outlines the development of an observational tool, 'consultancy observations', for use when practitioners in Early Years settings have concerns about particular children in their care. The methodology facilitates the development of a shared reflective capacity, allowing staff teams to think together about a child's whole experience in their setting. This process encourages staff teams to consider their feelings and actions towards the child in question, gaining a deeper understanding of what the experience is like for the child. Often, members of staff gain insights into children's particular vulnerabilities and strengths. Through thinking and talking together, *reflecting*, staff behaviours change in subtle ways, thus changing the child's experience, for the better.

## Background

The Pen Green Centre in Corby, Northamptonshire, is a fully integrated provision for children and families, combining early education, health and social care, which opened in 1983. The Centre offers the following:

- Nursery provision for 320 children from nine months to four years old across five nursery spaces
- Family Support, including a home visiting service
- Children's Centre services, including a group work programme, ranging from a support group for mothers suffering from postnatal depression to a baby massage class or messy play session
- Adult Education enabling parents to gain basic qualifications such as IT, functional skills or an Introduction to Childcare
- Research, training and development, within which practitioners can access accredited undergraduate and postgraduate education (Whalley *et al.*, 2013)

## Psychodynamic theory

Historically, we have drawn on psychodynamic theory to support our work in groups with parents and children and our understanding of relational development. The theories that we have found particularly helpful have been as follows:

- 'Holding' (Winnicott, 1965): describing the emotional Holding parents can give their baby by Holding him or her in mind
- 'Containment' (Bion, 1962): describing the parent taking in the baby's distress, understanding it and responding so that the baby feels emotionally looked after and 'Contained'
- 'Attachment' (Bowlby, 1969): considering how adults and children form and develop reciprocal relationships

As a result of learning about and drawing on these theories, alongside a psychotherapist, we began to introduce 'reflection' and 'pre-flection' times at the beginning and end of group sessions where we were working with parents, infants and children up to three years of age. These times were used to reflect on the functioning of the group and to think about how we might prepare ourselves for the group ahead. This was a way of keeping links between the weekly sessions, therefore Holding parents and children 'in mind' (Winnicott, 1965). Sometimes during these sessions, it seemed as though we spoke about what appeared to be an issue, and then without doing anything tangible, the issue disappeared. The psychotherapist, who was working alongside us, used to say that merely by talking and thinking about something, in other words 'reflecting', "...change would occur". Staff members, although perplexed initially, soon saw the value of working in this way.

As an organization, it became important to 'skill up' more staff members in understanding psychodynamic theory.

## Research projects and interventions

Over time, different approaches were taken to 'skill up' staff members in relational and psychodynamic theory:

1999: A psychotherapist was employed to work in the Growing Together groups and offered monthly supervision to staff.

2002: A consultant child and adolescent psychiatrist was introduced to support practitioners to think about the complexities of their work with vulnerable families and process their emotions. This was arranged on an ad hoc basis as and when it was needed.

2000–2004: A research project was completed to consider children's Emotional Well-being and Resilience (Laevers, 1997). The project identified the importance of the Key Person (Elfer et al., 2003), transitions (Griebel & Niesle, 2003), separations (Ainsworth et al., 1978) and good supervision (Hawkins & Shohet, 2000). Through the project, our Pedagogic Strategies (Whalley & Arnold, 1997) were further developed in recognition of an emotional pedagogy to include relational aspects between practitioners and children. Links between parents' Attachment status and their child's emotional well-being were identified (Charlwood & Steele, 2004; Arnold, 2010).

2005: A seven-week training programme was run at Pen Green, by the Anna Freud Centre, exploring Parent-Infant Mental Health. Within this course, practitioners had the opportunity to hone their observational skills through observing using the Bick Tavistock method of observation (Bick, 1964).

2008: The consultant child and adolescent psychiatrist that we had been working with since 2002 was systematised and booked on a termly basis to support practitioners. This intervention is still in place.

2008: A psychologist and expert in group relations and organisational consultancy was introduced to support the Centre Leadership Team to develop their ability to understand and make use of organisational dynamics in identifying new approaches to challenges faced by the organisation. This intervention still takes place every six weeks.

## The emotional roots of learning: the beginnings of consultancy observation

In 2012, "The Emotional Roots of Learning – A Young Child Observation Course" was set up in conjunction with Janet Shaw, a child psychotherapist from the Northern School of Psychotherapy, to take place at Pen Green. The aims of 'Emotional Roots' were to enable participants to

- Extend and develop their awareness and understanding of young children's emotional development
- Develop their observational skills
- Use psychodynamic concepts as a framework to understand children's interactions, behaviour and play

Emotional Roots runs over the course of an academic year with participants undertaking the following:

- Attending fifteen fortnightly seminars with other participants, facilitated by a child psychotherapist
- Carrying out a Young Child Observation for an hour each week for the duration of the course
- Engaging in a 'work discussion' where participants bring an observation of themselves at work to the fortnightly seminar group
- Reflecting on and discussing psychodynamic papers during the fortnightly seminars

## The Young Child Observation

The Young Child Observation must be made in a setting that is not the participant's own of a child they do not know. Participants are required to undertake the observation using the Bick method of observation (Bick, 1964).

Using this method, participants do not make notes whilst observing, but try to pay 'free-floating attention' to the child and to become aware of the feelings evoked in themselves as observers (Bick, 1964). The observation is written up as soon afterwards as is possible, in its 'raw' form with no analysis or interpretation.

## Fortnightly seminars

Fortnightly seminars are facilitated by a child psychotherapist who, as seminar leader, creates a safe space for discussion within a psychodynamic frame. During the seminars, the morning is given to reflecting on and discussing the psychodynamic literature that participants have read prior to the seminar. Concepts from the papers are linked directly with participants' observations and experiences (Shaw & Tait, 2014). In the afternoon, two participants have an opportunity to share their child observation and one participant their work discussion. The participant reads aloud her copy of the observation she has made, and the seminar group then reflects on the emotional content of the observation, the internal world of the child observed and how s/he relates to others in the setting. Similarly, the seminar group focuses on the emotional communication within interactions with colleagues, children and parents when the work discussion is presented.

Below is an example of an observation taken from Whyte (2003) that is similar to the observations taken to the seminar group. It is followed by a short analysis, identifying themes with the observation.

## Fragment of an observation

"Did she have to go to work?" asks Meagan's mum. Kirsty nods her head again.

"Do you want a cuddle?"

She puts her arms round Kirsty and holds her gently. Meagan comes over. Her mum says to Kirsty, "Meagan misses her mummy sometimes as well. But your mummy will come back for you. You'll see her later".

Meagan has been listening. She puts her arms round Kirsty, gives her a hug, then moves away. Meagan's mum says to Kirsty, "Will we go over to the hospital and see what's wrong with this baby?"

She points to a doll lying on the bed. Kirsty suddenly comes to life. She bounces over to the bed and Meagan's mum follows. "What's wrong with the baby?" she asks.

"She had a fall", replies Kristy.

"Oh dear, what has she hurt?"

"Her leg...and her arm".

"Oh, we'll need to put on a bandage".

She starts to bandage up the doll's leg (Whyte, 2003).

## Analysis: themes

In this short extract, a number of themes can be seen:

- Kirsty allows herself to be 'Contained' (Bion, 1962) when she is distressed.
- Meagan's mother puts Kirsty's distress into words; it begins to be possible to think about it.
- Meagan is in 'identification' with her mother (Sandler, 1987).
- Kirsty is being helped to manage her distress at her mother leaving by symbolically caring for the baby.
- Psychical pain is represented as physical pain. The symbol is meaningful for Kirsty (Shaw & Tait, 2014).

## A small scale research project

It was important that, as an organization, we understood the impact this training was having on staff members. A small scale research project was undertaken in the hope of identifying how Emotional Roots had impacted participants personally, professionally and organizationally.

Altogether, twenty participants had undertaken the course from Pen Green. Nine of those participants had either left the organization, retired or were off sick, leaving eleven potential participants for this research. Preliminary information was requested from those eleven and was received from ten participants. Of those ten, six indicated that they were happy to take part in an interview in order for us to understand their 'experiences in as rigorous and detailed a manner as possible' (Denzin & Lincoln, 2000, pg. 782).

The six participants were approached, and the project was discussed with them.

We discussed the following:

- What the project would entail, based on 'full and open information' (Denzin & Lincoln, 2000, pg. 138) to enable them to give informed consent should they wish to take part
- Their right to withdraw at any time
- Their right to have a copy of the interview transcript within a week of the interview
- Their right to withdraw parts of the interview or restrict its use

In effect, we had applied '...a system of moral principles to prevent harming or wronging others, to be respectful and to be fair' (Sieber, 1993, pg. 14).

Semi-structured interviews were carried out with six participants still employed within the organization, allowing the 'interviewees freedom to digress and raise their own topics as the interview progresses' (Elliott, 1991, pg. 80). Although the cohort interviewed was small, it was necessary to allow enough time to carry out the interviews and allow for '...the time needed to consider what has been said during the interview, to go though notes, to extend and clarify points' (Bell, 1999, pg. 143).

It was decided that in order to elicit narrative evidence in a creative way, we would draw on the idea of 'surprising the unconscious' (George *et al.*, 1985). To do this, two of the semi-structured interview prompts were as follows:

- Please give me three adjectives that describe your experience of Emotional Roots.

Once the adjectives were given, the participants were asked the following:

- Please give me a specific example from your experience that illustrates your adjective.

This method seemed to take participants to a 'feeling' place. One participant commented, "Oh, my goodness that gets me right to the nub of it". It evoked emotion in participants and during the discussion participants became very animated and in three instances cried for varying reasons. The technique really did seem to surprise the unconscious (George *et al.*, 1985).

The three most common adjectives supplied were as follows.

### Challenging
"The reading material...the academic nature of some of the papers...some of the content as well".

### Interesting
"I found it was interesting as I found I was very focused...it helped me gain a deeper understanding of theory".

### Thought-provoking
"Raising your awareness of own feelings and own mind...also asking those questions you might avoid".

Other adjectives were awakening, enlightening, stimulating, exciting, deep, reflective, emotional, scary, demanding, and useful.

## Findings

The findings were overwhelmingly positive, with all participants reporting the positive impact the course had on them both personally and professionally:

"I had heightened my awareness of why people behave as they do, including myself – you can find yourself not getting so cross".

"Reminded me again of my early experiences and how they still impact on who I am, how I behave, what's important to me and how I manage".

"I am more connected to my emotions since doing Emotional Roots".

"It definitely made me consider other ways of analysing and taking into account how I'm reacting to things...it goes everywhere with you".

"I think I've been more reflective about the way my 'baggage' and 'being' at the moment can influence how I work with others and be aware of that".

"Helped so much in work – I know what makes me shut off".

"I feel more knowledgeable; I feel I can link my learning to children in nursery now".

"It made me think about boundaries".

"Deepened my understanding and gave me new strategies and techniques to use and share with my colleagues".

"I am far more in tune with children".

"It's the permission to 'feel' – it's just so powerful... makes me much better at my job".

In relation to whether they felt the course had impacted on the organisation, the responses were far less positive, with participants stating:

"No, not so..."

"I can't say it's embedded across the Centre as I wouldn't know".

"Not enough I don't think...It's not wide enough yet, but there are people that are seeing it and value it...we've got to drive it forward".

Participants reported feeling as though they understood the complex theories when they were in the seminar group with other participants and the psychotherapist, but when they returned to practice, they found it hard to articulate their learning and share these ideas with colleagues. In a team where a senior member of staff, as well as a practitioner, had undertaken the training, this was not the case. In this particular team, the ideas were brought to the team discussions and reflection time. This seemed a critical point. One participant commented, *"Learning has to be kept alive and we need to make an effort for that to happen"*. In order for learning to be kept alive, it was important we considered the following:

- Planning strategically across the organization, ensuring more than one person from each team undertook the training.
- Ensuring senior leaders and practitioners from the same teams took discussions and ideas back to their teams on a regular basis.
- Finding a way to embed this understanding across the organisation.

In addition to finding out the impact the course had had on participants, two additional themes emerged from the interview data: 'Reading Material' and 'Love'.

## Reading material

In relation to reading material, the following statements were made:

- "Reading it once isn't enough".
- "I found some papers demanding…and left [reading] it until the night before, which was a bit late to take on board".
- "Some papers were really challenging, and I would still say I haven't got my head around the concepts…didn't feel confident".
- "Some of the theory I found quite…I wasn't sure about…I wasn't convinced".
- "Other [papers] I found less easy to embrace. I struggle with the idea of a two-year old having an understanding of sexuality".
- "The reading was a massive commitment".

Participants seemed to struggle with both the 'intangible' theoretical content and the time commitment of reading and marking up papers ready for the seminar group.

## Love

Comments made that either directly or indirectly indicated strong feelings, identified by some participants as love were as follows:

- "I loved her from the first moment…I still love her".
- "I was astonished at how attracted I felt to him…how much I cared about him".
- "I felt bereft at the idea of letting him go".
- "Almost everybody had a soft spot for their child…really were more than curious… relationships almost".
- "I fell in love with him the moment I saw him…he was just so beautiful, I really loved him so much".

Participants seemed to feel a real emotional connection to the child they were observing, almost from the beginning, without ever having met them before and without interacting with them during the observation period (Page, 2011). This was interesting and something that was not expected. The participants who had made these statements were then asked to elaborate. Several of the participants spoke about how they believed the particular study child knew that they were being observed and that the observer was 'there for them'. One participant described how on her second observation, she went into the setting and her study child was alongside another child. The other child looked up and waved at my colleague. The study child then hit him on the arm and said "Hey, she's here for me". This was fascinating. The child understood and was able to articulate that she knew the person who had never spoken to her was 'there for her'. This led us to consider how it feels for children in settings. Do they 'know' at some level if someone there is an advocate for them? Do they 'know' when they are not liked? What impact might that have on them? This realization was the beginning of our conceptualization of 'consultancy observations' (Ringer, 2008).

## Pilot: consultancy observation

Through discussions, we decided that it would be appropriate to pilot this method of observation in the nursery setting when staff had concerns about children in their care (Elfer *et al.*, 2003). We hoped that it would be a way to consider children's behaviour, staff members' feelings towards particular children and the reasons behind the behaviours and the feelings. It was important to ensure the following:

- People undertaking what we termed 'Consultancy Observations' had undertaken the Emotional Roots course.
- Observations would not be undertaken with children that were known to the observer (the organization is large, so it is possible to ensure this happens).
- Observations would be written up as soon after the observation as possible, with no analysis.
- Copies would be made for all members of a team and taken to a team meeting.
- The person who had undertaken the observation would read through the observation (like in the seminar group) in the team meeting.
- The team would discuss the observation.

## Joseph: a case study

The domain that Joseph attends offers 50% of its places to children eligible for two-year funding (DfE, 2014). With this high proportion of funded two-year olds, it requires the staff to be deeply thoughtful. They need to think about creating an emotionally supportive environment and rich opportunities for cognitive challenge to promote children's learning and development (Whalley, 1994; Whalley, 1997; Whalley & The Pen Green Team, 2007; Arnold, 2012; Mairs *et al.*, 2013; Whalley *et al.*, 2013; McKinnon, 2014).

Joseph was concerning both his Key Person (Elfer *et al.*, 2003), known in this organization as a Family Worker (Whalley & The Pen Green Team, 2007), and the rest of the team. His Family Worker had spoken about Joseph in both her individual supervision and team meetings. It felt appropriate to undertake a consultancy observation to consider Joseph.

The Family Worker reported that Joseph kept "pushing, pushing, pushing other children". There was almost an element of desperation in the way the practitioner articulated his actions. The staff team cared deeply about getting it right for him, but at the same time, they were finding his behaviour really challenging. It had become hard for some members of staff to 'like' Joseph when he was pushing and hurting children in their key groups (Elfer *et al.*, 2003). A senior leader who did not know Joseph was asked to undertake the observation.

## Excerpt from the observation of Joseph

"Joseph walked away from the water tray and wandered over to the babygym (which comprises steps, bridge and slide). He pulled at his wet sleeve. Joseph climbed up the steps and walked down the slide; he repeated this action several times. Joseph climbed to the top of the slide and joined Rosie on the bridge. Rosie looked at Joseph and smiled. Joseph walked past her and walked down the slide. Joseph again climbed up the slide, he met Rosie at the top; he pushed Rosie and stood and stared. He pushed her again. Rosie sat down at the top of the slide, Joseph pushed her. Rosie slid down followed by Joseph. Joseph reached the bottom of the slide and turned his head. He looked directly at Claire (a worker). Claire was reading a story. She did not react to Joseph; she had not seen him push Rosie. Joseph turned and looked at me. He smiled. He then went back to climb the steps of the babygym. Alice was sitting at the bottom of the slide. Joseph came down the slide and pushed Alice. He immediately turned to look at Claire. Claire did not see. Joseph looked at me and smiled. I felt that he was waiting for a reaction".

## The discussion

The senior leader who had undertaken the observation read the observation out to the staff team. Together the staff team and senior leader talked, and some comments made during this discussion were the following:

- "He was seeking our attention".
- "We had missed him".
- "He was trying to get us to notice him".
- "I missed him...I really missed him".
- "All the children he's hurting are smaller than him".
- "He's getting negative feedback from us".
- "What can we do differently?"
- "How can we make sure we don't miss him?"

The team thought about whether Joseph was acting 'bigger' and 'stronger' than he was. Was he feeling vulnerable himself? They considered whether he was acting in a way to make Rosie feel vulnerable, locating that feeling in her, rather than in himself? Was his behaviour a 'defence against anxiety'? (Klein, 1952).

The team identified that Joseph seemed to be seeking adult attention, and in the day-to-day running, that had not always been noticed. Together they thought about their responses to Joseph and how they could be mindful of him in the space and facilitate the adult connection he seemed to be needing.

## What about Joseph?

Through the process of undertaking and discussing the observation, the team began to see Joseph's vulnerability and his need for them. This allowed them to begin to think about him in a different way. The team talked about it being easier to 'be with' him. He was not pushing nearly as much.

## Staff reflections

Prior to the observation, some staff members were very sceptical about the method and voiced this. One practitioner said to the senior leader that she really thought she had "gone mad this time".

A short time after the observation had been carried out and discussed, the team reflected on the fact that Joseph was not pushing nearly as much. They reflected that actually they were thinking about Joseph differently and therefore possibly behaving towards him differently. The senior leader who had undertaken the observation fed back that she had noticed staff, for instance, touching Joseph gently as they passed him by. This was something that had not happened during the observation. The changes in their behaviour seemed to be out of their conscious awareness (Fonagy et al., 2005). The staff team appeared to have become more emotionally available to him, which for Joseph would have been a Containing experience (Bion, 1962).

## Making sense

This methodology seemed to give staff the permission to really feel and voice the feelings they had about Joseph. They were able to both feel and express the negative emotion they were feeling when he was pushing children they were responsible for. Earlier in this paper, we considered practitioners 'loving' children they did not even know (Page, 2011). This felt like the other end of the spectrum where, rather than it being frowned upon, staff were actually encouraged to voice their more negative feelings about Joseph. This was in order for them to honestly think about their feelings about Joseph and therefore begin the process of understanding his world and being able to respond to him more effectively.

## An ethical consideration: what to share?

Historically at Pen Green, we have always shared all our observations with parents. In the psychodynamic tradition, when undertaking infant observation training, the raw data of the observation is not shared with the parents of the child being observed although, of course, consent to observe the child is gained from the parents. In the same way, the raw data of Joseph's observation was not shared with his family. It was felt that the raw data would not benefit the family in any way and could potentially cause distress. However, Joseph's Family Worker spoke with Joseph's parents about her concerns for him. She shared that she would be considering Joseph in both her supervision and team meetings, and identified this as an opportunity to think together about how to support Joseph most appropriately. Dialogue at Pen Green is iterative, and therefore the discussion and debate about individual children with their parents happen on a daily basis (Prodger, 2013 in Whalley *et al.*, 2013; Arnold & Cummings, 2013 in Whalley *et al.*, 2013).

In moving forward, it was decided that all parents would be informed that their child may be observed and considered in team situations in order to ensure staff teams were responding to their particular child in the most appropriate manner, the focus being the staff team's understanding of a child's experience and *their own* responses.

## Locating consultancy observations within a framework of support

As an organisation, it was important to locate consultancy observations within the existing and developing framework of support for staff members. The complexity of the work that was being undertaken in each of the nursery domains and in the Family Support team had increased with the introduction of the two-year-old, government-funded places (DfE, 2014). We needed to ensure staff were supported consistently and coherently, and were able to address the emotional aspects of their work as well as the practical ones.

We held a team training day, and part of the time was given to considering 'Spaces and Places for Thinking and Feeling' (Tait & Gallagher, 2013). We were keen for all staff members to consider the different forums they could access to ensure that they felt well supported in undertaking the complex work they were engaged in.

The different forums were identified and discussed in groups.

- **Supervision**
  'Reflective supervision' (Morrell, 2003; Finlay, 2009) occurs for each individual member of staff on a monthly basis and is an opportunity for personal and professional development discussions, including sharing concerns about children and families staff members are engaged with.
- **Coordination Meeting**
  A Coordination Meeting occurs twice each month. The purpose of the coordination meeting is to share information, across the Centre, about families receiving intensive support. This is the forum for staff to go to if they

need decisions to be made, or if they need to share factual information with other domains. This ensures families are not 'lost' across the organization and that all domains working with a family are aware of other support/ services they are receiving. Feedback from some participants has been that it has really helped them to understand the legislation and the processes that occur when families are referred to social care (Griffiths-Baker *et al.*, 2013).

- **Safer Practice Meetings**
  A Safer Practice Meeting is an opportunity for workers to call a meeting to discuss situations they are concerned about. These concerns, in this instance, are often based on a 'gut feeling'. In one instance, a member of staff described how, when working in a group at the Centre, she felt "uncomfortable with one of the dads". At the time the worker was not able to articulate what her discomfort was about or where it came from. Following the Safer Practice Meetings, the worker was able to share her feelings and concerns with the other staff and the group was able to think together about this situation and how to support the mum. It transpired that the dad was a perpetrator of domestic violence.

- **Work-Based Discussion Group**
  A termly work-based discussion group is facilitated by a Consultant Child and Adolescent Psychiatrist. This forum adopts a psychodynamic approach where the workers are able to reflect on the emotional impact their work is having on them, giving permission to staff members to acknowledge and understand their feelings in relation to the complexity they are working with. One member of staff spoke about how it felt to acknowledge how hard it was to engage with a mother who had neglected her own child and support her to parent more effectively.

- **Consultancy Observation**
  The consultancy observation that had been undertaken was shared on this day with staff members from the whole organisation. The particularly sceptical member of staff, referred to earlier, stood in front of the whole staff team and talked about how she had been initially sceptical and thought her manager was "going mad". She then reflected on what happened and how, through thinking together, they began to see Joseph's vulnerability. This was very powerful to hear. With hindsight, this seemed to be a catalyst for other staff teams to request consultancy observations when they had worries or concerns about a particular child.

## Conclusion and implications for the organisation

This technique enables staff to reflect together on a child's whole experience and promotes the idea of reflection and 'the potential for each group member to develop his or her own internal reflective space' (Ringer, 2002, pg. 231) in addition to the development of a group reflective capacity. We will continue to embed 'consultancy observations' throughout the organization for the benefit of the children attending the setting. We will begin to offer 'consultancy observations' and opportunities for organisational reflection both within our own organisation and elsewhere. In addition to this, it will be important to continue to offer an Emotional Roots course, 'skilling up' practitioners in their observational skills and understanding of psychodynamic theory. Finally, we will implement an 'Advanced Emotional Roots Course', for previous participants, 'to keep the learning alive'.

## References

Ainsworth, M., Blehar, M.C., Waters, E. & Wall, S. (1978) *Patterns of Attachment: A Psychological Study of the Strange Situation*. Hillsdale: Erlbaum.

Arnold, C. (2010) *Understanding Schemas and Emotion in Early Childhood*. London: Sage.

Arnold, C. (Ed.) (2012) *Improving Your Reflective Practice through Stories of Practitioner Research*. Abingdon: Routledge.

Arnold, C. & Cummings, A. (2013) Engaging in a dialogue with parents about their children's learning. In Whalley, M., Arnold, C., Orr, R. & The Pen Green Centre Team (2013) *Working with Families in Children's Centres and Early Years Settings*, 29–45. London: Hodder Education.

Bell, J. (1999) *Doing Your Research Project* (3rd ed.). Maidenhead: Open University Press.

Bick, E. (1964) Notes on infant observation in psychoanalytic training. *International Journal of Psychoanalysis*, 45, 558–566.

Bion, W. (1962) *Learning from Experience*. London: Heinemann.

Bowlby, J. (1969) *Attachment and Loss: Volume 1*. London: Hogarth Press Ltd.

Charlwood, N. & Steele, H. (2004) Using attachment theory to inform practice in an integrated centre for children and families. *European Early Childhood Education Research Journal*, 12 (2), 59–74.

Denzin, N.K. & Lincoln, Y.S. (Eds.) (2000) *Handbook of Qualitative Research* (2nd ed.). London: Sage.

Department for Education (DfE). (2014) *Early education and childcare statutory guidance for local authorities*. London: DfE. www.gov.uk/government/publications (Accessed 14 March 17).

Elfer, P., Goldschmied, E. & Selleck, D. (2003) *Key Persons in the Nursery*. London: Fulton.

Elliott, J. (1991) *Action Research for Educational Change*. Buckingham: Open University Press.

Finlay, L. (2009) *Reflecting on 'Reflective practice'*. PBL Paper 52. Milton Keynes: Open University. Available at www.open.ac.uk/pbpl (Accessed 16 September 2015).

Fonagy, P., Twemlow, S.W. & Sacco, F.C. (2005) A developmental approach to mentalizing communities: I. A model for social change. *Bulletin of the Menninger Clinic*, 69 (4), 265–304.

George, C., Kaplan, N. & Main, M. (1985) *Adult Attachment Interview*. Unpublished manuscript. Department of Psychology, University of California, Berkeley.

Griebel, W. & Niesel, R. (2003) Successful transitions: Social competencies help pave the way into kindergarten and school. *European Early Childhood Education Research Journal*, Series No. 1, 25–33.

Griffiths-Baker, S., McFarlane, C., Elliott, R. & Potts, J. (2013) Family support for families with young children. In Whalley, M., Arnold, C., Orr, R. & The Pen Green Centre Team (2013) *Working with Families in Children's Centres and Early Years Settings*, 95–108. London: Hodder Education.

Hawkins, P. & Shohet, R. (2000) *Supervision in the Helping Professions* (2nd ed.). Maidenhead: Open University Press.

Klein, M. (1952) *Developments in Psychoanalysis.* London: Hogarth Press Ltd.

Laevers, F. (1997) *A Process-Oriented Child Follow-Up System for Young Children.* Leuven, Belgium: Centre for Experiential Education.

Mairs, K. & The Pen Green Team (Arnold, C. Ed.) (2013) *Young Children Learning through Schemas.* Abingdon: Routledge.

McKinnon, E. (Ed.) (2014) *Using Evidence for Advocacy and Resistance in Early Years Services: Exploring the Pen Green Research Approach.* Abingdon: Routledge.

Morrell, M. (2003) Forethought and afterthought – two of the keys to professional development and good practice in supervision. *Social Work Review*, Autumn/Winter 15 (1/2), 29–32.

Page, J. (2011) Do mothers want professionals to 'love' their babies? *Journal of Early Childhood Research*, 9 (3): 310–320.

Prodger, A. (2013) Sharing knowled with families using our nursery: The Family Worker role. In Whalley, M., Arnold, C., Orr, R. & The Pen Green Centre Team (2013) *Working with Families in Children's Centres and Early Years Settings,* 15–28. London: Hodder Education.

Ringer, T.M. (2002) *Group Action: The Dynamics of Groups in Therapeutic, Educational and Corporate Settings.* International Library of Group Analysis. London: Jessica Kingsley Publishers.

Ringer, T. M. (2008) *Group Action: The Dynamics of Groups in Therapeutic, Educational and Corporate Settings.* International Library of Group Analysis. London: Jessica Kingsley Publishers.

Sandler, J. (1987) *Projection, Identification, Projective Identification.* Madison, CT: International Universities Press.

Shaw, J. & Tait, C. (2014) The Emotional Roots of Learning Training at the Pen Green Centre for Children and Families. Presentation at the 24th European Early Childhood Education Research Association Annual Conference, *Universal, Targeted or Individuated Early Childhood Programmes.* Crete, Tuesday 9 September.

Sieber, J. (1993) The ethics and politics of sensitive research. In Renzetti, C. & Lee, R. M. *Research Sensitive Topics,* 14–18. London: Sage.

Tait, C. & Gallagher, T. (2013) *Spaces and Places for Thinking and Feeling – Team Day Presentation.* Corby: Pen Green Centre.

Whalley, M. (1994) *Learning to Be Strong.* London: Hodder and Stoughton.

Whalley, M. (1997) *Working with Parents.* Abingdon: Hodder and Stoughton.

Whalley, M. & Arnold, C. (1997) *Effective Pedagogic Strategies, TTA Summary of Research Findings.* London: Teacher Training Agency.

Whalley, M., Arnold, C., Orr, R. & The Pen Green Centre Team. (2013) *Working with Families in Children's Centres and Early Years Settings.* London: Hodder Education.

Whalley, M. & The Pen Green Team. (2007) *Involving Parents in their Children's Learning* (2nd ed). London: Sage Publications.

Whyte, C. (2003) Struggling to separate: Observation of a young child in a playgroup. *Infant Observation*, 6 (2), 128–142.

Winnicott, D.W. (1965) The Theory of the Parent-Infant Relationship (1960), in The Maturational Processes and the Facilitating Environment. *The International Psycho-analytic Library*, 64: 1–276. London: Hogarth Press Ltd and the Institute of Psycho-analysis.

## Chapter 9

# Universal and specialised groups for children under three and their families

*Lorna MacLeod and Elaine Young*

## Introduction

In this chapter, we discuss information about the group work programme at Pen Green, specifically regarding groups for 0–3's and their families. We explore the importance of developing relationships with all the important adults in the child's life and working in a thoughtful and respectful way which enables successful and sustained engagement with parents. For this work to happen, we describe the range of services and groups available throughout the whole week both within the Centre and in the local community. We also consider the responsibilities and qualities of a group leader (Figure 9.1 and Figure 9.2).

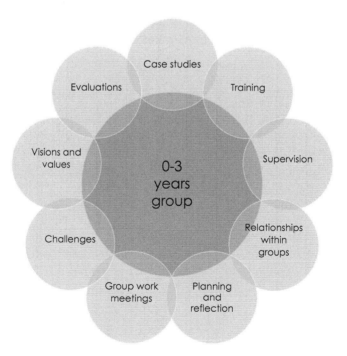

*Figure 9.1* Responsiblities of a group leader in the 0–3 groups

| | | |
|---|---|---|
| supportive | friendly | welcoming |
| creative | imaginative | approachable |
| honest/open | sensitive | trustworthy |
| confident | committed | well-prepared |

*Figure 9.2* Qualities of a group leader

At Pen Green, groups are usually run by two group leaders and a volunteer. We know that group leaders are most effective when they respect each other's differences and encourage each other's strengths. This is represented in Figure 9.2 describing the qualities of a group leader.

Benson wrote:

> Reasons put forward in literature for using co-leaders include the advantages of support, sharing feedback on each other's performance, time to observe more closely, modelling co-operative leadership. ...

> (Benson, 1987, pg. 42)

## Groups at Pen Green

We provide universal groups for all families to use, as well as more targeted provisions for those families that need a more specialist support. We know that for the targeted services to be accessible and acceptable to the most disadvantaged families, they need to have a universal gateway. In this chapter, we outline the range of groups families with children under three years can access, as well as demonstrating the difference the services make for families.

### Universal groups

Universal groups have open access for families to attend.

### Targeted groups

Targeted groups are a particular kind of closed group with a specified aim. The majority of these groups run for a limited length of time.

From our experience of running groups, we know that it is important to be aware of how families may access the services we provide. We offer a wide range of groups throughout the week and at the weekends, thus

*(Continued)*

enabling families to make choices as to which group they choose according to their needs. Nevertheless, we would also expect workers to be aware
that family's needs may change over time and that the groups we provide
need to support these changes. Families may attend a universal group first,
and as they build up trusting relationships with workers, they may be able
to share challenges they are currently facing that could be better supported in a targeted group. Workers can then refer the family to the most
appropriate group for them.

### Example from practice

Dianne shares her experience of Growing Together, which is a universal group
specifically for children from birth until three years old providing an opportunity to be reflective whilst playing alongside your child. She explains what is
important to her and why she comes.

> "I really enjoy coming to the group each week, it's a chance for the children
> to play and for me to enjoy adult company. Not feeling judged at my low
> times gives me confidence to come back. Last week I was feeling very low
> but forced myself to come to the group, my mood soon changes and this
> helped for the rest of the day, I had more energy to get through the day.
> When I come to the group I talk to other parents and that boosts my self-
> esteem. My confidence has grown because I'm getting out and socialising".

Although Dianne felt able to attend a universal group and did not need specialist support, this example illustrates that she still feels low at times and that the
companionship of other adults helps.

### Example from practice

Tina shares her experience of moving from Great Expectations to Social Baby.
Great Expectations is a targeted group for pregnant women to share their experiences and get support from a midwife and experienced group worker. Social
Baby is a universal drop-in group promoting understanding of a baby's development and building relationships. Tina was then referred in to the GAP group
(Get Ahead of Postnatal Depression), a group for women who are experiencing
postnatal depression, anxiety or distress after the birth of a baby.

> "He was about six months old, and I had started Social Baby because we
> went from Great Expectations to Social Baby and by being there, my feel-
> ings of anxiety started. It was like people were constantly watching me and
> although they weren't and I knew logically they weren't, I felt that everyone
> was watching to see how I was with Alan. I went to see the midwife in Great

Expectations, as it was a Wednesday, so I went to see her and broke down and said, 'Is it normal to hit rock bottom when he is six months old?' That's when she put me through to GAP because Social Baby didn't work for me at the time; it was too loud. I felt like I had to be watching him all the time. I can't describe how I am with Alan. I still do it now, not as much, but, like, you watch some people and they let their baby go off and I feel like I have to be right behind him all the time".

This example highlights how difficult it can be for some parents to transition from a targeted group into a universal drop-in group. As workers, we sometimes don't get it right for parents as we support and encourage them to try new experiences. We can, as workers, get caught up in our own enthusiasm for what we think is the right group for a parent to attend. Tina was able to talk with another worker, who listened to her, about this and considered what her needs were at that time. Tina then attended a group to help and support with anxiety. As practitioners, we should not expect that all groups are right for all parents. As Whalley and The Pen Green Centre Team (2001) point out, '...parents are not a homogenous group – their lives vary greatly and, therefore, the 'method of engagement' that works for one family will not necessary work for another' (pg. 36).

## Group work and community education values

All groups and courses that run at Pen Green work towards the same shared values for everyone to

- Have access to and be offered equal opportunities and choices;
- Respect each other's beliefs, behaviours and values;
- Offer a welcoming place where individuals feel safe, included and able to express themselves in confidence;
- Be sensitive and take time to understand each person's learning journey and life circumstances;
- Learn from each other and value what each of us has to offer;
- Be concerned about and support individual learning routes and help sustain learners on their journey;
- Enable learners to realise their own potential and feel safe enough to take risks;
- Encourage people to feel they have the power to challenge and change things (MacLeod & Young, 2013, pg. 72. Originally taken from the Pen Green group work booklet, unpublished).

For our 0–3 groups, we also have the following additional principles:

- A dedicated 0–3 Group Coordinator
- Specific training for group facilitators and volunteers

- The use of planning and documentation relating to the Early Years Foundation Stage (EYFS) (DfE, 2012)
- The use of child development frameworks including 'well-being' (Laevers, 2005), 'involvement' (Laevers, 2005) and 'schemas' (Athey, 2007; Arnold, 2010) to inform our thinking

## Professional development in order to work in groups

We offer professional development and training in group work at different levels.

### Basic training in group work

Here are some questions that we pose to prospective group workers and volunteers when they do our 'in-house' basic group work training: "Why do you want to be a group worker?" "Why do you think we provide a group work programme?" We ask them to think about their vision and values in relation to group work and what is important to them. Then we ask them to think about what the roles and responsibilities of a group leader would be. We spend time reflecting on the way we run groups here and emphasise the importance of the relationships we build with the families who attend our groups.

Here are some thoughts from group leaders and volunteers who have recently completed the training:

Why be a group leader – visions and values?

- For experience and to learn new things
- Passion for working with children and adults
- To make a difference to people's lives
- To offer support and to listen
- Commitment and satisfaction
- Meeting a variety of people
- Team work within the group and across the centre
- For our own enjoyment

How do you implement these visions and values?

- Greet families and make them feel welcome
- Offer a drink, either tea or coffee
- Provide a safe environment for adults and children
- Offer experiences that are varied and exciting
- Offer a listening ear
- Plan for individual children depending on their interests shown in the group alongside discussions with parents about what their child likes to do at home
- Remember adults' and children's names
- Prepare and plan for the group

### A second tier of development in working in groups

We also offer a second tier of training for group workers which follows on from the practical side of running groups to understanding groups at a deeper level, including group dynamics. This training covers more complex topics and encourages group leaders to reflect on the dilemmas that occur in groups, drawing from their own experiences and those of their peers. The aim is to develop a better understanding of groups and explore strategies that could be used to help support the running of their group.

### Studying for a master's module in group work

We then offer a master's-level group work module for those staff that lead targeted therapeutic groups. This module looks in detail at group work theory and provides the staff with the opportunity to carry out a small-scale research project in relation to one of their groups.

## Relationships within groups

We know from our experience that the initial welcome that families receive is crucial and that this needs to be right from the outset if we want families to come back the following week. We also recognise that having consistent group leaders each time is vital for establishing relationships with all families. In group work, 'there are multiple relationships and interactions to be understood' (Northen & Kurland, 2001, pg. 24), and group leaders are adept at using their skills to do this. While the group is running, group leaders need to be able to scan the room to see what is happening and to notice if any of the parents appear to be isolated. They may always sit on their own on the edge of the group and may not often engage in conversation with many others in the room. This is when the group leader can try to gently include parents into the conversation and begin building up relationships with them.

## Ending the group each week

Group leaders have to keep to boundaries regarding the end of the group, as this can be a stressful time for parents trying to encourage their children that it is time to go. Group leaders are subtle and sensitive as they tidy up the room and acknowledge that people are leaving and that they will see them next week. This is often an opportunity to check out with the parents how it was for them and their child, especially if it was their first time attending. With all of this in place, we find that parents don't just attend for a few weeks but choose to come for months or years and then come back with their younger children.

In the following case study, Hannah shares her experiences of attending many groups including the following:

- Community Drop-In – a universal group open to parents and carers with children under the age of five
- Messy Play – a universal group that provides an opportunity for children's learning and development to be supported through play experiences with a wide range of tactile materials
- Infant Massage – a universal group for parents to learn how to massage their baby and an opportunity to socialise with other parents
- Adult Infant Drop-In – a dedicated space which is open every day for parents and carers with infants and toddlers, in which a wide range of appropriate play experiences are provided for the children to explore and investigate

### Example from practice

Hannah has two sons, Jack who is three years and nine months old, and Sam who is eleven months old. Hannah has been attending the 0–3-year groups here at Pen Green for 8 years now. Initially, Hannah was a nanny for a local family, and she brought the one-year-old child she cared for to Wednesday morning Community Drop-In. He is now nine years old. Hannah then went on to use the services at Pen Green with her own children.

Initially, Hannah began attending groups at Pen Green because they were convenient. The groups she attended ran on the days she was caring for the children she nannied. Then, when she had her own children, she used a wider range of groups from when they were babies. Adult company was an important aspect to her: "At Infant Massage, I met two mums and I am still really close to them. I feel I have made a lifelong friend with both of them". They have a great deal in common: "They have both had their second babies at the same time as me". Hannah notices when other parents at groups seem isolated, and she makes an effort to talk to them, which is something she has observed staff doing. Hannah is also clear that she attends groups "for the children's interactions". She values the relationships made with staff and with other parents and appreciates the fact that "all the staff still ask after Jack" (even though he no longer attends the group).

Enjoyment and learning for the children are also important to Hannah: "Jack really loved it when they put paper on the wall in Messy Play and they had the paint out with rollers. They got to roller the wall and it went everywhere but he loved it. They stuck all this white paper to the wall and they had rollers and paint brushes, and they didn't care. He was down to his vest and he really loved it". This play made a link with what was happening at home: "I think we were doing decorating at home at the time, so he got a chance to do it here, I think this was the most enjoyable experience for Jack he really enjoyed it and talked about it for hours afterwards. I do it here so I don't have to do it at home; it keeps my house tidy". Hannah brings spare clothes so that the children can get messy: "I don't want to bring him here and keep telling him not to get wet, don't go near the water as that is not part of the experience is it?"

This case study demonstrates the importance of building relationships with families and shows that if the welcome is embedded in practice from the start, families may attend for many years. Hannah uses the group work programme to complement her family's individual needs and circumstances. She talks warmly about the relationships she has made and how she values the groups that we provide and the experience they offer her children (Figure 9.3).

### Example from practice

In contrast to Hannah's experiences, Natalia shares her experiences when she and her child attended Growing Together and then when she attended the GAP group, which she attended without her child.

Growing Together is a group for parents to attend with their children from birth through to their child's third birthday. The group supports parents in developing their relationship with their child and provides opportunities for parents and workers to think together about the children's development (see Chapter 10 for more information on Growing Together).

GAP, as previously described, is a group for women who are experiencing postnatal depression, anxiety or distress after the birth of a baby.

"If I go to Growing Together, I don't really mind not talking to the group leaders because we're just getting on with playing. In the GAP group, it's really important 'cause if we say something and don't get any acknowledgement from a group leader, then you just feel, 'why am I in this group' and

*Figure 9.3* Room set up in preparation for a drop-in session

then you're not going to come back to the group. I'm telling you my deepest darkest secrets, so I need to know that you are bothered or that you are actually listening otherwise I might not bother making the effort".

This example highlights one of the dilemmas faced by leaders whose groups are for children and adults together. To know how and when to intervene with either conversation, support or guidance takes a level of confidence and skills. In a group, specifically for adults, the group leaders' approach may differ as the nature of the relationship can be at a much deeper level. Knowing when to include a silent member of the group and when to calm down a vocal member of the group is a finely balanced approach. These skills of subtle intervention by the group leader are developed through supervision, training and experience, and we have to take risks and do not always get it right first time.

Most of the groups we run in the week are attended by mothers and female carers with only a small percentage of fathers who attend. However, we also run a group on Sunday mornings which is exclusively for fathers and male carers. Although specific fathers' groups work for some fathers, they are not necessarily what every father wants. Ghate *et al.* (2000) observed '... men's groups are by no means appealing to all fathers as borne out by the small number of fathers who attend (pg. 40).

### Example from practice

In the following example, Alex shares his experiences of attending groups during the week at Pen Green which fit better into his working week than attending the Sunday group.

Alex is married and has two children: Emma who is four years old and Jake who is two years old. He has been attending the 0–3-year groups for 4 years now, sometimes with his wife and sometimes on his own depending on their shifts at work.

Alex mentioned attending 'Growing Together', 'Messy Play' and 'Community Drop-In', and also that his wife took both children to 'Baby Massage'. He has an important link with the centre as his mum is a member of staff. He explains that, "With Growing Together, my mum, who was part of the team who ran the group, introduced us to the group. It was also within walking distance from home and this helped when I was working as my wife could make her own way there as she doesn't drive".

Alex has been attending 'Growing Together' for four years and appreciates the provision both for the children and for his family: "My son Jake has been able to interact with other children, learning to share and play together as well as build his confidence. I come to the group so that Jake can develop skills to help him in the future when he moves to nursery, and he enjoys playing with the various activities".

He goes on to say that, "My confidence has increased as I talk to the other parents, especially those whose children are playing with Jake, which helps to break the ice. I don't feel isolated, however, I am quite often the only male in the room. We enjoy playing with the activities together and by watching him play and interact with other children, I can see his likes and dislikes and learn from this".

Alex also values the relationships with staff: "I enjoy talking with the workers and getting their professional insight on things Jake is doing which I may not notice. I find this sort of interaction with group leaders extremely insightful and helpful. It let me see my children's play in a whole new light and meant that I could tailor their play at home to be suited to them, providing toys that they would get the most out of".

Alex spoke about 'Messy Play' and, "loved the idea of them [his children] having the freedom to express themselves and be creative in any way they wished, with anything that was on offer to them. Having this freedom at home can be much harder as I find messy play can be restricted at home due to not wanting things to get covered in paint or soaked with water etc. Messy Play has taught my children a lot about how to interact with things and how they work and feel, in a way they would not have been able to experience at home". He continued, "With my daughter, it was playing in the sinks and painting, but with my son, it was being out in the garden in the mud and soaking everyone with the hose".

There was one book in particular that his daughter enjoyed and which helped her to learn numbers: "Every Growing Together session we would read the book together, counting the animals and items and pressing the noisy buttons. To this day, she loves reading and is top of the class for reading and maths. It is without doubt that part of her success is down to her interactions at a young age through these groups.

"With my son, he is very hands on and has loved playing outside ever since he was able to. He loves searching for bugs and does not mind getting dirty. One thing he does love in the Drop-In and Messy Play groups is the water. Something that always sticks out for me is how he loves to play with the hose. He is able to change the head on it so at all times it was a stream and then a shower. To see his fascination with it and how he would intelligently use a different type of stream for different purposes shows that he is using this tool to constantly learn. He is only two years old, so he is still attending groups and will do so till he starts nursery, so he still has much to learn".

Alex felt welcome when coming to these groups, even though as he himself pointed out he was quite often the only male there. The fact that Alex and his family had an overall good experience meant that he has continued to attend over a period of years.

Ghate *et al.* (2000) when conducting their study on fathers' engagement with children's centres found that '...a warm welcome and a relaxing atmosphere could make fathers feel both comfortable and that they belonged despite being in the minority' (2000, pg. 41).

## Supervision

It is our belief that everybody is entitled to supervision. This model has evolved over time, and we expect all prospective group workers to have completed the basic group work training before they run a group. They will be equipped to run a group then as during the training they will also have covered roles, responsibilities and rights of group leaders. Supervision is offered on a monthly basis to group leaders with their co-leaders. It is a process where group leaders have the opportunities to reflect on their practice and voice any worries and concerns they may have. The supervisor focuses on supporting the group leaders emotionally and practically. It is an opportunity for discussion, challenge and reassurance within a safe environment. This model promotes peer supervision for all who run the group, including workers and volunteers together. Our 0–3-year group coordinator facilitates these supervisions for our universal group work provision. For our targeted group work programme, the level of supervision needs to be more specialist, therefore we employ a qualified psychotherapist. This gives the opportunity for workers within these groups to be self-reflective and to explore group dynamics at a deeper level. 'The primary focus of group supervision is the support of group members practically and emotionally, assisting them to share and develop their understanding and skills in working collaboratively with children and families' (John, 2011, pg. 26).

## Planning and reflection

Group leaders who co-lead in the groups which are specifically for 0–3's and their families use a planning and reflection sheet each week. This is a tool to enable group leaders to document how they plan for individual children's interests by observing how and what they play with in the group, then linking what they have observed to the Development Matters in the EYFS (DfE, 2012) as well as to the key concepts of 'Involvement', 'Emotional Well-being' and 'Schemas' (Laevers, 2005; Athey, 2007). This process enables group leaders to plan which resources to provide each week. There is also space on the planning sheet for reflecting on what went well and what did not, what you might change and also a space for the parent's voice, which may be a conversation you had with the parent or something you need to follow up with them the following week. Debriefing time for the team at the end of the group is used to add to the planning sheet and to think deeply about practice, reviewing and evaluating what they do. What is even more important than filling in the planning sheet is the conversation during the debrief about what was going on in the room for children, parents and staff.

Whalley and The Pen Green Centre Team (2001, pg. 32) wrote, 'Having time to think and reflect on the work they do is critical if early childhood educators are to become increasingly rigorous and insightful in their practice'.

From our experience, we know that by providing rich and meaningful experiences for the children who attend our groups, we can support and extend children's thinking by observation and planning. We may only see individual children once a week, but the value of documenting their learning will provide links between sessions and consistency in the provision that we offer for them (Figure 9.4).

Nutbrown (1999, pg. 35) states that, 'Continuity and progression in children's learning can best be achieved if the children – as people and as learners – are respected as central to and active in the learning process in which they are engaged. Learning opportunities must be meaningful and motivating to children.'

*Figure 9.4* Group leaders reflecting on the session and documenting the children's experiences

## Group work meetings

The group work programme at Pen Green is categorised into strands depending on the type of group. These strands are as follows:

- Parents involvement in their children's learning
- 0–3 years groups
- Adult and infant mental health
- Family support/health/supporting family life
- Adult education/community learning

Each of these strands has a worker who leads the team in terms of training, supervision and representing them at the monthly group work meeting. These monthly meetings are the forum for reflecting on what we are currently offering in terms of group work, what is going well, what we may need to change, staffing issues, training, budgets and evaluating our services. This is also the time when new group proposals that are submitted from centre staff, parents and governors are discussed and a decision made as to whether they can run or not depending on the above issues, and also if there is a need for that particular group.

## Evaluations of the group work programme

Workers in the Centre evaluate the whole group work programme three times a year, and all the 0–3-year groups are included within this. We have developed an evaluation tool which is one way that enables the voice of service users to be heard. This tool has been devised with parents' input and is reviewed as an ongoing process. This allows for development and change. The tool has been validated by The Centre for Excellence and Outcomes in Children and Young People's Services (C4EO). Each time we evaluate the groups, we do this across a whole week. The evaluations are given out in each group that week by the group leaders for families to fill in, and alternatively this tool is also available online through our webpage. All the forms are then collated by each 'strand leader' gathering the quantitative and qualitative data. Strand leaders hold responsibility for overseeing particular areas of the group work programme, for example 0–3 groups, Family Support groups, Adult-Infant Mental health groups. The data, once analysed, are then used to inform future provision by the group leaders, governors and the Centre Leadership Team. Information gathered enables us to implement changes to our practice both in the short and long terms. We are aware that this is one of many ways in which to engage with parents to get their views. We also have Termly Parent forums at Pen Green (offered morning, afternoon and evening), and this may offer an alternative opportunity for parents to feed back what they think of the groups and to share their ideas.

## Examples of actions from previous group evaluations

*Example one* – Families from the Tuesday morning 'U2 Can be messy' group said that they can't use the soft room alongside attending the group as it is always booked out.

*Response to the feedback* – We have now booked it for families using this group from 9.30 to 10.00 on Tuesday mornings so that it can be used before the group starts.

*Example two* – Families have suggested that we run a grandparents group and also a group for toddlers in the afternoon.

*Response to the feedback* – These requests will be taken to the next monthly group work meeting for further discussion and consideration.

*Example three* – Families using the community drop-in group on Wednesday mornings requested if they could bring their school-aged children to the group in the school holidays.

*Response to the feedback* – We considered the resources, the environment, staffing and produced appropriate risk assessments and then opened the group up to school-aged children up to the age of eight years during the holiday periods.

We also link the evaluations to the data we collate from registers. By looking at the attrition rates of attendance, we can provide a cost-effective, efficient service that relates to the needs of our community. Regular evaluations help us to be reflective about our practice and to question whether we are getting it right for service users. Pen Green is a fully integrated centre and we receive our funding from many different streams. We are accountable to our families and funders/ commissioners who set our Key Performance indicators and periodically monitor us to ensure that we are meeting these outcomes. We have overarching structures and requirements that we have to adhere to, including Ofsted themes, which we take into account when planning groups. We are always mindful of the dilemma of weighing up the needs of children and families and the needs of external factors.

Despite all of these efforts, sometimes parents are not satisfied with what we offer.

### Example from practice

Over the summer period, some group leaders had been asked to move rooms. This was part of a larger plan to allocate rooms to specific focus areas, for example Adult Education. The music group had been running every Wednesday morning in the Young Parents group room from 9:45 to 10:15 a.m. Following the music group, the parents could stay on if they wished and move in to the large group room next door for the community drop-in.

*(Continued)*

I discussed with the 0–3 group coordinator the need for the music group to move rooms and considered possible rooms for the group to move to. The 0–3 coordinator discussed it with the team and it was agreed that we would use the garden area of the large group room during the summer and then trial the music group in the Family Room.

The first Wednesday the music group was due to run in the Family Room, I came to reception to receive fourteen written complaints from parents. The music group had been on in the large group room, not the Family Room, as had been planned, alongside all the resources set up for the community drop-in session. Parents shared their feedback with me explaining the music group had not worked in the large group room, as the children had been distracted by all the experiences that had been set up in preparation for the drop-in session.

I immediately met with the group leader and we discussed the session and the feedback I had received. The group leader had not been clear the Family Room had been suggested as an alternative so had used the large group room. We talked about the use of the Family Room and whether this would be a suitable space to facilitate the music group in future weeks. She thought it could work in the Family Room. As many of the parents were still on site in the community drop-in session, the group leader went and found them. She explained I had read their complaints and suggestions. The group leader suggested trialling the Family Room the following week.

This example highlights we do not always get it right for families, but we welcome their feedback and try, where possible, to accommodate their ideas. As many groups were moving rooms, we knew not all families would be happy about the process, but on this occasion, we had not included families in the discussions or asked for their ideas. The room the music group leaders used did not work for all the families, and they felt confident to express their views. They knew that their views had been listened to and appreciated a new room being allocated.

## Challenges for the future

Alongside our regular reviews and consistent evaluation processes, we continue to ensure that our group work programme is ever evolving. We do, however, have new and ongoing challenges. Some of these are listed below:

- Conflicting demands of funding and the needs of the community
- Ensuring that all group leaders have the same opportunities regarding training and supervision, particularly when the majority of the team are part-time workers and volunteers

- Promotion of the group work programme for families in our community who may not currently access the groups we provide
- Capturing the voice of the child in the evaluation process
- To continue to keep our group work timetable up to date alongside our daily Facebook updates and website

## References

Arnold, C. & The Pen Green Centre Team (2010) *Understanding Schemas and Emotion in Early Childhood*. London: Sage.

Athey, C. (2007) *Extending Thought in Young Children: A Parent-Teacher Partnership* (2nd edn.). London: Paul Chapman Publishing Ltd.

Benson, J.F. (1987) *Working More Creatively with Groups*. London: Tavistock Publications.

DfE (Department for Education) (2012) *Development Matters in the Early Years Foundation Stage (EYFS)*. Cheshire: Crown Copyright.

Ghate, D., Shaw, C. & Hazel, N. (2000) *Fathers and family centres. Engaging fathers in preventative services*. Policy Research Bureau. York: YPS, Joseph Rowntree Foundation. www.jrf.org.uk/report/how-family-centres-are-working-fathers (Accessed 16 March 2017).

John, K. (2011) *Staff Supervision in Children's Centres: Guidance on Policy and Practice*. Corby: Pen Green Centre.

Laevers, F. (2005) *Deep Level Learning and the Experiential Approach in Early Childhood and Primary Education*. Leuven: Research Centre for Experiential Education. https://vorming.cego.be/images/downloads/BO_DP_Deep-levelLearning.pdf (Accessed 13 September 2016).

MacLeod, L. & Young, E. (2013) Developing a Groupwork Programme to Respond to the Needs of Local Families. In Whalley, M., Arnold, C. & Orr, R. (Eds.) *Working with Families in Children's Centres and Early Years Settings*. London: Hodder Education.

Northen, H. & Kurland, R. (2001) *Social Work with Groups* (3rd edn.). New York: Columbia University Press.

Nutbrown, C. (1999) *Threads of Thinking* (2nd edn.). London: Paul Chapman.

Whalley, M. & The Pen Green Centre Team (2001) *Involving Parents in Their Children's Learning*. London: Paul Chapman Publishing.

## Chapter 10

# Growing Together

## A group for parents and carers with infants and toddlers

*Cessie Cole and Tracy Gallagher*

If you walked past the window of a 'Growing Together' session at Pen Green, it might well appear like any other parent and toddler group. However, if you attended the group, you would quickly realise that the staff are working with parents and toddlers in a more intensive way. As the name implies, we encourage parent and child to 'grow together', based on the Attachment relationship ideas of John Bowlby, which were first published in 1969.

Growing Together is not didactic, but it is a regular forum for meeting, playing with children and talking together to increase parents', staff's and children's awareness of how to communicate better with each other. That improved communication may be occurring is evidenced by

- Arriving at a more satisfactory outcome to any conflict or concern
- Extending learning and knowledge about the parent/child relationship
- Noticing relational interactions within the group

This chapter focuses on Growing Together in 2016 to highlight its evolution in the past decade, whereas the initial works describing Growing Together have been in print for some time (Norton *et al.*, 2013).

In this chapter, we would like to give a flavour of a Growing Together session, from our pre-brief meetings to our debriefs; explain the process of filming; and give examples of how families have used the group, as well as how we, as teams, always aim to progress our learning, influenced by Psychodynamic theory. We will illustrate, with examples from practice and a case study, how we have tried to remain a consistent place for families to attend with their children, as well as show how we feel we have developed since our inception.

A graphic representation of the flow of activities in a Growing Together session is given in Table 10.1 (see Figure 10.1).

Growing Together is an open group that welcomes all parents and children from birth to their third birthday, where we hope to have an impact on families by raising their awareness of and insight into the parent/child relationship and support parents in understanding how their child is learning and developing.

*Table 10.1* A graphic representation of the flow of activities in a Growing
Together session

| Growing Together team | Growing Together team, parents and children |
| --- | --- |
| Set up | |
| Pre-brief | |
| | Welcome and Hot drink |
| | Filming and Review |
| | Tidy up |
| | Bubbles |
| Debrief | |
| Learning and Evaluation | |

*Figure 10.1* The layout of the room prepared for the Growing Together session

Although our work is deeply embedded in a theoretical base that informs what
we offer families, Growing Together does not aim to teach parents any theory
regarding children, relationships or the unconscious. We do, however, aim to
teach parents about the child development theories that we find helpful to think
about when we are considering how children learn and develop.

The original Growing Together groups were set up in 1999 as a result of a
three-year research project that was carried out in the nursery. The research
focused on Parents' Involvement in their Children's Learning (PICL). The aim
of the Growing Together group was to bring the findings of the research into
practice for parents and carers with children from birth to their third birthday.

The group was conceptualised based initially on our understanding of the child development theories, which are fully described in other chapters of this book, as well as other publications from Pen Green. In addition to those ideas, a Psychodynamic theoretical framework from an Object Relations background was also added into the thinking behind creating Growing Together groups. One such idea, for example, is Winnicott (1971), who published his description of Holding. The Holding environment refers to the whole psycho/physiological system that protects, supports, cares, contains and envelops the baby. It is crucial for the baby's survival and therefore requires reliability in the responsiveness to provide that environment for the baby. The impact of maternal Holding for a child creates the circumstances that nurture the emotional growth of a child. The child is unable to manage this process for themselves. They need an adult to manage this on their behalf in the early stages of life. Ideas like Holding link the physical nurture of a child with their emotional growth. So, Growing Together thinking links the Child Development theories with Psychodynamic ideas to encourage full consideration of both in the groups.

Another Psychodynamic theory that our groups are based on is that of Attachment (Bowlby, 1969). This describes a pattern between a care-seeker (usually an infant/child) and care-giver (usually interpreted as a responsible adult). The care-seeker, under circumstances of uncertainty or fear, seeks out the care-giver for reassurance, proximity and soothing behaviours to allow the care-seeker to feel able to function. (Separation and illness are the most common examples where Attachment behaviours are displayed.) If the care-giver does not respond, then a child can feel that they are too fragmented to be able to cope with the external world. There are various categories from this theory, which have been devised to articulate an understanding of the behaviours a child is displaying to its parent/carer. These categories connote a secure or insecure Attachment pattern. Most parents come to the groups with an idea of the importance of having a bond with their child. Attachment, though, specifically focuses on the relationship between parent and child when a child experiences duress and seeks out their Attachment figure, usually the mother. Schaffer and Emerson (1964) and Rutter (1972) have extended this to suggest that children have multiple Attachment figures, often within the family network.

Since the inception of Growing Together, the internet, television programmes and social media have given people access to limitless, and sometimes unreliable, information about having babies, bringing up children and the psychological issues involved. This appears to encourage in parents the idea that there is a right and a wrong way to do things, promoting judgemental thinking about being a parent.

We, however, come from a very different orientation. We are keen to encourage parents to develop their own ideas and intuition about the relationships between parents and children. Of course, we have our ideas and training, but the discussions we have with parents are to encourage them to consider what would be appropriate for their child in the circumstances.

## A Growing Together session

It is extremely important to our staff teams that we are as consistent as possible in our attendance at the groups, and it is a commitment we all undertake at the outset, acting as a 'secure base', as described by Bowlby (1969).

### Multidisciplinary team

The aim is to have a team of four in any session, and from the beginning, we make clear our names, our range of skills, our roles outside Growing Together and that parents can approach us for information, a chat and support with their children during the session. Each of our two Growing Together teams is multidisciplinary in training and experience in Early Years work with children and families. So, apart from their work in Growing Together, they fulfil other roles in Pen Green where their roles focus on different areas. Therefore, when they come together in a Growing Together team, the mix in skill sets is enriched by their individual perspectives, as well as the background knowledge and experience that they present into the blend in any of the three teams. The make-up of each team ranges from a Researcher who teaches and writes in the field, the Centre Group-work Coordinator, a Family Support worker, people with various skill sets from the Early Years Team and a Deputy Head of Centre. The psychotherapist is a regular weekly member of the two teams. Once the team members have each done the Growing Together training involving what the group entails, the theoretical basis of Growing Together thinking, as well as training in iPad filming techniques to produce portfolios, then the person is ready to be in the staff team. If any one of us is going to be away on annual leave or is ill, then the first people called on to replace them will be from another Growing Together team. That way, we aim for consistency of approach.

Over time, parents get to know us well and know that we will tell them in advance if we will miss a session. So, they expect us to be consistent in our attendance, and we try to make that as dependable as possible. If we have four people in the team, then parents and children can create relationships with the staff in whichever way they want and with whomever they are most drawn to talk to.

### Set-up

The staff team sets up the room together, laying it out in the same way each week. This is for reasons of familiarity, as well as to offer children the opportunity to return to what they prefer each week and develop from there. It also

*Figure 10.2* The layout of the room showing some of the resources used in the group

allows parents to select what they feel most comfortable around. For example, some parents dislike sand but are glad for their children to experience it. Each week, we offer sand, water, play dough, drawing, books, cars, trains, play animals, dolls and dressing up, as well as a baby corner with treasure baskets, cushions, rugs, mats and mirrors and a doll's house. The baby corner is the only sedentary area (Figure 10.2).

### Pre-brief

Having set up the room, the team sits down to discuss the approaching session a quarter of an hour before the start. We remind ourselves of significant situations from the previous week, so that we are in tune with the parents who are expected to attend.

### Session

This lasts ninety minutes, but we do not structure how it proceeds. After offering the parents a hot drink when they first arrive, we encourage them to let their children decide what they wish to play with and we support them in doing so. Parents can use the staff however they wish. For example, if a parent finds it difficult to move around the room and play with their child, we can be alongside them for a time, talk about it, share our observations of their child's preferences and so on. We prefer parents to feel relaxed and available to their children, and not feel watched, or worse, feel judged by us. We also choose a family to film in each session. That film process will be described more fully below.

## Bubbles

Ten minutes from the end of the session, we discreetly cover up the water and start some very basic clearing of the floor space. If the children have stripped down to their nappies/pants in order not to get their clothes wet, then this is the time they get dressed. We finish by blowing bubbles. Each child has a pot of bubbles, which they blow with their parents, before returning them to the box to be reused in subsequent sessions. (Once, a child who was four and in the Growing Together group until their third birthday, came back to collect their younger sibling who was now attending the group. She asked me what we were doing, and I replied that we were clearing up after the session. She immediately turned to the cupboard where the bubbles were stored and asked if she would then have bubbles!)

## Debrief

When the families have left and we have cleared up the space, we all sit down and debrief together for at least fifteen minutes. We share what has struck us during the session, conversations we should know about, how the filming had been and so on. If a parent has told us something significant, we remind them in the session that we share things as a team to improve the support we can offer. They are made aware that we are not going to gossip about them, but talk about the significant aspects of what they've said. That way, we can have more than one outlook on what has been shared. Parents build up trust in us, and we are extremely careful with personal information, which is their business, but we attempt to support them through whatever they are experiencing. During the debrief, we also reflect on the experiences the children have had and document this on a planning sheet; relating the experiences to the Early Years Foundation Stage (EYFS) (DfE, 2014), this then also helps us to plan for the following week's session.

## Training

Before they start working in Growing Together, staff members are all inducted to familiarise themselves with the group, its aims, operations and the psychological ideas embedded in our work. We have Growing Together groups and try to meet three times a year as one large team to learn around a chosen theme. This can either be practically oriented training, like exploring our Evaluation process, or it can be theoretically based, like extending our knowledge of Attachment theory.

## Filming in the sessions

When a parent and child feel settled and comfortable enough in a Growing Together session, we offer them the opportunity to be filmed. We take about a five-minute film of the parent and child, when the child is fully involved in their play, and then look through it with the parent, having a full discussion about what they observe going on in the film. There are many subtle glances, expressions and movements that may well have been missed while the action was going on. These movements can be cues between parent and child, signals that communicate feelings and emotions between them as well as behaviours that might not have been too obvious. The parent and staff member watching the film together can produce a very rich experience and conversation which aims to work out what the child is communicating and understanding in the room, reflecting the relational connections between them. When the staff member and parent watch the video, it can be watched at normal speed and also one frame at a time. This enables the worker and the parent to look very closely at what has gone on in the film. Parents often comment on seeing much more when they view the film a frame at a time. If appropriate, a worker may introduce some theory to the parent. By discussing the theoretical concepts with parents, we are able to develop a dialogue and shared understanding of the child's experiences.

The parent then selects six images from the film, which we put onto a portfolio. Then they add some words, usually chosen from the discussion that happened while viewing the film together, to complete that portfolio. This process takes the whole time in a Growing Together session, which is ninety minutes. Like our overall thinking behind Growing Together, this illustrates our wish as a staff team not to be the experts, but to use our expertise to encourage the parents making choices based on their knowledge of their own child. We take a stance of combined observation and discussion to facilitate the parents' creation of their own portfolios of their experience at Growing Together.

Another theory that underlines the filming of our families at Growing Together is Mentalization (Fonagy et al., 1991; Fonagy & Target, 1997). Mentalization describes the ability to imagine that others, as well as oneself, have mental states of their own thoughts, feelings and desires. From infancy, the child is constructing a representation of the care-giver's mind to explain the behaviour of the care-giver to the child. It has both a self-reflective and interpersonal aspect. For a parent, therefore, this involves being a person who models being curious and interested in trying to understand what is going on for their children. This imagined mental state's position towards others can contain a sense that is frequently described as someone has really "got" you.

Filming families in Growing Together sessions opens up another approach for the parent to wonder and be curious about what their child might be thinking, feeling and experiencing. Observing the film, with the staff member who did the filming, encourages parental interest and confidence to work out a deeper understanding of what their child is trying to illustrate and communicate.

## How it happens

After a parent and child have attended the group for four to six weeks, we hope that they feel familiar with the staff, the room layout and how the group is run. It is then a good time to suggest being filmed for the first time. The parent will be aware that they will be offered this opportunity, and that if it comes at an inconvenient time, for example, if the child is off-colour after having injections or the parent is feeling unwell themselves, then they could choose to be filmed another week instead. It is also made clear that there is no obligation to be filmed if they don't want to be. When Growing Together started, we used a video camera and then sat in the corner at a desk where the computer was to view the footage with the parent. As a result, we could not be mobile. In recent years, we have converted to using an iPad and so can move freely around the room to view the film wherever the parent wishes to be. Usually, that is determined by where the child wishes the parent to be. The widespread use of iPads these days means that parents and children are not fazed by seeing it being used in the room each week. Viewing others being filmed, and enjoying the process in the room, makes the filming accessible to the rest of the group, too. Often, parents show others their portfolio at the end of the session.

## Process

Staff would run through the filming process and remind the parent that the person filming will wait until the child is engaged in some play, and then film them for about five minutes. After that, the staff member would sit in the room with the parent and look through the footage. Then they would run through it again, stopping at any point the parent wished. We can freeze any part of the film to see what is going on more clearly, move forward and back until the parent gets the exact image they desire, and take six such images. Then we put the images onto a template with space below for the parent's words. These could be their thoughts and feelings about what they have witnessed, or reflections what they have learnt from the filming, or whatever. The staff tend to remember key words and ideas that are mentioned during the filming, so that if a parent is struggling with what to say in the template, we can prompt their recall. Once the six images and words are inserted, we print out a hard copy for the parent to take home, keeping another for our records. We have a display board in the Growing Together room to illustrate the

*Figure 10.3* Parent and worker viewing a completed portfolio

variety of portfolios. Parents are acquainted with these from their first visit, so they are clear about examples of the filming. This process is intended to be as collaborative as possible, right to the point that we often ask the child if it is alright to be filmed. They frequently want to see what the parent is viewing and usually enjoy seeing themselves on film! There have been occasions when a child has refused to be filmed and the staff member has waited until another week to suggest it again (Figure 10.3).

### Aim

The main impact of filming, and then watching it with the parent, is for staff and parents to see how much detail there is of the child's behaviour, responses, interests and general manner of operating in the group, and also how their couple relationship is being enacted on film. This is the material on which the conversations and learning are based.

- Reviewing film increases powers of observation, noticing and general attunement (Stern, 1985) within the parent-child relationship. It is very powerful, as the iPad is the third presence, the "other", for the staff and parents to base their comments on. This allows us to gather multiple perspectives of the child's experience (Raban *et al.*, 2003).

- Once parents notice what their child is expressing, the film conversation can evolve to include the exchange of cues and responses, or not, between parent and child.
- Choosing the images, and conversing with staff while doing so, boosts parents' confidence about their knowledge of their child and of what their child is thinking, feeling and trying to express at any point (Fonagy *et al.*, 1991) as explained earlier. Often parents will extend what is happening in the video with examples of how the child displays variations of those behaviours at home.
- Discussing the video and the images provides an opportunity to consider in detail with the parents the children's learning and development, making links to children's emotional well-being, their deep-level involvement and their schematic play.

Many parents are amazed at how much they notice and understand, as well as what they might have missed. This is not a criticism, but a reflection of how rich the clues and cues are in any parent-child relationship. As these are frequently patterned and repeated, there are numerous occasions to notice, discuss and learn. That is why we give parents their portfolio and offer copies for key people in the children's lives, e.g. a granny who takes regular care of the child, or the other parent. We encourage mothers to bring dads to the group if they are free to come so that they can see what happens at Growing Together and bring the children themselves on occasion. We have many dads who come to Growing Together, which is great for the children and to see how children relate to the other parent.

When we carry out a subsequent filming of a family, we start with previous portfolios of the family to remind us all of what the child was doing, what happened during filming and raise curiosity in the parent as to what might emerge this time.

### Frequency of filming

As a team, we take turns filming each week, keeping a record of who films whom, when and so on. Over time, the staff team will try to film each family that attends, so it is not a case of just one person filming a particular family. It is a collaborative process that is enriched by multiple perspectives on filming and review.

As a minimum, our aim is to film the child as an infant, then as a toddler, and finally, before they leave at their third birthday. Many children get filmed more often, depending on staff availability, family attendance and IT issues of internet connection, printers and so on. We have training sessions to improve staff members' confidence about filming; for example, cropping pictures when other children are in the image, enlarging a part of the picture to illustrate why it was chosen, and being able to blur the faces of other children in the image. Present-day issues about filming children were not at the forefront of our thinking with regard to Safeguarding when Growing Together started in 1999.

When a family is preparing to leave Growing Together, we will plan a final filming and take an image to put on a leaving card for that family from us, the staff at Growing Together. The children often don't understand that they are leaving Growing Together and what that means, though the parents, of course, do. So, having a card and portfolio at home allows the child to look at them whenever they want.

Since special relationships can sometimes form between family and staff members, based on the conversations had and so on, it makes sense for the final filming to be done by that member of staff.

## A unique perspective from a parent/team leader on filming at Growing Together

We in the Growing Together teams are always keen to note any parents who have attended the groups regularly and seem to have really engaged with the ideas and thinking. We then might consider asking them if they would like to have some training and join us in one of the teams in future. That would be when their children had finished Growing Together and they might be free to consider Growing Together from a different perspective. One such parent, Claire, did just that and now works in a Growing Together team, so we asked her if she would like to write a piece about what that experience had been like for her. This is the powerful piece she wrote:

> "When I first attended Growing Together, I was looking for somewhere that both my daughter and myself could socialize with other families.
>
> "I immediately felt at home within the groups (I accessed two different sessions). I was filmed two or three times and enjoyed meeting new friends, but I can remember the powerful moment like yesterday that changed my thinking about my child, and when I truly got what Growing Together is all about.
>
> "Almost everyone that knew my daughter and me would talk about how confident she was from an early age. She would burst into the room, saying good morning to everyone, happily chat to other parents, and children. I often joked she didn't really need me there.
>
> "When looking at a piece of film slowed down, we realized that every minute or so Layla would quickly glance up at something and then carry on playing. It wasn't obvious at all and it was only when we looked frame by frame that we could see she was even doing it, it took us a minute to work out she was watching and glancing at me almost the whole time.

"I must admit this felt a little strange to me, I would have said I know my daughter's personality very well, and coming from an early years background I loved to watch her play and would have said I knew her inside out – how did I not realize how key I was to her confidence! This was not a negative experience but a very powerful one for me, and a realization that perhaps she was not the overconfident child we all thought she was.

"I was working within the centre when a space became available for a staff member in Growing Together. I jumped at the chance to become involved, and feel really passionate about being part of it. As a member of staff, I always enjoy the filming process and the discussions with parents that follows. Having been a parent joining groups I feel mindful of parents that are new to a group, or perhaps not in a group of friends, or that may feel isolated in any way. Alongside my colleagues I particularly enjoy reflecting and discussing the interactions between families and theories like group dynamics – this is a subject I find very interesting."

### Regular feedback measures

We use regular feedback measures to find out how families are interacting with Growing Together, how we are reaching them and how effective we are in achieving outcomes beneficial for family relationships. The paperwork we use in Growing Together is not just a form-filling exercise. We have compiled our Initial and Evaluation forms to be the basis of a conversation with parents from which we can document parents' feedback. Either we fill them in during the conversation, or the parents do so themselves, whichever they prefer.

After about four weeks of attendance, we fill out an initial form with families, built around an initial conversation with them. We explore what families want from Growing Together and ask about the strengths and vulnerabilities of the parent-child relationship. Issues around the birth story, medical circumstances, sleep and eating patterns, as well as the perceived Attachment between the parent and child, are explored. That way, we can return to that initial form at any point with the parent and see how things are developing during the Growing Together experience. We also have an evaluation form that is completed at regular intervals and particularly when the family is filmed. In the evaluation forms, we use measures of progress, based on which we can produce statistics about the families we are reaching and how we are affecting them, so that we can all learn and develop our practice.

In each Growing Together group, we also have a Data Collection form where we document the dates when the families are filmed, complete forms and evaluations, as well as when the children are due to finish the group, so we can plan when we film each family. On these forms, we also document when we have filmed material, which we can send on to the Nursery if they have a child who also attends Growing Together. That is done through secure computer software used in the Centre.

## Starting at Growing Together

**Date:**

We ask parents to fill in this short form as the beginning of their time at Growing Together. We are not looking for 'right' answers to these questions, but we'd like to know where you are starting from in the group, and then we can look back at it together over time in the group to see what the journey has been like – particularly by the time you leave when your child reaches their third birthday.

First of all, we are interested in **getting to know** you and your child.

- What would you like us to call you?
- What would you like us to call your child?
- Do you need reminders of our names, too?

What made you choose Growing Together:

- For you?
- For your child?

We call the group Growing Together because the focus is on the relationship between you and your child. **Our aim** is for the relationship to grow and strengthen, so it would help us to have your views at the beginning. As we only see you and your child for an hour and a half a week,

- What would you like us to keep in mind about your child?
- What would be useful for us to know about you?
- What has been easy, as well as tough, about making a relationship with your child so far?

Could you put an X on the line below, between 1 and 10, to describe where you are now?

Use the boxes as a guide.

| 1 | 2 | 3 | 4 | 5 | 6 | 7 | 8 | 9 | 10 |

| I find my child difficult to be with. I worry about going out of the house with my child. | I try to spend time with my child, but it's a struggle. Some days are better than others. | I enjoy being with my child. We share things together and have fun. |

As you look at the room and resources available here, what do you think you and your child might be spending lots of time involved in?

We will look back at this over time, together, but when you come to the group, please talk to us about your experiences with your child at any time.

Thank you for sharing this information with us. It is our usual practice to share information from our families with our immediate team members, but not more widely without your permission.

**Evaluation Form**

Name:                                          Date:
DOB:                                           Age:    yrs    mths

When did you start coming to Growing Together?

1.  (a)  Tell me about the experience of watching video footage of
         your child's play:

    (b)  Where would you place yourself on the following scale on
         your first video?

| Too nervous to learn from it | Less nervous, but started to learn from it | Felt and learnt nothing in particular | Quite enjoyed, and learnt from it | Really enjoyed learning from it |
|---|---|---|---|---|

    (c)  Where would you place yourself on the same scale on your
         last video?

| Too nervous to learn from it | Less nervous, but started to learn from it | Felt and learnt nothing in particular | Quite enjoyed, and learnt from it | Really enjoyed learning from it |
|---|---|---|---|---|

2.  (a)  Tell me about your own well-being – has Growing Together
         had any impact on it? (For example, have you felt more posi-
         tive about yourself as a parent?)

    (b)  If you have gone away feeling any better about your parent-
         ing, what sort of things did you try out or consider at home?

3.  (a)  Think about any support you may or may not have felt in the
         group:

    (b)  How have other parents supported you?

| Not at all | A little bit | Not considered it | A bit | A great deal |
|---|---|---|---|---|

    (c)  How have staff supported you?

| Not at all | A little bit | Not considered it | A bit | A great deal |
|---|---|---|---|---|

*(Continued)*

(d)  How have other people's children supported you?

| Not at all | A little bit | Not considered it | A bit | A great deal |
|---|---|---|---|---|

4. Thinking about the relationship with your child, tell me what was helpful/unhelpful to you in this group?

Helpful things could be:

Unhelpful things could be:

5. You may remember filling in the scale, below, when you joined Growing Together. Would you do it again for us now, please?

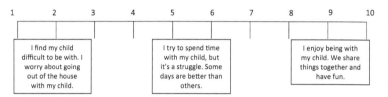

| 1 | 2 | 3 | 4 | 5 | 6 | 7 | 8 | 9 | 10 |

I find my child difficult to be with. I worry about going out of the house with my child.

I try to spend time with my child, but it's a struggle. Some days are better than others.

I enjoy being with my child. We share things together and have fun.

6. Do you have any other comments you would like to share with me about you and your child's experience coming to Growing Together?

Thank you for sharing this with us.

**Growing Together Data Collection**

| Name | DOB | Initial Form | 1st Filming | Permission Form | 2nd Filming | Images to link with Nursery | Final Filming | Evaluation Form | Card | Comments |
|---|---|---|---|---|---|---|---|---|---|---|
| | | | | | | Dates | | | | |
| | | | | | | | | | | |
| | | | | | | | | | | |
| | | | | | | | | | | |
| | | | | | | | | | | |
| | | | | | | | | | | |
| | | | | | | | | | | |
| | | | | | | | | | | |
| | | | | | | | | | | |
| | | | | | | | | | | |
| | | | | | | | | | | |
| | | | | | | | | | | |
| | | | | | | | | | | |
| | | | | | | | | | | |
| | | | | | | | | | | |
| | | | | | | | | | | |
| | | | | | | | | | | |
| | | | | | | | | | | |
| | | | | | | | | | | |

## Examples of attachment ideas in a **GT** group

We have chosen three examples from practice: one from an infant and mother, one from a toddler and the third from a 2+ year old about to leave Growing Together for Nursery.

A key idea from Winnicott is that security within the attachment relationship is the basis for a child to feel free to explore their external world through play (Winnicott 1971). What we offer in Growing Together is an environment for a child to take gradual steps away from a reliable adult and still have access to that adult. This enables the child to experience the parent as a secure base for itself (Bowlby, 1969). Most parents come to Growing Together to give their child access to other children and learn how to interact with them. However, what we encourage is that parents experience how crucial the security of the relationship between a child and their Attachment person is in order for the child to develop the confidence to interact with other children. So, it is not just a set of skills for a child to acquire, but for parents to realise that the Attachment figure is key to the success of this social step.

### Example from practice

A mother with a ten-month old was about to slip out of the room to go to the toilet, and asked a staff member to keep an eye on the infant. The staff member agreed to it, but encouraged the mother first to tell her child where she was going, and that she would be back very soon. The parent was unsure about letting her child experience any distress at seeing her leave.

A discussion then ensued about preparing the infant in such a way that the infant would feel able to bear the separation, as well as anticipate her mum's return. We feel that soothing the child and reassuring them that the mother would return soon and that the child would be fine is preferable to the child's panicking on discovering they were on their own and their world then disintegrating.

Further to this experience, when the mother was filmed for the first time she was very surprised at how often her infant looked at her and needed to find her when she was negotiating and experimenting with her environment. Thus, we could return to that conversation and connect the two together.

### Example from practice

A mother, who was going through periods of treatment in hospital, was having to leave her child (20 months) with granny overnight. The mother

(*Continued*)

came to Growing Together and talked about how distressed she had been to hear that her child asked for her at night in her absence, and she felt extremely guilty.

We discussed how her child knew to ask for her mother when she needed her and seek reassurance from her – it showed that the child anticipated her mother making it all okay for her. Granny could be a substitute, but was a stand-in until the child could be with her mother. The mother could hear this reframe with some confidence rather than have her guilty feelings emphasized.

## Example from practice

A child (31 months) was extremely articulate, well attuned with her mother and loved coming to the group. She knew exactly what she liked to play with and could express it to her mother, who would respond fully, and they enjoyed attending the group 'Growing Together' together. Suddenly one day, the girl shrieked and screamed for her mother, who was some metres away. They had a cuddle, and the little girl then resumed her play. It emerged that she'd told her mother that another child had shown her a toy lion and gave out a huge roar, scaring and panicking her into immediate meltdown. The speed with which the mother responded, the cuddle given, and the reassuring explanation all allowed the girl to resume her play, and her state of contentment returned quickly.

These three examples from practices illustrate how children at different stages of development can experience Attachment distress in different ways, leading them to seek the reassurance they require to continue with exploring their worlds. We also see how this reassurance can be given in a variety of ways.

Bion's idea of Containment (1962) is crucial to understanding the examples given. Bion's theory is that an Attachment figure can *hold* its child's distressed and unmanageable feelings, which are often displayed as rage, fury or upset. The parent can contain these uncomfortable feelings while supporting their child to find a way through them. It is not about snuffing out those feelings, or suppressing them, or disapproving of them so they go underground. It might feel embarrassing for a parent to see their child behave in a way that can be socially frowned upon, but if we can explore why this might be happening and offer alternative explanations about what the child might be communicating, as well as how to respond to these feelings, then maybe a child and its parent can develop a deeper way of relating between themselves. This could be learning that both parent and child could take into future relationships as well.

## Then and now

The group has evolved from its origins, as recalled by a mother. Sarah came to the group in 2002 and attended again in 2015 with her daughter, Kira. Sarah and Kira finished coming to the Growing Together group in December 2015 as Kira turned three.

In 2002, Sarah came to the group as a young Mum with Conner, her three-month-old first son. When Sarah returned to the group in 2013, the first thing she did was to show us, a new staff team, a portfolio she had brought from her initial experience in Growing Together. We thought this would be a rich opportunity to see what her perceptions of the group had been originally and how they had altered, or not, over time.

When I told her about this, she immediately said: "It hasn't changed!" and, "I didn't think I'd come back in ten years' time." What emerged was that what had changed was her availability and thinking as a mother.

## Then

Sarah recalled being very nervous and anxious about coming to Growing Together for the first time. She had been recommended it by her midwife as Sarah had felt low, isolated and "depressed", she told me. "I didn't know what it would be like", so walking in the first time was pretty scary.

- Room layout: Sarah recalled the room looked much as it does now, that the group was very busy then and she could even remember some of the staff's names.
- Asking questions: Sarah was "too shy" to ask questions of the staff, but she really liked them asking her "how my week had been" and how she was doing each session.
- Other parents: Sarah felt relief at getting to know other parents and starting to feel less isolated. But she also commented that the group used to be much bigger and a bit intimidating at times. "It took time to feel okay", and settle in the group.
- Filming: Sarah had been extremely nervous when it was her turn to be filmed and was very keen not to have her own face included in the pictures. She had "wanted to hide away". (Some were in black and white and some were in colour, apparently!)
- Conner's favourite play things: Sarah immediately said he liked the water play best, and then recalled he'd loved the doll's buggy.
- Bubbles: "Conner loved the bubbles", as did Sarah, and even now Conner will apparently offer to blow bubbles for Kira at home. Sarah attributes this to his early love of bubbles from Growing Together.

*(Continued)*

- <u>What she has got from the group</u>: Sarah was clear that it got her out of the house and got Conner in touch with other children. They could spend time together, but with others around her. She felt she needed to develop some confidence and did.

## Now

Sarah returned to the group very keen to show us she now had a daughter. She said she was not nervous or anxious but excited to return to the group as she knew what to expect, and wanted to show us the original portfolio.

- <u>Room layout</u>: Sarah quickly commented on the fact that the two big tables had gone, the water tray was still there with the same big water funnel toy in it, that the chairs which had been red had been changed and even that a large photo on the wall was still there. She noticed that we had added a doll's house, but commented that the doll's blue buggy, which Conner had loved, had gone. She recalled a lot of detail about the room layout.
- <u>Asking questions</u>: Sarah said that as she was not a new mum this time (she has three children), it made a difference. She was more confident to ask the staff questions.
- <u>Other parents</u>: Sarah feels she has made some real friends in the group this time. If Kira got involved in something with another child that required Sarah to get involved, then, "I would just talk to the other parent and sort it out".
- <u>Filming</u>: Sarah said it was easier to be filmed now. When I asked her about her face being in the film and portfolio, she replied, "Now I don't care, I just get on with it." She talked of taking the present portfolios home and showing them to Conner as well.
- <u>Kira's favourite play things</u>: Kira also likes the water, but she is very interested in playing with the dolls, too.
- <u>Bubbles</u>: Sarah was clear that Kira was interested in blowing the bubbles herself from when she was a newly walking toddler.
- <u>What she has got from the group this time</u>: Sarah thinks she is more confident about spending time with Kira, knows what Kira likes and can be there with her.

## How does this interview inform us at Growing Together?

We think that Sarah's responses to the questions reflect a confidence in both how she parents and in choosing how to parent. These are directly related to her knowledge of herself and her child, even though she wouldn't use technical terms to describe her parenting knowledge. She is able to read how Kira is presenting at any time and what she might be communicating to Sarah about what she needs from her. Sarah has grasped the idea that if she gets some personal support for herself in the group, she is then more available for her child. She exchanges ideas with other mothers in the group about what Kira is communicating and how Sarah responds to her.

There are things that Sarah does as a parent that are second nature to her now, which wasn't the case before. She is aware that thinking and imagining how Kira might be feeling affects how she parents her. She takes for granted now that how she herself feels affects her relationship with Kira and that Kira will pick up cues, both consciously and unconsciously.

## Sarah's recent Growing Together journey

### Timeline

Sarah and Kira started at Growing Together in January 2013, when Kira was about four weeks old. Table 10.2 shows when they were filmed in the session and when the feedback was documented. In total they were filmed eight times.

Sarah completed the Growing Together initial form in March 2013. What emerged from it was Sarah's fear of not bonding with her daughter. That would have been a repeat of her experience with her first son at the outset. But she could articulate that that had not occurred and she felt "proud" of her relationship with Kira because from the start, she could acknowledge a pleasure in being with her.

In one of the filming sessions, Kira was filmed as she was crawling. She hadn't been doing this very long, and it was clear to see that Sarah was immensely proud of Kira's new skill. The images Sarah chose on the portfolio clearly depicted Kira being mobile in the room. Sarah chose the words to accompany the images and

Table 10.2 A table showing when filming occurred and filming was documented

| Start | Filmed | Initial form | Evaluation | End |
|---|---|---|---|---|
| January 2013 | February 2013, April 2013, June 2013, October 2013 | March 2013 | December 2015 | December 2015 |
| | February 2014, June 2014 | | | |
| | September 2015, December 2015 | | | |

commented on all the choices and decisions that Kira appeared to be making about where to go and what to pick up. (What Sarah was starting to be confident about was mentioning how she thought Kira was feeling. She thought Kira was feeling proud of herself. Sarah reflected on this and went on to say that, as her Mum, she was proud, too. The congruence of these emotions was enriching their relationship.)

Sarah and Kira were filmed again, after they had been attending the Growing Together group for some time. In the images Sarah chose of Kira, you could see she was really confident as she explored the resources available in the room. At this time, Sarah was able to consider the experiences Kira was having in the group and reflect on those which she had particularly enjoyed. Sarah was once again very aware of how Kira was experiencing the group and what she was feeling as her mum.

Having given the reader a flavour of how filming might start and progress over time at Growing Together, then it is often the case that parents like Sarah will come into a session telling us how the child has continued to do at home what they did in the session, for example. Sarah would come in and tell us funny stories about Kira hiding things from her brothers for them to find, or enlisting them to come and sort out something for her that she couldn't manage herself. She would volunteer how Kira would get her older siblings to help her in setting up and doing whatever she wanted to achieve in her play at home.

There were occasions when Sarah used Growing Together as a place that she could bring Kira but she needed to talk through other concerns on her mind that week. Then there were occasions when she would arrive and just want to discuss Kira and maybe be filmed. Attending a weekly group for nearly three years allows parents to be very honest about how much energy and attention they feel able to share with their child. That will vary according to how life is at any one time for that family. We always feel pleased if parents make the effort to attend Growing Together when they might otherwise choose to stay at home feeling low or distracted about something. Their child can be in the group and get what they need and maybe the parent can receive the same. That will often lead to the parent being able to be more available to their child in the group and at home afterwards. It is a key aim for us at Growing Together to encourage parents' ideas, thinking and experience in the room that they can draw on and promote in their relationships with their children at home.

Over the weeks of attending Growing Together, both mother and child got more confident in the space, and building up a familiarity with the provision, staff and other parents and children using the space. Sarah made some connections with other mothers that have endured as relationships she has outside the group, too. Two families in particular had children that also started in the Pen Green nursery at a similar time to Kira. They all finished at Growing Together around the same time and arranged a date afterwards when they could all three come back for a final Growing Together and meet up in that space.

## Why have a psychotherapist in the group?

All the professionals working at Pen Green have expertise in child development or adult learning. Pen Green employs a psychotherapist in Growing Together to open up an extra dimension for staff and parents to recognise and understand psychological and emotional relational issues that are at work between parents and children, both conscious and unconscious. This provides additional perspectives when interacting with families. Psychodynamic psychotherapeutic ideas work in the area of possibility of viewpoint – it is not an orientation of certainty. We observe people and relationships to try and understand what might be happening, so we can discuss those ideas with people to enlarge their confidence to make differences in those conversations and relationships with people.

Getting used to theoretical ideas when perceiving external events, as well as wondering about how we feel and respond internally, widens the team's understanding of what we witness at Growing Together. One such theory that informs our work is that of Melanie Klein's ideas of Projection and Projective Identification (1946 & 1952). These are the names given to describe an unconscious way of dealing with anxiety. Projection is when a baby experiences impulses that she cannot hold or manage inside herself, so they are split off and propelled into the other, which is usually the mother. Projective identification is a more complex form of this idea of projection. If a baby is experiencing very intense anxiety, then whole aspects of the self that are too painful will be projected into the other person. It can give the baby the illusion of having defended against the source of anxiety. The other person may then start to act as though they have taken in the unwanted part, experiencing those feelings of intense anxiety themselves. So, a general example of this might be a mother saying that their child had known they had just got to sleep and then they started to cry intending to spoil the mother's sleep. The stressed mother projectively identifies her baby as her persecutor rather than being able to separate her own personal experience from her baby's.

The following example of a mother-child situation in Growing Together illustrates how having a psychotherapist in the team allowed us to explore these dynamics of projective identification to help us in our thinking. On this particular occasion, our staff team felt blocked by experiencing someone else's feelings on their behalf, as well as angry and defeated:

### Example from practice

A mother with a two-year-old daughter used to come to Growing Together with some of her friends and their children. This mother was very sociable with her friends, but could appear suddenly to be quite brusque

(*Continued*)

and angry with her child when, each week, the little girl would grab toys from others. The girl cried and got angry with her mother's response.

We, as a staff team, felt quite alienated by the perceived anger between mother and child, and were unable to think clearly about this situation, or about how we could fruitfully start a conversation with the mother. This was unusual.

In debrief, we shared what we saw and felt about the mother and child's reactions, and then connected them to how we ourselves felt. We began to wonder if our own feelings were related to the feelings being displayed, i.e. that we were experiencing the mother's feelings that she could not manage at that point (Projective Identification, Klein, 1930s and Counter Transference, Bion, 1962). Once we, as a team, had disentangled our own feelings and responses from the frozen ones we had experienced in the room, we felt freer to consider what might have been experienced in the room and how to think more creatively about it. We then wondered if the child's anger affected the mother's feelings and if both of them felt isolated and unable to reach each other. We hypothesised that each might well feel one way internally, but look different externally.

So, the next week, the mother was asked for her thoughts on the grabbing incident from the week before. Immediately, she got tearful and talked about the embarrassment of her daughter's behaviour and how she feared judgement from other parents. She was asked to guess what her daughter might have felt, and she was amazed to realise that her own feelings were too overwhelming for her to consider her daughter's. That discussion led us to consider if her daughter might be feeling alone, unable to engage her mother or to manage her feelings so she could be feeling overwhelmed. This elicited the mother's wish to help her daughter through such feelings. We wondered together why her daughter might be grabbing toys, and if she could be feeling jealous of her mother socialising with her friends and fearing she might not notice her. If that might be the case, then any behaviour that got her mother's attention could feel desirable to the child, but it all then spiralled downwards between them. We spoke about how her daughter could not possibly be consciously aware of how she felt, let alone be able to articulate it. But if the mother could think about it, anticipate it and generate some ideas about how to respond differently, then a whole range of alternatives could be considered.

As the psychotherapist in the group, I am perceived and used in different ways within the group, by the team, parents and children.

- **Some parents** seek me out for expertise they feel I have in psychological and emotional aspects of the relationship between the parent and the child. Some of my discussions with parents are pretty functional (what ideas I might have about potty training), some are apparently chat (especially with parents that find it extremely challenging just to walk over the threshold of Growing Together), and others are specifically about concerns they have about their child, their relationship with the child or with their partner – for example the end of a couple relationship, or when a key person in the family dies, moving house and so on. I listen to these and try to keep a particular ear open about how this information might be impacting the child-parent relationship.

- **Children** often seek me out by establishing rituals with me. That can be about how they enter the room and first see me, what play or toy they might want me to get involved with, and even how to get their parent to come and play with them. They can also sometimes look at me and I can see that they fear I may want to talk to their parent, or in some way take the parent away from them. Then I just voice that to the parent and move away for a time. I like to repeat my name to children and they often are intrigued with my name and photo round my neck. That is because I want them to feel they can call me and get my attention easily, rather than just think I'm "a lady" over there. There are clearly some children that feel my main function is to open the cupboard with the bubbles and I'm perceived as "the bubble lady"!
- **Staff** use me in different ways. We are a team and we all do the jobs of setting up, distributing hot drinks, having conversations and engaging families each time, as well as filming and observing behaviours and relationships in the group.
- My role is to move in and out of engaging with the team during the work, and to step back to reflect on the dynamics in the group as a whole. When team members during debrief bring their thoughts about what has gone on between specific families and staff interactions, my role is to explore with them what might have been going on. Then we can process it from our understanding about what has been happening and how they have been feeling. They can question me, try to take their ideas further with me acting as a sounding board, as well as ask about relevant theory and technical terminology.
- I feel that relationships are always works in progress, highly influenced by our childhood relationship with our key Attachment figure. As we grow into adulthood, our external and internal circumstances influence us and our attachment circle widens, adding templates for how we learn to relate to others. Attachment has a great deal to tell us, for example about the partners we choose (Clulow, 2009), while neurobiology informs us that our neural developmental pathways can be altered right up to old age.

## The Early Years Specialist in the group

The Early Years Specialist in the group has a deep knowledge of child development theory and extensive experience working with young children and their families. The Early Years Specialist will work with the parent to help them understand about their child's learning, make links with the experiences the child is having at home and support the parent with thinking about future learning opportunities.

The Early Years Specialist will bring a range of skills and knowledge to the group.

- **Some parents** will talk to the Early Years Specialist regarding their child's play and what they are interested in and when they observe their children deeply involved in experiences (Laevers, 1997, 2005). Parents may ask specifically about the patterns they are noticing in their child's play and want to consider how they most appropriately support their child's experiences (Athey, 2007; Arnold & The Pen Green Centre Team, 2010; Mairs & The Pen Green Centre Team, 2012). Parents may feel challenged by their child's play, for example a parent in the group found it quite difficult when their child became very interested in throwing things. His interest in the trajectory movement of the objects was clear to see but not always easy to accept with very young babies in the room. The Early Years Specialist talked about the child's interest and was able to suggest possibilities for the child in the group. We introduced a number of nylon sponges for the child so he could explore his interest in throwing things but in a safe way around the smaller children.
- **Children** will include the Early Years Specialist in their play and ask them for resources and support with what they are doing. The Early Years Specialist will play alongside the children, supporting their learning opportunities.
- **Staff** will consider children's interest and explorations, identify children's schematic play and make plans to further support the learning opportunities, planning the environment and ordering resources.

## The Family Support Worker in the group

The Family Support Worker in the group has a secure knowledge and skill base in supporting families within the Centre, within their home and within the wider community. The Family Support Worker will support parents in a variety of ways depending on the needs of the individual families that attend the group. The Family Support Worker will be an advocate for the whole family and often make links for the family with other services on offer within the Centre.

- **Some parents** will talk to the Family Support Worker about complexities at home; the worker may provide practical information such as phone numbers for specific support, assisting to make links with external agencies or general advice on being a parent.
- **Children** will connect with the Family Support Worker as they are greeted on arrival and supported to access the resources on offer. Children will see the worker relating to their parent and they soon see them as a trusted familiar adult within the group.
- **Staff** will use the expertise of the Family Worker to link with other agencies and offer advice re: housing, benefits, etc.

## The Researcher in the group

The Researcher in the group helps us to make the links with current theory to our practice in the Growing Together group. The researcher will link with the team to write about the work in the group and support the team with producing material for case studies and presentations.

- **Some parents** will talk to the researcher about their role as a parent and more specifically about the community education and adult learning opportunities within the Centre.
- **Children** will connect with the researcher as a resourceful adult who is interested and intrigued by their learning and development.
- **Staff** will use the researcher as a link person between the practice of the integrated Centre and the work within the onsite research, development and training base.

We are all learning all the time in Growing Together. There is never a session when we have not felt that our own learning has been expanded, altered, or affected in some fashion. Experience and reflection always keep the Growing Together experience fresh for us.

We would like to finish with a small anecdote that we as a team, as well as the mother concerned, found amusing. This mother had attended Growing Together pretty regularly for nearly two years with her son, so the room, staff, toys and provision were very familiar to him. One Friday at home, the mother told her son they were coming to Pen Green that day. He responded by asking what they were attending. She replied describing Growing Together. He scoffed in reply, saying:

"That's not Pen Green, it's the Centre of the Universe!"

We would not consider our group to be as lofty as that, but we all had to laugh at how we had apparently gotten framed in this child's head!

## References

Arnold, C. & The Pen Green Centre Team (2010) *Understanding Schemas and Emotion in Early Childhood*. London: Sage.

Athey, C. (2007) *Extending Thought in Young Children: A Parent-Teacher Partnership (2nd edition)*. London: Paul Chapman.

Bion, W. (1962) *Learning from Experience*. London: Heinemann.

Bowlby, J. (1969) *Attachment and Loss. Vol 1: Attachment*. London: Hogarth Press.

Clulow, C. (2009) *How Attachment Shapes Family Relationships: A Guide for Practitioners*. London: Tavistock Centre for Couple Relationships.

Department for Education (DfE) (2014) *The Early Years Foundation Stage: Setting Standards for Learning, Development and Care for Children from Birth to Five*. London: DfE.

Fonagy, P. Steele, H. & Steele, M. (1991) Maternal Representation of Attachment during Pregnancy Predicts the Organization of Infant-Mother Attachment at One Year of Age. *Child Development*, 62, 891–905.

Fonagy, P. & Target, M. (1997) Attachment and Reflective Function: Their Role in Self-Organization. *Development and Psychopathology*, 9, 679–700.

Klein, M. (1946) 'Notes on Some Schizoid Mechanisms (1946)', in *Envy and Gratitude and Other Works* 1946–1963, ch. 1, pp. 1–24, London: Vintage.

Klein, M. Heimann, P. Isaacs, S. & Rivière, J. (1952) *Developments in Psychoanalysis*. (Also in Karnac Maresfield Reprints, 1985.) 'Notes on Some Schizoid Mechanisms'. This 1952 version gives the same definition as the 1946 version but adds a definitive sentence: 'I suggest for these processes the term "projective identification"'.

Laevers, F. (1997) *A Process-Orientated Child Monitoring System for Young Children*. Belgium: Centre for Experiential Education.

Laevers, F. (2005) *Deep Level Learning and the Experiential Approach in Early Childhood and Primary Education*. Leuven: Research Centre for Experiential Education. https://vorming.cego.be/images/downloads/BO_DP_Deep-levelLearning.pdf (Accessed 13 September 2016).

Mairs, K. & The Pen Green Centre Team (2012) *Young Children Learning Through Schemas: Deepening the Dialogue about Learning in the Home and the Nursery*. London: Routledge.

Norton, F. Woodhead, J. Gallagher, T. Benford, J. & Cole, C. (2013) *Working with Families in Children's Centres and Early Years Settings*. London: Hodder Education.

Raban, B., Ure, C. & Waniganayake, M. (2003) Multiple Perspectives: Acknowledging the Virtue of Complexity Measuring Quality. *Early Years,* 23 (1), 67–77.

Rutter, M. (1972) Childhood Schizophrenia Reconsidered. *Journal of Autism and Childhood Schizophrenia*, 2 (3), 315–337.

Schaffer, R. & Emerson, P. (1964) 4 Stages of Attachment in Infants (4th stage is about multiple attachments) from a Glasgow Research study.

Stern, D. (1985) *The Interpersonal World of the Infant*. New York: Basic Books.

Winnicott, D.W. (1971) *Playing and Reality*. London: Routledge.

## Chapter 11

# The 'Being Two' project
## Disseminating good practice locally and nationally

*Kate Hayward, Andrea Layzell, Michele Duffy and Tracy Gallagher*

In this chapter, Kate Hayward begins by outlining the challenges facing pedagogues following the expansion of two-year-old funded places. She goes on to describe the 'Being Two' project developed by Pen Green to address these challenges by enabling nursery teams to reflect on and develop their work with two-year olds and their families. Tracy Gallagher shares a case study explaining how practitioners in the 0–3 team at Pen Green reflected on their practice and developed their work with a specific focus on one particular aspect of the Early Years Foundation Stage (EYFS) learning and development (DfE, 2014).

Andrea Layzell and Michele Duffy then illustrate this work, describing how they involved the childminder network in professional development and training opportunities within the Pen Green locality. Tracy Gallagher shares an example from practice to highlight how the Pen Green staff within the 0–3 team analyse data to inform and develop their work with young children.

## The Pen Green 'Being Two' project by Kate Hayward (Case study by Tracy Gallagher)

### Two-year-old funded places: the challenge

From September 2014, the widening provision for two-year olds whose family circumstances met certain eligibility criteria meant that many nursery teams were expanding their provision for the youngest children for the first time. At Pen Green, having thought so carefully about our 0–3 provision across the Centre and having worked with two-year olds in our nurseries for over thirty years, we knew that this would be challenging. The pedagogical considerations for each unique child are of course important, and we were acutely aware that very young children needed a specific and particularly sensitive and responsive approach to their care and learning needs and, importantly, Family Workers needed a very close relationship with each child's family.

### Building on our previous learning

We had been involved in supporting pedagogical reflection within teams for some years, through our professional development programmes, 'Parents Involvement in their Children's Learning' (PICL) and 'Making Children's Learning Visible' (MCLV). Practitioners were encouraged to attend these programmes in pairs so that they could work together through the projects with their staff teams over three months of review and reflection. The project work involved reviewing their own practice in relation to the principles of working with children and their families that have been developed at Pen Green, and the completion of case studies with families. They were then able to create action plans for developing and improving their practice within their own staff teams.

Through this work and drawing on our continually developing Pen Green practice, we were well placed to apply for Department for Education (DfE)

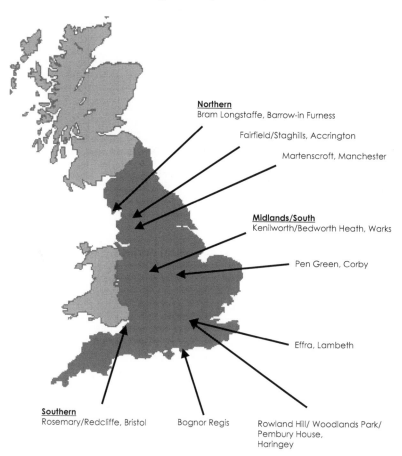

## Early Years Teaching Centres
### working with 2 year olds

**Northern**
Bram Longstaffe, Barrow-in Furness

Fairfield/Staghills, Accrington

Martenscroft, Manchester

**Midlands/South**
Kenilworth/Bedworth Heath, Warks

Pen Green, Corby

Effra, Lambeth

**Southern**
Rosemary/Redcliffe, Bristol          Bognor Regis          Rowland Hill/ Woodlands Park/ Pembury House, Haringey

*Figure 11.1* Map showing location of project centres

funding to develop a programme of support for practitioners working with two-year olds in other Early Years settings. Having built a network of Early Years Teaching Centres through a project, previously funded by the DfE, we knew that the best way to support and sustain pedagogical development was through an ongoing network of practitioners who are encouraged to support, inspire and challenge each other.

### Developing a network of 'Being Two' associate centres

The Centres we had worked with as Early Years Teaching Centres were in some of the most deprived areas of the country. While many of these areas had large numbers of families eligible for funded two-year-old places, the nurseries in the locality were of variable quality, struggling with high staff turnover, low pay and poor prospects within the setting.

The focus of the Being Two project was to improve the quality of experiences in settings for two-year olds and their families, and to support better outcomes for children and families through developing local professional development networks with Early Years settings in each area. We drew on the principles and approach developed through PICL and MCLV and created the 'Being Two' professional development project approach, specifically looking at practice developments with those who were working with two-year olds and their families.

There were nine 'Being Two' project Centres including Pen Green, and each worked with eleven or more Early Years settings in the first year and twenty-two or more settings in the second year, supporting the practice development of a total of 2,290 practitioners working with two-year olds (Figure 11.1).

## The 'Being Two' Pen Green approach

The strands of PICL and MCLV were combined to enable practitioners to focus on the following.

### The Image of the Child

A concept developed in Reggio Emilia. Creating a shared 'Image of the Child' enables staff teams to own and articulate what it is they are working towards supporting and developing in children. Malaguzzi (Penn, 1997, pg. 117) described their image of a child as being 'rich in potential, strong, powerful, competent and, most of all, connected to adults and children', and this is used as a stimulus for staff to come up with their own 'Image of the Child'. The process gives staff teams the joy of focusing on their pedagogy and the outcomes for children that they are passionate about. This is a powerful process and a far cry from the usual pattern of professional development training where knowledge is imparted about 'best practice'. This was a starting point in the 'Being Two' project and gave even the most reluctant and fearful teams a sense of who they were and what they were working towards.

## Use of video

The power of video as a tool for analysis, reflection and dialogue has been instrumental in the development of both pedagogy and work with families at Pen Green (McKinnon, 2007). In the 'Being Two' project, practitioners invested in filming equipment, getting to grips with iPads and cameras with video facility that could allow them to edit footage and share films with colleagues and, importantly, also with parents to reflect on the children's development and learning.

## A focus on pedagogy to support the 'Image of the Child'

Once teams had established their 'Image of the Child', they could then consider their role as practitioners in supporting this image. What pedagogy supported their Image of the Child? For example, if they wanted to support children to be confident, what did they need to do to promote this for each child? With the help of video reflection, staff teams could begin to challenge themselves on their pedagogical approach, not from an imposed set of 'must dos' but from a considered position of reflection against their own set of values and beliefs.

## Peer observations

As a development of this focused reflection, we encouraged pairs of practitioners to observe each other through videoing an aspect of practice or an interaction with a child, when and where the practitioner being filmed was comfortable enough with the process. This was a huge challenge and a part of practice that needed to be built up. It can be horrible to see yourself on video and even more difficult to examine your pedagogical support through watching what you did. However, many practitioners stated that they were surprised at how many positives came out of this. It was an opportunity to celebrate the effectiveness of the adult support, as well as an opportunity to raise questions about the individual or group of children's learning needs and to talk about how these needs could be best supported.

The ethics of the process were paramount. If a practitioner was uncomfortable with what was recorded, it was deleted. As staff became more familiar with the process, however, they began to see beyond the discomfort of seeing themselves on video and to see the potential of the film clips in enabling dialogue with families and staff about the children. In addition, Pedagogical Strategies could also be used to look at and discuss the pedagogical engagement in adult-child interactions (you can find out more about this work in Chapter 7).

### Reflecting on children's progress with families

For several years at Pen Green, we have tussled with the challenge of recording and reflecting on children's progress in a way that does not lean towards 'tick boxing' against developmental statements. In developing the electronic assessment aspect of MCLV, we were keen for the assessment judgements to be made by each Family Worker in dialogue with families to reflect a professional judgement about the child's learning and development and to celebrate progress over time. The individual child graphs generated after the assessment judgements are made lend themselves to reflection by the adults supporting the child's learning and can be used to raise questions from the data.

### Case study of Isobella

The following case study identifies how Lesley, Isobella's Family Worker, and Joanne and Stuart, Isobella's parents, dialogued together to produce her MCLV assessments and what the assessments were able to show them.

Isobella attended the Couthie from when she was nine months old. Lesley worked closely with Joanne and Stuart to document her learning, her achievements and her progress. Isobella was deeply interested in mark making at home and when she was in the Couthie. Lesley knew from Stuart and Joanne that Isobella liked to 'draw' and 'write' when at home and when with her grandparent. Isobella didn't attend the Couthie every day, so Lesley knew it was really important for her to have access to these resources on the days she did come to the setting. Lesley would always make sure that there was a mark making area set up for Isobella when she came to the Couthie. Lesley was keen to make sure the area was full of interesting resources for Isobella to explore as soon as she arrived. Lesley talked with Joanne and Stuart about Isobella's interests at home and closely observed Isobella in the Couthie. She would then plan experiences and new opportunities related to her interests and current curiosities. Lesley discussed with Joanne and Stuart Isobella's first MCLV assessment, and when it was completed, she analysed the graph. Lesley noticed that Isobella was working at age-related expectations. She completed the second assessment, and on analysis, she noticed that although Isobella had continued to make progress in all of the prime areas, there was no recorded difference in her physical development on her MCLV graph. This raised questions and challenges for Lesley and Isobella's parents. On completion of her third assessment, Lesley noticed that there was rapid progress in all three prime areas. It was obvious to Joanne, Stuart and Lesley why there had been such a shift. After the second MCLV assessment, Isobella had been diagnosed with a significant sight

*(Continued)*

impairment and had received her new glasses. Isobella was wearing her glasses every day, and the difference this made to Isobella's learning and development was phenomenal. In the Couthie, Lesley saw Isobella was able to walk with confidence; she was able to more easily move around the environment and access all that was on offer to her. She was totally at ease in the Couthie and self-assured to explore and experiment. Stuart, Joanne and Lesley all recognised the difference the glasses had made to Isobella, and the MCLV graphical image clearly depicted the amazing progress Isobella had made (Figure 11.2).

The graph itself does not tell the story of Isobella's development; however, the graphical image is useful for demonstrating her progress. The context of her learning and development is critical, drawing on Joanne and Stuart's knowledge of Isobella and Lesley's rich documentation of Isobella in the Couthie.

All settings within the Being Two project used the MCLV assessment software to reflect on the progress the children made over a two-year period. The individual child graphs were important in enabling focused discussions with families about children's learning and in including other professionals in these

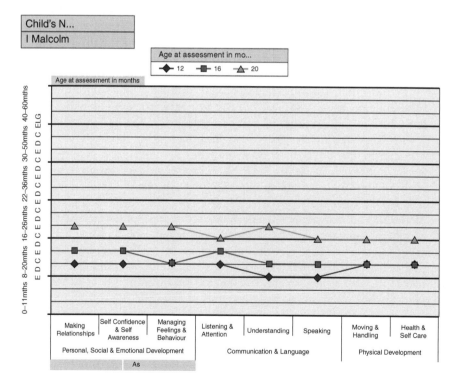

*Figure 11.2* Isobella's MCLV graph showing her progress and the areas where she is emerging (E), developing (D) and confident (C)

discussions, who were also involved in supporting the child. In addition, group and cohort graphs could be generated, which enabled staff teams to look at certain groups and to raise questions about areas of strength and areas for development, aspects that may be supported very well and certain aspects that may present more of a challenge. Staff discussed why this might be so, with ideas ranging from the support the children were being offered in the setting, the environment that was created (particularly the outdoor environment), the process of assessment and, with much discussion, the appropriateness of the Early Years Outcome statements themselves.

## Developing a differentiated pedagogy

The analysis of assessment data and the video reflection with families about each child's learning supported practitioners in the project to develop a differentiated pedagogy to meet the needs of each and every child. Case studies of children were developed with their families, and these were shared and celebrated. Being Two case studies were on the Pen Green website in order to celebrate the learning with a wider audience. Where it was found that a child was making less progress than might be anticipated, there was a real commitment to understanding why this was the case. We drew on the frameworks of Involvement (Laevers, 1997) and Well-being (Laevers, 1997), as well as Schemas (Athey, 2007) that are used at Pen Green to share with parents and understand a child's learning interests and approach to learning. A focus on children's well-being and emotional development was particularly important as the project was focusing on two-year olds, and this gave rise to many discussions about settling-in practices and Family Worker or Key Person roles.

## Developing the Key Person approach

Many settings within the Being Two project had key worker systems, but they did not always seem to be about the relationship between the worker and the child and the family. They often seemed to serve an administration function and to be a mechanism for bringing children together into groups at the end of a session. Some practitioners felt that every pedagogue needed to be able to support each child in the nursery and talk with all parents.

While, of course, it is important for all staff to know all children and families, the specific role of a Key Person as developed by Elfer *et al.* (2011) is crucial in supporting the very youngest children. The role as developed at Pen Green is outlined in Chapter 4 in this book.

We supported reflection among the Being Two settings about their key worker/person role with case study exemplars and discussions around home visiting, getting to know the whole family and the important adults in children's lives, and sharing documentation and discussions about the child's learning with each household where there is shared care across and between families.

## Working across a locality

The staff in the settings in the Being Two project were supported through network meetings as they progressed through the project work. They came together to share their experiences and struggles and to celebrate their learning. There was also an opportunity to share assessment data across and between settings and, importantly, to connect with the Primary Schools where the children were going to move to in the September of each year. This sharing and questioning of data through the development of respectful relationships between professionals led the way to greater clarity about children's progress and how settings could work more effectively together to provide seamless transitions for children across the EYFS (DfE, 2014).

## The Being Two project at the Pen Green Centre for Children and their Families by Andrea Layzell and Michele Duffy (Example from practice by Tracy Gallagher)

The team working with the youngest children at Pen Green, in the Nest and the Couthie, had expanded during the short time before the Being Two project in response to additional local demand for places for eligible two-year olds. Work with two-year olds was already well established at Pen Green, but we recognised the need to think about the additional challenges of increased demand and greater numbers of children. Pedagogical support for the younger children needed to be approached sensitively. We were, by then, working with children from nine months to three years in each of those pedagogical spaces. We needed to both maintain ratios and have a balanced group across the age range in each space.

The opening of the new space for under threes, named by parents as the Couthie, resulted in a need to increase the staff team. Any rapid expansion of team members brings its own challenges: the main ones being ensuring that values and work practice are embedded and sustained across the whole team. The Being Two project offered a focused opportunity to reflect on practice, both as individuals and in terms of an expanded environment and team. The proportions of two-year olds in the spaces increased, so we had to reflect on working closely with both the families and the children, who were at a developmental stage perceived by some as demanding. Previous work to establish the team's 'Image of the Child' was revisited, ensuring that the current team had ownership of this key principle. We also reflected on the experience for children and practitioners, as the cohorts shifted to include a greater number of two-year olds entering the provision with experience of family challenges. We recognized that both staff and family were aspiring to ensure developmental progress at an appropriate level to ensure the children entered school with the skills and knowledge to reach their full potential.

The team was supported in this work with a careful and detailed analysis of the data provided by the software for individual children and cohort information that enabled us to see the strengths and areas that required additional focus within the team.

The following example from practice shows how the analysis of the data can be useful to consider individual children and groups of children in the setting.

The 0–3 team produced the MCLV assessments, in collaboration with the parents, for all the children in their Family Group. When the graphs were produced, we gathered together as a team to look at all the graphs and analyse the data. Staff looked at individual graphs for the children in their Family Group, thinking about the progress they had made and reflecting on the areas that children were not achieving so well. The staff then identified individual action plans for the children that required additional support. As a team, we then looked at the sets of cohort data, asking questions about children's progress across each cohort, scrutinising the data and looking for unusual patterns. Looking at one cohort of children, we identified that 'Speaking' was the aspect where that particular group of children were doing least well. Additionally, it was apparent from the cohort data that this aspect was significantly low for boys. We discussed together what we could do to support this aspect with the children in the Nest and Couthie, and put in place a range of different actions:

- We reflected on the environment and the skills of the team in supporting children's early communication and language development.
- We provided professional development for a staff member, training her in supporting children's early communication and language development; this worker became the communication champion in the team and was then able to disseminate her learning to her colleagues in the Nest and Couthie.
- We set up small group work for children with a specific focus on encouraging communication and language development relating to children's current interests.
- We planned 1:1 work with the communication champion and specific children to give them enhanced opportunities.
- We purchased additional resources, thinking about the indoor and outdoor environment with a specific consideration to the interests of the boys.

The example from practice demonstrates the value of having planning time for the team to come together to view the MCLV data, asking questions of the data and considering implications for their practice.

Michele (at that time, a Senior Family Worker with the under-threes team) and Andrea (at that time, Project Coordinator) worked closely together with the development of the project in Corby and the surrounding area, engaging group providers and childminders working with two-year olds in and around Corby. Training days supported the building of networks in the locality, where dialogue and sharing of experience strengthened a growing reflective practice amongst providers.

## Local childminders embraced the Being Two project

Historically, in the United Kingdom, childminders have provided care and education for significant numbers of the under-three population accessing care, and local childminders were perceived as a group who would provide a number of the newly funded two-year-old places, working with small ratios of one childminder to three young children. Some of the project childminders worked with larger numbers of children when supported by childminding assistants, but all worked in their own homes. The Northamptonshire Childminding Association had provided support and training for childminders in the county, and the consultant working locally from the association engaged in the project as a means to provide a sustainable approach beyond the life of the funded project.

Aspects of the project, such as discussions to establish their own Image of the Child, were immediately embraced by the childminder participants, but other aspects, such as video used as a tool to support pedagogical reflection, presented challenges that were logistically difficult for lone workers. This was overcome with childminders such as Carmel McNeill and Beth Cain, who'd established a close working relationship prior to the project, supporting each other in undertaking videoed peer observation in groups or by visiting each other's homes. One childminder, Michelle Thompson, described how a video of children baking biscuits enabled her to reflect on the conversation she had with the children at play and how she might differentiate those aspects of conversation more effectively.

During the project, some of the childminders were inspected, receiving improved Ofsted grades, as the practitioners used the frameworks to reflect about their work. One childminder, Diane Houston, whose grade from Ofsted improved to Outstanding, described the Being Two Project as "...very informative and influential" on the process of inspection and her practice.

Peer observation, where childminders discussed their own practice with others, provided some of the childminders the means to deepen their awareness of how they interacted with the children they cared for, some seeing themselves as increasingly professional and resulting in a growing self-confidence (Justine Brierly and Louise Williams).

Many of the childminders who attended the training were enthusiastic from the very start of the programme. I believe others showed a degree of resistance, perhaps anticipating that they would be expected to work in the same way as Pen Green, a very different provision to their childminding setting. However, as the work progressed, they began to see that we understood childminding. We used the experience and knowledge of an outstanding childminder, Julie Denton from Bradford, who had studied for many years at Pen Green. Julie became a member of the tutor team on the project (Hayward *et al.*, 2016). Our vision was that we would work towards the group, developing the best practice that was appropriate for their setting, using frameworks that gave all participants the opportunity to consider how they might best be adopted. The group reflected on aspects including the way they engaged with parents, moving away from perceiving the relationship as sometimes unequal, to recognising that working in a flexible yet professional way paid dividends in the way they understood the two-year olds in their care.

Fiona McLaughlin enthusiastically adopted MCLV and the software to map to share children's progress with parents. She said, "parents love MCLV and being able to make sense of it. [A parent said] '...at last something I understand about how my child is learning'". Within the whole project, the MCLV software was used by settings not only to track children's progress but also to assess cohort progress and staff strengths. The childminders found that individual graphs were much more useful in a setting where 'cohorts' of similarly aged children were small. The childminding element of the project developed some of the participants' perception of self and professionalism. Several childminders saw that a Foundation Degree was an appropriate next step as they succeeded in the project expectations, with two of them, Carmel McNeill and Michelle Thompson, enrolling on the Pen Green Foundation Degree, which gave them the opportunity to deepen their understanding of the frameworks they were implementing in their practice.

Carmel and Beth reflected on their experience of being involved in the project. They had been involved with Pen Green for many years, attending the childminder group at the Centre and accessing training. Carmel told me that "Being 2 gave me the confidence in myself to further my own professional development, which I'm not sure I would have done before". Beth recounted, "when people now ask me 'what do you do?' I say confidently, 'I am a childminder, I am a professional childcare provider'".

Andrea reports that, "My own experience of working with the childminders in Corby and the surrounding areas was extremely positive. Working with group provision was sometimes frustrating, as enthusiastic practitioners sometimes returned to the workplace and found implementing their learning was a huge challenge, without their leadership team 'buying in' to this way of working. As well as my own professional heritage being grounded in childminding, I found that the childminders were able to implement their learning and reflection with no such third-party barrier, and that the professional discussions with the group often resulted in a growing awareness and understanding for all of us".

## Conclusion

In conclusion, we found that the methods we used in the Being Two project enabled practitioners the opportunity to identify, for themselves, what areas they wanted to develop in their practice. The practitioners were able to take time to consider their practice with young children and develop a differentiated pedagogy. The network meetings facilitated practitioners coming together to share project work; this proved an effective method of identifying the celebrations and the struggles, and in turn, strengthening the support they offered each other sharing their own thoughts and ideas. The childminders embraced the project work and implemented new ways of working; this enabled them to fully participate and enhance their own professional development.

## References

Athey, C. (2007) *Extending Thought in Young Children: A Parent-Teacher Partnership* (2nd edition). London: Paul Chapman Publishing Ltd.

Department for Education (DfE) (2014) *Early Education and Childcare Statutory Guidance for Local Authorities.* London: DfE. www.gov.uk/government/publications (Accessed 16 September 2016).

Elfer, P. Goldschmied, E. and Selleck, D. (2011) *Key Persons in the Early Years* (2nd edition). Oxon: Routledge.

Hayward, K., Cotterell, T., Smith, J., Layzell, A. and Denton. J. (2017) Developing PICL in Primary Schools, Children's Centres and in Childminder Settings. In Whalley, M. and the Pen Green Centre Team, *Involving Parents in Their Children's Learning: A Knowledge Sharing Approach* (3rd edition). London: Sage.

Laevers, F. (1997) *A Process-Orientated Child Follow-Up System for Young Children.* Belgium: Centre for Experiential Education.

McKinnon, E. (2007) Deepening the Dialogue with Parents, in M. Whalley and The Pen Green Centre Team, *Involving Parents in Their Children's Learning* (2nd edition). London: Paul Chapman, 156–173.

Penn, H. (1997) *Comparing Nurseries Staff and Children in Italy, Spain and the UK.* London: Paul Chapman Publishing.

# Index